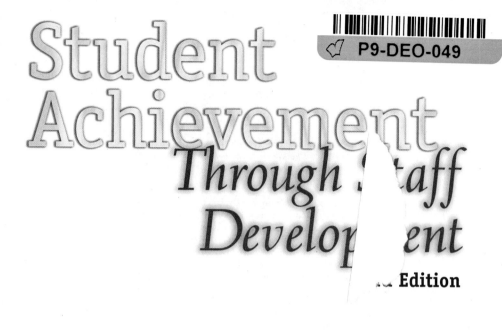

Student Achievement

Through Staff Development

Edition

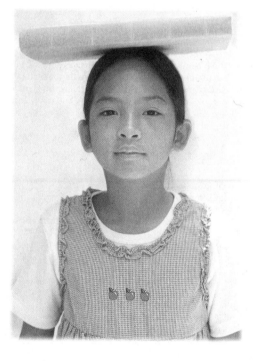

Association for Supervision and Curriculum Development
Alexandria, VA USA

Association for Supervision and Curriculum Development
1703 N. Beauregard St. • Alexandria, VA 22311-1714 USA
Telephone: 1-800-933-2723 or 703-578-9600 • Fax: 703-575-5400
Web site: http://www.ascd.org • E-mail: member@ascd.org

This book was previously published by Longman, Inc.

Cover art copyright © 2002 by ASCD.

ASCD publications present a variety of viewpoints. The views expressed or implied in this book should not be interpreted as official positions of the Association.

All Web links in this book are correct as of the publication date below but may have become inactive or otherwise modified since that time. If you notice a deactivated or changed link, please e-mail books@ascd.org with the words "Link Update" in the subject line. In your message, please specify the Web link, the book title, and the page number on which the link appears.

Printed in the United States of America.

s09/2002

ASCD Product No. 102003
ASCD member price: $24.95   nonmember price: $29.95

Library of Congress Cataloging-in-Publication Data
Joyce, Bruce R.
   Student achievement through staff development / Bruce Joyce
and Beverly Showers ; foreword by Michael Fullan. -- 3rd ed.
      p. cm.
   Includes bibliographical references and index.
   "ASCD product no. 102003"—T.p. verso.
   ISBN 0-87120-674-9 (alk. paper)
   1. Teachers—In-service training—United States. 2. Continuing
education—United States. 3. Career development—United
States. 4. Academic achievement—United States.   I. Showers,
Beverly. II. Title.
LB1731.J69 2002
370'.71'5--dc21

                                                    2002008421

11 10 09 08 07 06 05 04 03 02   10 9 8 7 6 5 4 3 2 1

Student Achievement
Through Staff Development
3rd Edition

Part I
Linking Staff Development and Student Achievement

Chapter 1

Although there are many purposes for staff development, we concentrate on the development of professional communities that influence student learning through changes in curriculum, instruction, or the social climate of the school.

Chapter 2

We examine several staff development efforts where inquiring professional communities have made considerable changes in student learning. In all cases the communities used the knowledge base on curriculum and instruction, engaged in intensive staff development, studied implementation, and tracked student learning.

Chapter 3

Consulting the knowledge base is a major part of staff development design. We make a brief introduction to studies of curriculum and instruction that can be a resource for staff development content and that can help students become more effective learners.

Part II
The Structure of Staff Development

Chapter 4.

The essence is teaching students to be more powerful learners, a function of our professional repertoire in curriculum, instruction, and ways of building social climate in our schools.

Chapter 5.

How do educators expand our repertoires so that we can reach more and more students? We review the literature and consider the staff development environments that work for us.

Chapter 6.

No matter how good the content of staff development, making things happen for students is the ultimate goal. To do so, we need to study the changes we make and the effects on the capacity of our students.

Chapter 7.

We study our students and how they learn. Clinical (teaching) practice is informed by our inquiry. How do we do this? We include an example where kindergarten teachers are learning how to teach their students to read.

Part III
People, Organization, and Leadership

Chapter 8.

We are people with various personalities and ways of growing. Who we are affects how we respond to the learning environments that are provided to us. We need to design a staff development environment that propels all of us into higher learning curves, into states that benefit us both personally and professionally.

Chapter 9.

School leadership is critical to the nurturing of staff development that affects student learning. We look at the cases of two principals. The first is a model of the great principal and professional. The second is caught in an ethos of helplessness.

Chapter 10.

We examine three recent studies on leadership. We examine a school with extremely high and extremely low student learning, the ethos of school districts with very high and very low student learning, and staff development directed at teachers as individuals, school faculties, and school districts.

Chapter 11.

We close with a look at the current standards advocated for staff development and how those standards would change when student achievement is the goal. We recommend policy at the organizational level.

. . . . . .

Foreword

By Michael Fullan

Bruce Joyce and Beverly Showers continue to provide the state-of-the-art ideas on the role of staff development and its link to improved student achievement. This third edition of *Student Achievement Through Staff Development* contains numerous clear examples of powerful cases of improved student achievement.

First, the authors establish that student learning for all should be the only goal for staff development. They then demonstrate the very close linkages between staff development, the development of professional learning communities, changes in curriculum, instruction and climate, and the cumulative effects on student learning.

They use case examples to test the propositions, showing clearly how the content and process of staff development can alter the functioning of classrooms and schools. Joyce and Showers provide ideas for "designing training and peer coaching," "moving from workshops to the classroom," and "inquiring about and evaluating what students are learning."

In addition to sharpening the focus on staff development and student learning, this new edition pushes much further into the critical importance of the larger infrastructure. There are new chapters and analyses on (1) the states of growth of people, (2) creating communities in districts and schools, (3) the role of leadership at the school and district levels, and (4) policy implications for national standards for staff development.

The overall result is that *Student Achievement Through Staff Development* is a comprehensive guide that establishes the core agenda for staff development—one that weaves together classrooms, schools, districts, and state policy—all for the benefit of students. The findings and cases ring true with my own analyses of successful reform. Joyce and Showers remain the definitive authorities on staff development's role in affecting the key conditions that influence greater student learning for all.

—Michael Fullan is Dean, Ontario Institute for Studies in Education, University of Toronto, 252 Bloor St. W, 12-130, Toronto, ON M5S 1V6 (e-mail: mfullan@oise.utoronto.ca)

· · · · · ·

Preface
to the 3rd Edition

The field of staff development has trouble changing (an irony, because change is its business); and yet it is poised to change as never before because of increases in the knowledge base and pressures from within the field and outside it.

Inside the field just about everyone is weary of brief workshops that do not affect practice. Yet, they continue to dominate offerings. Similarly, what Michael Fullan has termed a "bombardment" of initiatives to improve schools—initiatives that exist largely on paper and absent of the staff development to make them work—has worn us all to a frazzle. Yet the bombardment continues.

Outside the field the publicity given the National Report Cards and the cross national studies of educational achievement has unnerved the public and led to the "high stakes" testing programs that are making test-preparation a major curriculum area.

Yet, slowly and clumsily, knowledge continues to accrue and school districts here and there generate fine programs that provide satisfaction and growth to professional educators and increased learning to students. Staff development ultimately depends on the individual development of all its members, as described by Joyce, Calhoun, and Hopkins (1999), in *The New Structure of School Improvement*.

Staff development knowledge has reached the point where any school district can build a staff development program that enhances professionalism and supports curricular and instructional change that accelerates student learning in the personal, social, and academic domains. Just imagine, for example, what we can do with social studies in a post–September 11, 2001, world.

Let's just do it!

Bruce Joyce
Beverly Showers
September 2002

. . . . . .

Part I

Linking Staff Development and Student Achievement

Not just anything called staff development will generate increased student learning. But some kinds of professional development can produce substantial gains—and in relatively short periods of time. These build learning communities of teachers and administrators who use the knowledge base to shape initiatives while studying curriculum, instruction, and student response on a formative basis. In Chapter 2 we present detailed case studies in which the inquiry process is apparent. In Chapter 3 we look at aspects of the knowledge base on which curricular and instructional initiatives can be built.

Student Learning as the Goal: Learning by Everyone as an Ethos

"Staff development and student achievement" is the topic of this book and foreshadows the intertwined facets of the topic.

We focus on student achievement as the product of formal study by educators—study oriented directly toward improvements in curriculum and instruction and accompanied by continuous examination of student learning.

Our proposition is that if a teacher or a community of teachers

- engages, for a dozen days during the school year, in the formal study of a curriculum area or a teaching strategy that is useful across curriculum areas, and
- regularly studies implementation and consequent student learning, then
- the odds are that student achievement will rise substantially.

This book revolves about this proposition. We believe it is based on ample evidence, and we invite you to join us in inquiry regarding the effects of staff development oriented to student achievement. After all, schooling is about student achievement. We are in business to teach students to become more powerful learners. Thus a major part of the core of this kind of staff development is the study of curricular and instructional forms that help students reach higher states of growth.

Relationship to the Curricular and Instructional Knowledge Base

In most school districts, only limited time is available for staff development. We focus on concentrating that time on the repertoire of curricular and instructional strategies where the knowledge base promises that students will learn more content and skills *and* will increase their ability to learn more in the future.

We deal also with methods of staff development that enable educators to develop the knowledge and skill that lead them to implement what they've learned, to track student learning, and to modify learning environments on the basis of results. Although staff development offerings can reasonably be oriented toward helping teachers become aware of issues and options and provide knowledge about alternatives, we concentrate solely on staff development methods that increase knowledge *and* generate the classroom skills and practices that expand the active teaching/learning repertoire. (See Chapters 2 and 3 for descriptions of many such practices.)

This book is for teachers, school administrators, and central office personnel—those people who can create learning opportunities for themselves and their colleagues in their workplaces. We deal with how to generate systems of staff development centered around student learning and the dynamics of building professional communities. We present case studies of school districts and relate evidence from formal research that will introduce the knowledge base and illustrate the concepts employed to help educators design programs of staff development where increasing student learning is the central goal.

The Essential Elements of Staff Development Focused on Student Achievement

Four conditions must be present if staff development is to significantly affect student learning:

● A community of professionals comes together who study together, put into practice what they are learning, and share the results.

● The content of staff development develops around curricular and instructional strategies selected because they have a high probability of affecting student learning—and, as important, student ability to learn.

● The magnitude of change generated is sufficient that the students' gain in knowledge and skill is palpable. What is taught, how it is taught, and the social climate of the school have to change to the degree that the increase in student ability to learn is manifest.

● The processes of staff development enable educators to develop the skill to implement what they are learning.

The continuum is also useful when considering various strategies and policies that are intended to affect student learning by changing the school environment. We emphasize staff development that influences what is taught, how it is taught, and the social climate of the school *because* the school environment is proximal. A curricular/instructional change, mediated through well-designed staff development, can have a major and rapid effect on student learning.

The Concept of Effect Size

We use the concept of "effect size" (Glass, 1975, 1982) to describe the magnitude of gains from any given change in educational practice and thus to predict what we can hope to accomplish by using that practice.

To introduce the idea, let us consider a study designed to test the effectiveness of an inductive approach to a botany unit against an intensive tutorial treatment. Researchers gave all students a test at the beginning of the unit to assess their knowledge. They then divided the students into two groups based on achievement. The control group studied the material with the aid of tutoring and lectures on the material—the standard treatment in those schools for courses of this type. The experimental group worked in pairs that were led through inductive and concept-attainment exercises emphasizing classification of plants.

Figure 1.1 shows the distribution of scores for the experimental and control groups on the post-test, which, like the pretest, contained items dealing with the information in the unit. (For a more extensive treatment, see Joyce, Calhoun, & Weil, 2000.)

The difference between the experimental and control groups was a little above one standard deviation. The difference, computed in terms of standard deviations, is the *effect size of the inductive treatment*. Essentially, what that means is that the experimental group's average (50th percentile) score was where the 80th percentile score was for the control group. The difference increased when researchers gave a delayed recall test 10 months later, indicating that students retained the information acquired with the concept-oriented strategies somewhat better than information gained via the control treatment.

Calculations like these enable us to compare the magnitude of the potential effects of the innovations (teaching skills and strategies, curriculums, and technologies) that we might use in an effort to affect student learning. We can also determine whether the

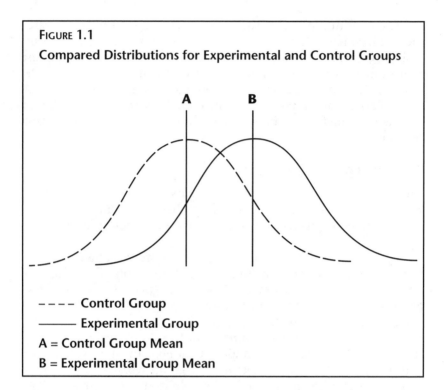

FIGURE 1.1

Compared Distributions for Experimental and Control Groups

– – – – **Control Group**

———— **Experimental Group**

A = **Control Group Mean**

B = **Experimental Group Mean**

treatment has different effects for all kinds of students or just for some. In the study just described, the experimental treatment was apparently effective for the whole population. The lowest score in the experimental group distribution was about where the 30th percentile score was for the control group, and *about 30 percent of the students exceeded the highest score obtained in the control.*

Although substantial in their own right, learning and retention of information were modest when we consider the effect on the students' ability to identify plants and their characteristics, which was measured on a separate test. The scores by students from the experimental group were *eight* times higher than the scores for the control group. The implication is that the inductive treatment enabled students to apply the information and concepts from the unit much more effectively than did the students from the tutorial treatment.

Also, different types of effects need to be considered. Attitudes, values, concepts, intellectual development, skills, and information are just a few. Consider the example of early reading. Two treatments might be approximately equal in terms of learning to read in the short run, but one treatment might affect attitudes positively and leave the students feeling confident and ready to try again. Similarly, two social studies programs might achieve similar amounts of information and concepts, but one might excel in developing positive attitudes toward citizenship.

Again, as we describe some practices and the effects that can be expected from them, we should not concentrate on magnitude of effects alone. Self-instructional programs that are no more effective than standard instruction can be very useful because they enable students to teach themselves and can be blended with teacher-delivered instruction. Broadcast television, because of its potential to reach so many children, can make a big difference even in areas where a program is only modestly effective in comparison with standard instruction. *Sesame Street* and the *Electric Company* are examples. They are not dramatically more effective than the best 1st grade instruction in reading, but they produce positive attitudes and augment instruction handsomely, enabling a certain percentage of students to virtually teach themselves.

Some procedures can interact productively (or unproductively) with others. Doses of one-to-one tutoring have a large effect size (Bloom, 1984) and might interact productively with some teaching strategies such as procedures to help students study words and build phonetic and structural word-attack skills, as in the case of Marilyn Hrycauk's Early Literacy Program and Success for All (see Chapter 2). On the other hand, "tracking," or strict ability or achievement grouping in a school, can reduce the effectiveness of any procedure.

Measures of learning can take many forms. School grades are of great importance, as are measures of conduct, such as numbers of referrals to special education, suspensions, and so forth. In fact, staff development programs should give close attention to those measures, as well as to some simple measures, such as how many books students read (as in the example of the Just Read program in Chapter 2). Analyzing the content of student work is important, as in the study of writing quality, and will be more important as educators increase their emphasis on portfolios and products. (Of special relevance to this book, qualitative measures, such as portfolios, require careful design and considerable amounts of staff development if they are to pay off.) Curriculum-relevant tests (those that measure the content of a unit or course) are important. Finally, schools can analyze the traditional standardized tests to produce estimates of effect size.

A Call to Arms

In this book, we make the case that staff development and student achievement are crucially, causally linked and that the knowledge exists for designing and implementing programs that make a difference in the lives of students. We illustrate our argument with case studies that echo Ron Edmond's (1979) plea: "How many effective schools do you have to see to be persuaded of the educability of your children?" And we will challenge you—teachers, administrators, central office personnel, and district and state policymakers—to put in place a staff development system that nurtures learning communities, injects new knowledge and life into classrooms, and engages students in increasingly successful learning experiences.

Testing the Proposition: Cases in Point

> Good faith efforts to establish goals and then to collectively and regularly monitor and adjust actions toward them produce results. (Schmoker, 1996)

Let's examine a number of cases of schools, districts, and programs that generated effects on student achievement. In each school and district, educators reached into the research base on curriculum, instruction, and social climate to select and develop the content of staff development. We selected these cases to try to bring alive the process of building the communities, selecting the objectives, identifying the content for the focus of initiatives, and generating initiative-related staff development with its embedded study of student learning. The cases are varied: Some center around specific aspects of curriculum, some generate safety net programs for students at serious risk, and some redesign curriculums. Several are nested within broad staff development/school renewal efforts. They are not, by any means, the *only* successful programs, but they provide insight into the staff development elements that were critical to their success. Four characteristics are obvious from the outset:

● *Content.* These programs all brought educators together to study content in curriculum and instruction. We believe that only content dealing with curriculum and instruction or the overall social climate of the schools is likely to *considerably* improve student learning. And the content has to be substantial. Minor variations on curriculum, instruction, or social climate are worthwhile, but cannot be expected to result in sizable changes in student learning. (See Chapter 3 for a survey of curricular and instructional approaches that have substantial effect sizes.)

11

● *Staff Development*. All these programs provided extensive staff development to all school personnel who were critical to the implementation of their new initiatives in curriculum and instruction. These staff development programs created ongoing systems in which goals for student learning were set, training in new content was provided, time and structure for collaborative work were embedded in the schedule, and student data were collected and analyzed in a continuous cycle.

● *Implementation*. Content of the highest quality must be implemented to change student learning. All these programs developed adequate training and organized the teachers and administrators to implement the content of the programs. Furthermore, teachers and administrators formally studied implementation and used results to inform the next cycle of planning, training, and implementation. In other words, staff development did not end until transfer was achieved—the faculties were actually using their new skills and knowledge to affect the learning environments of the students.

● *Goals and Inquiry*. An understanding of goals and how to achieve them was kept central. For example, all had specific student learning goals in mind and measured learning outcomes on a formative and summative basis. Periodic *formative* measures were embedded in the curriculum to determine student learning and, at intervals (as semester or year-end assessments), teachers took stock of progress students had made (the measures were *summed*).

Taken together, these cases test the proposition on which this book is based. We believe they inform our argument that developing communities of teacher researchers can generate and sustain initiatives that raise student achievement. The cases are as follows:

● *Case 1*. Just Read, which generates independent at-home reading for K–12 students.

● *Case 2*. Second Chance/Read to Succeed, a safety-net literacy initiative for upper elementary, middle school, and high school students with literacy problems.

● *Case 3*. Success for All, a program to improve reading achievement, especially in low-achieving inner-city schools.

● *Case 4*. The River City School Improvement Program, a districtwide staff development program directed particularly at low-achieving students.

● *Case 5.* University City, an initiative directed at the improvement of writing and reading in a traditionally high-achieving district.

● *Case 6.* The Schenley School Project, an unusual effort in Pittsburgh, Pennsylvania, where the outstanding teachers of a sizable district provide extensive support to the rest of the faculty.

Case 1: Just Read

Let's begin with a curricular initiative where we can trace an inquiry from the recognition of a problem to the development of a districtwide effort that produced favorable effects on student learning (in that district and in several others that pursued the same course of action). Central office personnel, principals, and teachers were key decision makers in the program; parents and students were involved as "co-action researchers" in this first experience with Just Read. The setting was the U.S. Department of Defense Dependents Schools (DoDDS) in Panama (see Joyce & Wolf, 1996; Wolf, 1994). Throughout, staff development played a central role, helping district- and school-level planners study the literature on literacy, develop data collection instruments and data management procedures, develop action plans, and study progress. These procedures or their equivalent are important when confronting *any* complex problem, and Just Read attacked a problem that plagues many schools and school districts.

The Beginning

The dialogue began one day at a meeting of teachers, principals, and central office personnel. Someone began speculating about how much independent reading (at-home reading of self-selected books) the students were doing, and a lively discussion ensued. Everyone had an opinion, and everyone was surprised at the variety of those opinions. The estimates of independent reading ranged from the belief that most of the kids read widely to the belief that most read almost nothing except school assignments. Some thought that good readers read widely but poor readers do not. Some thought that females do most of the reading. A few people thought that independent reading was a function of the socioeconomic status (SES) of the families. A few others suggested that there was a perverse SES effect in that the wealthier parents kept the students so busy that there was no time for reading. A couple of teachers suggested that the "sustained silent reading" program had made independent readers of virtually all the students. Several believed that literacy was just losing out to television; many disagreed about whether the TV battle was over.

The interchange intensified when someone suggested that an initiative be made to increase reading—arguing that whether kids read is an important responsibility of schools. Several argued that the school's business is to teach the kids to read but that it is the parents' and children's responsibility to ensure they read independently.

A task group was formed, not to design an initiative, but to gather information for reflection. Frequently strong initiatives begin with the suspicion that there is a problem or simply a puzzlement—in this case, the first action is to clarify the picture.

The task group proceeded to dig into the literature and generate a local study around the questions and puzzles that emerged from the discussions.

The studies on reading from the National Assessment of Educational Progress were a big help (e.g., Donahue, 1999; Donahue, Flanagan, Lutkus, Allen, & Campbell, 2001; National Center for Educational Statistics, 1998). First, they indicated that the average U.S. 4th grade student read only four minutes a day out of school, including newspapers, magazines, and books. Over half of the students read nothing at all out of school. Students in grades 8 and 12 read even less. Only about one in seven high school students visited a library, including the school library, during a given week for any purpose; many did not visit the library at all during the school year. The assessment of competence indicated that more than a third of the 4th grade students were unable to read upper elementary grade textual material fluently and with high comprehension. Further, scores on reading competence were similar for grades 4 and 12 in the sense of the numbers of students possessing the basic levels of skill needed to understand typical grade-level instructional materials. Substantial differences between the genders existed, with males reading less and scoring lower (on average) than females. More recent studies have made similar findings (Santapau, 2001).

Examining the literature on literacy revealed strong evidence that wide reading is essential for developing competence in both reading and writing and that ensuring that students read widely is therefore a vital part of the language arts curriculum (see reviews by Calhoun, 1997, 1998). In reading, practice leads to greater fluency, comprehension, and growth in vocabulary. Thus increasing independent reading will improve the quality of a student's reading and writing.

Collecting Local Data: First Empirical Inquiry

The task group collected data for 14 weeks in one elementary school by asking the students to fill out a "reading log" at the end of each week. The data were organized to display trends for each student, classroom, and the school. Thus trends could be seen at all three levels. Figure 2.1 contains the data for the 14-week "baseline" period.

FIGURE 2.1 Mean Number of Books Read Per Student During 14-Week Baseline Period, by Grade	
Grade	**Mean No. of Books**
One	21
Two	35
Three	10
Four	4
Five	3
Six	3

Judging from the data collected in the 14-week period, the average DoDDS 5th grade female would read about nine books per year and the average male about four—both above the national average. Puzzling to many task group members was the finding that SES did not appear to be a factor. Even more puzzling was that estimates of competence in reading (measured by the California Test of Basic Skills [CTBS] battery) were not significantly related to reported amounts of reading ($r = 0.15$). Some of the highest-scoring students read very little except for school assignments.

All were disturbed by the low reported amounts of reading by both boys and girls, but they continued to argue about whether the schools could make a difference.

Developing an Initiative

Reflecting on the results and, especially, the importance of independent reading to other types of growth, the task group brought the issue to the schools, and the Just Read initiative was born. They decided to begin in the elementary school that had first participated in the baseline study, examine its results, and possibly devise an approach that could be used in all of the elementary schools. The objective was to markedly increase the amounts of independent reading among all students by mounting a campaign that would include the extensive involvement of parents.

The strategy was built on information gained from past research. Previous school studies indicate that initiatives that build in continuous formative assessment of progress are more likely to achieve and sustain implementation. A substantial school/home connection helps a great deal; and, in this case, parents and students are as important consumers of data as are professional staff members (Joyce, Calhoun, & Hopkins, 1999). The social climate appeared to be key to the development of a culture of readers.

Therefore, data collection received much attention. The collection of data—particularly the weekly student self-reports—was used throughout to help students, classes, and schools measure progress and hold celebrations of success. The data were collected and organized weekly so that leadership teams and study teams of teachers could reflect on them, classes and teams of students could see their progress, and individuals could see how much—and what—they were reading and writing. In addition, teachers offered guidance and encouragement based on data showing the types of books the students were reading. (Classroom libraries were augmented from the central school library and special purchases so that teachers could easily guide their students in book selection.)

Cultural climate was the primary vehicle. The project was started with an aggressive campaign to encourage parents and students to increase amounts of at-home reading. Meetings signaled the beginning of the campaign. Campaign newsletters included samples of books read and writing produced by the children. Paper chains, containing titles of books read, hung from ceilings and doors. Pizza parties and T-shirts, complete with Just Read logos and the like, motivated readers. Student writing, notes on books, and computer-generated book advertisements draped the school hallways. Parents generated ideas for reading projects, book clubs, trading fairs, and at-home writing projects.

Goals and celebrations maintained focus. Individual, classroom, and school goals were set. Students and teachers found ways to show progress—from statistical charts to chains of animals representing books read. Celebrations were held for individuals, classes, and schools. These celebrations included certificates, notes sent home, announcements in newsletters, celebratory parties, and a host of other devices.

The Effects on the Quantity of Reading

The first question, as the teachers and task force members counted the number of books read, was to estimate *whether Just Read increased the quantity of reading by the students.*

The 14-week period after the program kick-off (the first target period) was compared to the 14-week baseline to generate the first estimate of impact. The results are presented in Figure 2.2.

It appeared they were on the right track. The increases in the primary grades were gratifying to the task force members and school faculty, but they were not satisfied. The average 5th and 6th grade student increased to about a book each week. The task group discovered that individual differences among teachers affected the influence of the initiative, which proved important for future planning. Classes of some teachers increased reading as little as 50 percent, while in other classrooms the amount of student reading increased four to seven times over the baseline. The task group speculated that a thoroughgoing "all school, all district" effort would gradually reduce the "teacher effect" as regular reading became an ingrained habit across the schools, pulling along the classes where the initiative had less initial effect.

FIGURE 2.2

Books Read by Grade and Period: Comparison of Baseline and First Target Period

	Baseline		First Target	
	Mean	Range	Mean	Range
Grade 1	21	0–28	47	7–89
Grade 2	35	2–71	50	8–104
Grade 3	10	3–24	11	1–23
Grade 4	4	1–5	8	3–29
Grade 5	3	1–5	16	4–38
Grade 6	3	1–5	18	6–38

Adding Standard Test Results to the Picture

The objective was to induce the students, with the aid of their parents and cheerleading of their teachers, to increase their reading. They wanted to build a culture of readers (and not incidentally, writers). "Raising test scores" was not an objective. However, in the "pilot" elementary school, a study of standard test scores for the 5th grades indicated that the difference between student performance in the fall and spring administrations of the CTBS battery was substantial. The 5th grade mean had increased from the 48th national percentile to the 66th percentile. The effect size of about 2.0 was computed using comparable students in other schools as the control.

Writing samples from the case study students were submitted to analytic scoring using an instrument developed by the University of California at Los Angeles (UCLA) Center for the Study of Evaluation. Researchers compared writing during the baseline period and the first target period. For the elementary students, the average gain was about two and a half times the national average gain made in a school year. The gains cannot be attributed with certainty to Just Read, but the task force was curious enough to accompany the next year's effort, which included all the elementary schools, with a thoroughgoing examination. The goals of the exam were to determine the quantities of reading and writing generated by the initiative and to see whether there were systematic effects on standard test performance or on quality of writing. The 5th grade was chosen for the intensive testing program, although all grades were involved in the second year of Just Read. The effect size in quality of writing was over 3.0—the *average* student scored at the level of the *highest 10 percent* in the control group.

Nonreading was greatly reduced as the effort intensified and expanded. During the first quarter, 11.4 percent of 5th grade students recorded no books read. This dropped to 3 percent in the fourth quarter. Only 22 students read fewer than 10 books during the year. A quarter of the 5th grade students averaged more than 2 books per week during the year. The evidence appears clear that Just Read had an enormous impact on the amounts of out-of-school reading. Yet, from a technical stance, it is an easy initiative to implement.

The task group asked a number of questions about the program's effectiveness with different populations. They found that it was equally effective with boys and girls, for native Spanish speakers, and for native English speakers. They found that the program was as effective with students whose reading skills were poorest as it was with those with higher levels of skill, although the poorer readers, of course, read simpler books. The task group asked whether reading more had affected the quality of students' writing; they learned that gains in the quality of writing and reading comprehension increased to more than twice the national average gains. They found that the schools that most successfully implemented Just Read "pulled" low- to nonreading students into regular reading more quickly than those schools that started slowly (see Joyce & Wolf, 1996, for a detailed analysis).

This little school district worked from puzzle to puzzle to focus on a problem, create a viable solution, and study the effects both on the primary target, quantity of reading, and derivative targets, such as quality of writing. Embedded staff development—first by external consultants who specialized in curricular and instructional change and staff development and later by district coordinators—sustained the initiative. Most staff development took the form of discussions, modeling data collection and analysis, and modeling action plan development. Just Read illustrates a classic sequence of school improvement procedures but with unusually consistent use of data and support of efforts.

Case 2: Second Chance/Read to Succeed

Next let's turn to another endeavor in the literacy area and explore its origins and evolution. This effort involved building a curriculum, developing and organizing the staff development to implement it, and embedding an action research component to study its effects and improve it. The objective was to solve a common and serious problem—how to create a "safety net" curriculum for upper elementary, middle, and high school students whose literacy development prevents them from benefiting from the academic curriculum. These students are at extremely high risk for dropping out of school and are ill prepared to enjoy full cultural participation as adults.

Whereas many literacy initiatives are based on instructional materials and manuals for teaching, Second Chance/Read to Succeed* does not depend on a "package" of publishers' materials that can be substituted for older materials. Rather, it depends on extensive staff development to help teachers inquire into how older

---

* Note: The Second Chance/Read to Succeed cases are collaborative efforts among Bruce Joyce, Beverly Showers, Emily Calhoun, and teachers in Holtville, California, the Morse High School in San Diego, California, a variety of teachers and administrators in a dozen other districts and, more recently, Marilyn Hrycauk and teachers in the Northern Lights, Alberta, School Division #69.

students acquire literacy and then to develop the new repertoire of teaching strategies needed to implement the curricular framework. The initiative is a curricular/instructional approach in which many of the teaching/learning models are new to the teachers.

Beginnings

Few high school teachers have been prepared to teach reading, especially to beginning, struggling readers. A dozen years ago in Holtville, California, it became apparent during a general school renewal program that many of the middle and high school students were failing. Nearly all of those students could not read or write well enough to manage the core curriculum subjects. The schools had tried many of the packaged programs to help middle and high school students overcome their literacy problem, and those programs had failed. The decision was made to review the literature on literacy and, consequently, to develop and implement a curriculum designed for those students.

Some students experienced immediate success. Unfortunately, a crisis on measurement occurred in California at that time because of a controversy over testing. Reliable measures were not available; but teachers, administrators, and consultants were encouraged because of the evidence the schools themselves had gathered about student learning.

Shortly afterward, a high school in San Diego decided to address a staggering problem. Its entering 9th grade classes averaged a 5.3 grade level equivalent (GLE) score on the reading battery of the Stanford Achievement Test. Nearly 60 percent of those students entering 9th and 10th grades (about 1,000 in all) scored two or more years below the national average for grade level (see Figure 2.3).

The school conducted an extensive survey of the literature (see Calhoun, 1997), repeating the Holtville analysis and seeking information about the types of learning needed for older struggling readers. The review yielded an intervention with multiple dimensions, which Joyce and Calhoun, in collaboration with the Holtville teachers, worked into a curriculum. The components included

● *Increasing amounts of reading.* Extensive recreational reading was required of all students in the reading class.
● *Building sight vocabulary and studying word structures.* Teachers engaged in extensive vocabulary work with students because an expanded vocabulary is highly correlated with reading comprehension. Words were generated through reading (students identified

FIGURE 2.3 Ninth-Grade Reading Comprehension		
Grade Equivalency	**No. of Students**	**Percent of 9th Graders**
1.0–2.9	63	15%
3.0–5.9	134	32%
6.0–8.9	117	28%
9.0–12.9	79	19%
Post–High School	26	6%
Total	419	100%

words they needed to attack) and then classified and reclassified the words as the students concentrated on learning structural and phonetic concepts.

● *Building comprehension skills.* The initial focus on reading was to ensure that students developed high levels of reading fluency (much of which depends on high levels of reading practice). Cooperative strategies focused initially on lower-order comprehension (the factual recall of what is read). With increasing fluency, comprehension activities expanded to include higher-order comprehension tasks (identification of main ideas/central themes, inference/interpretation, etc.).

● *Writing practice.* Practice included frequent, short assignments relating to comprehension of reading materials. The teacher, with the entire class and with the assistance of students, modeled dictated writing, which was completed on selections the teacher read to the entire class. These collaborative writing sessions modeled various approaches to elaborated sentence syntax, as well as different types of writing.

Each year, the school organized about 20 sections of Second Chance with an average enrollment of about 25 students and a normal duration of one semester. In GLE terms, estimating from the Stanford Achievement Test, these students had apparently been gaining an average of roughly one-half year for the nine years they had been in school. Reading rates significantly improved for all students during the semester-long course; 45 percent of the students averaged growth of two GLE years or better during the four-month course.

Staff Development

As we mentioned earlier, few high school teachers are prepared to teach reading, and certainly most secondary teachers have not been prepared to help struggling readers. The Morse High School teachers were no exception. Staff development in the Second Chance reading program spanned a period of years and included recurring cycles of training, analysis of student data, and testing. The teachers studied the literature on literacy, saw many demonstrations of the components of the curriculum, practiced, shared their results, and studied student response.

Read to Succeed: An Evolution of Second Chance within the Northern Lights Districtwide System

We now turn to a district that has created a general staff development system oriented toward student achievement. Within that general system, one important strand built on the experience of Second Chance and generated a program called Read to Succeed.

Thus we discuss the inquiry in Northern Lights School Division #69 (in the United States, it would be called a district), located in the northeastern corner of Alberta, Canada. About 375 professionals and 180 teaching assistants serve about 6,400 students in schools scattered over an area five times the size of Rhode Island. Although the district is engaged in general curriculum improvement efforts in the area of literacy, here we are concerned with "safety net" initiatives, particularly the Read to Succeed program that capitalizes on the experience with Second Chance. Another program, the Early Literacy Tutorial, targets 2nd grade students who are struggling in reading (Hrycauk, 2002).

The Read to Succeed component is parallel to the Early Literacy Tutorial in that it addresses the needs of 4th to 12th grade students whose reading/writing competence is below the level necessary for success in the academic curriculum. The school schedules of those students are organized so that they continue to enroll in the basic academic subjects, but for 90 minutes per day, they are taught by teachers engaged in the study of curriculum and instruction for "overage beginning readers"—older students who have not even approached grade-level reading skills. Students are initially enrolled for at least eight weeks a semester, but they remain in the Read to Succeed program until they are at a level that permits them to succeed in the academic curriculum areas.

Curriculum

The components of Second Chance have been augmented to include the Picture Word Inductive Model (Calhoun, 1999; see Chapter 10) and more extensive formal attention to comprehension skills. The current components include

• Development of sight vocabulary from the students' listening-speaking vocabulary through the picture-word inductive model (Calhoun, 1997) and the study of words encountered through wide reading (Nagy & Anderson, 1987; Nagy, Herman, & Anderson, 1985).
• Wide reading at the developed level (Duke & Pearson, undated).
• The study of word patterns, including spelling (Ehri, 1999).
• Regular (several times daily) writing and the study of writing (Englert et al., 1991).
• The study of comprehension strategies (Garner, 1987; Pressley & Woloshyn, 1995).
• Weekly and monthly progress studies, by both teachers and students, including reading levels, sight words learned, phonetic and structural analysis skills acquired, information learned, and fluency in writing (Calhoun, 1999). Students study their progress and know whether they are ready for exit when they are independent readers of grade-appropriate text.

The Ongoing Study of Read to Succeed in Northern Lights

The information described here comes from 12 sections of several schools in the division involving 300 students, about 15 percent of the secondary school enrollment. The Read to Succeed teachers received 10–15 days of staff development and studied their implementation and the growth of their students by a variety of measures. These included standard tests (the Canadian Tests of Basic Skills or the Gates-MacGinitie battery) administered when they enrolled in Read to Succeed and again at the end of the academic year 1999–2000. The 20 schools of the district include populations of considerable variance in SES and ethnicity.

In this report, standard tests are the focus and are interpreted, first, in terms of the students' competence in reading (on entry) and, second, in terms of their progress. Complete data were available for 250 students in the 12 sections (some students changed schools, and some were not available for both testing sessions). For each student, learning history indexes were computed providing estimates of student progress compared with the national "average" student. Each of the 12 section teachers studied the growth of each student, the progress of the students in their section, and the progress of the Second Chance initiative as a whole.

Figure 2.4 comes from one class of 4th and 5th grade students and provides an example of the data that were accumulated in each section.

FIGURE 2.4
Pretest and Post-Test California Test of Basic Skills (CTBS)
Scores for 16 Students from One Section

Student Number/ Gender	Length (months)	Vocabulary Grade Level Equivalent (GLE)			Comprehension Grade Level Equivalent (GLE)		
		Initial	Final	Gain	Initial	Final	Gain
1. F	9	2.3	4.4	2.1	2.9	4.9	2.0
2. F	9	1.9	4.3	2.4	2.9	4.6	1.7
3. M	9	1.7	4.2	2.5	1.4	5.0	3.6
4. M	5	3.3	3.9	0.6	3.0	4.8	1.8
6. M	9	1.4	4.3	2.9	3.0	4.7	1.7
7. M	5	2.8	2.9	0.1	3.2	3.7	0.5
8. M	5	1.9	4.0	2.1	2.1	3.5	1.4
9. M	9	2.3	4.3	2.0	3.5	4.8	1.3
10. M	7	3.9	3.3	(0.6)	3.0	4.1	1.1
11. M	5	3.1	4.1	1.0	4.8	5.1	0.3
12. F	5	3.6	4.4	0.8	3.0	4.6	1.6
13. M	5	2.6	3.0	0.4	2.9	3.5	0.6
14. F	5	4.5	4.9	0.4	3.3	5.1	1.8
15. M	9	3.9	4.9	1.0	2.7	5.3	2.6
16. M	5	2.3	3.0	0.7	2.4	3.6	1.2

All of these students made substantial gains on either the Vocabulary subtest, the Comprehension subtest, or both subtests of the Canadian Tests of Basic Skills. In this class, there were just four females; thus, there is a big gender difference in enrollment, but no gender difference appears in effects. The mean gain on the Vocabulary subtest was 1.2 GLE and on the Comprehension subtest, 1.5. Gains relative to initial scores are particularly interesting. The initial scores for six students were in the average range of end-of-first-grade students (1.7–2.3). The average gain for this subgroup of students was 2.1. In their previous four or five years of schooling, the average gain for these six students had been around 0.25 per year, and the prognosis that that level of gain would rise would normally be poor (Juel, 1988). In national curve equivalent (NCE) terms, the average gain moved from about the 10th percentile to about the 35th percentile for the students' grade. In other words, the students were edging toward the competence of average students.

During this year, or half-year in eight cases, the student gains were twice the gain of average students for a year, and eight times their own previous average annual gain. For most of these students, another year of this magnitude of gain would bring them to where they "look like" average students, at least from a test score perspective. As it is, they have experienced a year of considerable growth and have reached a level in reading where, with effort, they can manage typical upper elementary grade academic tasks. As an aside, all these students were coded as having serious learning disabilities or communication disorders.

What was the progress of the students in all sections?

● The first objective was to help the students attain higher levels of learning, where, instead of falling behind more and more each year, they would progress at the rate of average students at the least, and—even better—begin to catch up. Three quarters of the students apparently succeeded. The gain scores of 56 percent of them (in GLE terms) were from one and a half to three times the gains of their "average student" agemates, whereas their entry scores indicated GLE gains of from one-fourth to one-half of the average gains of the entire population in their previous years in school. Another 18 percent gained as much or more than the average student gains each year.

● Gender was not a factor. Males and females made almost identical progress.

● Elementary and middle school sections made almost identical gains. Grade level of students within sections (some included students from two or three grade levels) was also not a factor. For example, 7th grade students in sections where there were also 6th and 8th grade students gained about as much as did 7th grade students in sections containing only 7th grade students.

● Scores on entry were not a factor. Gains were similar for students beginning at 2.0, 3.0, 4.0, and so on.

● Overall, progress of students with and without special needs codes was almost identical across all grades.

● The socioeconomic status of students was not a factor with respect to progress.

● Implementation was a factor. Where the conditions for implementation (such as a dedicated 90-minute period for Second Chance) and full use of the dimensions of the program occurred, at least 9 out of 10 of the students made large gains. Lesser conditions and degrees of instructional implementation resulted in lesser numbers of students who achieved the goal. Even in those cases, most students made substantial progress and, with a longer period of enrollment in the program, may succeed (an issue that will become clearer later). However, the effect size between the lowest and highest implementing sections was 2.8, despite the considerable gains by the low-implementing cohorts. The gains are reflected in the scores on the provincial tests on reading competence for the high-implementing schools. Figure 2.5 provides an example.

In the Northern Lights school district, Read to Succeed appears to be making inroads into a problem that previously appeared to be virtually insoluble. Without segregating the overage beginning readers from the core curriculum subjects, the district has been able to

FIGURE 2.5 School A, Grade Nine: Percent of Students Reaching Acceptable Level on Provincial Tests of Reading Compared with Students Across the Province				
	Year One	**Year Two**	**Year Three**	**Gain**
Percent of School Students	78.9	85.7	95.2	16.3
Percent of Provincial Students	83.9	84.5	85.5	1.6

increase their rates of learning, give them hope, and, with further effort, may rescue them from the terrible situation in which they have found themselves. Essentially, no student is "written off" as a hopeless case because they did not learn to read in the primary grades. However, the program is not regarded as a quick (one-year) treatment after which the students can be left to their own devices. They will be supported for the rest of their time as secondary school students and their progress reported over the next several years.

Many educators are discouraged about the prospects of the over-age beginning readers and what can be done to help them. We may have underestimated what is known and how that knowledge can be used. Research on curriculum for overage beginning readers appears to have reached the point where we can design curriculums that can reach those students and provide them with an opportunity to grow at normal rates and better.

Case #3: Success for All

Now let's examine a program that has been extensively used and carefully studied for almost 15 years. It focuses on literacy in the primary grades and may be nested in a broad and multifaceted staff development/school renewal program or, as is often the case, in a targeted initiative, particularly in low-achieving urban schools. In fall 2000, 1,800 schools (serving more than a million students) used the program.

The Success for All program is a complex initiative that combines an intensive reading curriculum with systematic diagnosis of learning problems, immediate and targeted tutoring intervention, cooperative learning, and family support teams. The staff development program continues throughout the year, with heavy emphasis on follow-up for implementation. The focus is on preventing the onset of the downward spiral that so often begins during the primary years and leaves the students unable to cope with the ordinary demands of the upper grades. The program developers aim at bringing *all* students to satisfactory levels on literacy measures, especially reading, and not accepting the losses that occur when normally distributed achievement occurs.

The program is eminently transportable because of the combination of a curricular system, adequate staff development, and the insistence on the formative study of student achievement. Most settings that adopt it realize effects.

The Center for Research on Effective Schooling for Disadvantaged Students at Johns Hopkins University (Slavin, 1990; Slavin et al.,

1996) is studying the program's efforts to improve primary education in inner-city schools. The multiyear effects of Success for All are consistent. Retention has been reduced greatly (from about 40 percent to 10 percent in some project schools and to nearly zero in the schools receiving the most intensive attention). Gains in reading are considerable across a variety of tests (effect sizes average about 0.4 on tests of growth in reading against comparable schools) (Hurley, Slavin, & Madden, 2000). As achievement rises, fewer students are qualifying for special education services.

Success for All has worked quite well in multicultural and multilingual settings and, with intensive efforts, has reached many students judged to be most "at risk." With such widespread use, implementation of the curricular and instructional pattern has inevitably varied, and effects have varied with degrees of implementation (Smith, Ross, & Nunnery, 1997).

The complex Success for All intervention is reminiscent of Spaulding's (1970) program for a similar population in North Carolina. Spaulding's most important academic goal was to raise aptitude to learn as measured by tests of ability or intelligence. He also used a combination of careful diagnosis, direct and immediate intervention, intensive reading instruction, and several well-tested models of teaching, including social learning theory, simulations, role-playing, and cooperative study. The ability indices (once popularly known as "IQ") of the average student in Spaulding's initiative rose about a third of a standard deviation after three years. The results are pertinent to an important question—the extent to which efforts to improve student learning do so by teaching content (such as literacy skills) or whether they succeed by improving learning capabilities such as those measured by IQ tests. This is not an either/or question. The importance of Spaulding's findings is that curriculum and instruction can be aimed at learning ability.

Success for All demonstrates what can be done with the intensive implementation of the available tools for teaching. While many districts agonize over the number of students who fail to learn adequately, this straightforward, relentless approach gets the job done with a combination of careful design and school personnel support to work through the stages of implementation.

Case 4: The River City Experience

The River City School Improvement Program focused on instruction, staff development, and organizing faculties for collaborative action. Schools entered the program as units. A condition of school participation was that 80 percent of each faculty had to vote to participate and the majority decision was binding on the entire faculty. All teachers in each participating school studied a set of well-tested models of teaching selected to increase the learning capacity of their students. The faculties were organized into study groups and elected councils whose responsibility was to examine information about the health of the school and to plan school improvement initiatives; Joyce, Murphy, Showers, & Murphy, 1989).

In some of the schools the need for school improvement was urgent. For example, in one of the middle schools, the students had such poor learning histories that only 30 percent achieved promotion at the end of the year before the project began. Scores on standard tests revealed that the average student in the school had gained only about six months' achievement for each year in school. (Ten months is average.) The school district had tried a number of initiatives to alleviate the situation, including special programs for "at risk" students, lowered class size, and increased counseling services, all with little effect. However, learning rates began to improve dramatically as the teachers learned to use models designed to increase cooperative activity, teach concepts, and to teach students to work inductively and memorize information.

By the end of the first year, 70 percent of middle school students achieved the standards required for promotion, and 95 percent earned promotion at the end of the second year. Judging from the standardized tests administered at the end of the second year, the average students in the school were achieving at a normal rate (that is, gaining 10 months of learning for 10 months of effort when compared to the U.S. population as a whole). Time lost in disciplinary action decreased dramatically, to about one-fifth of the amount lost before the program began. Helping the students learn a variety of learning strategies (which enabled them to educate themselves more successfully) probably reduced the incidence of disciplinary infractions. Students who experience success in the classroom have less reason (and less time) to express their dissatisfaction with school in socially inappropriate ways.

After consultants trained the faculties of the first three schools, a cadre of teachers disseminated the teaching strategies to other schools in the district. Results for the first nine schools on the Iowa Tests of Basic Skills were substantial. Each of the nine schools completed 8 tests for a total of 72 test scores. Forty of the 72 scores reflected gains of greater than four months over the previous year's results, and 20 of the scores reflected gains of between two and four months. It is important to note that faculties taught by a cadre of their peers learned new models of teaching as thoroughly, implemented them as frequently, and gained equally successful student outcomes as faculties taught by outside consultants.

The large effects on student learning occurred rapidly—in the first year of implementation, once again demonstrating the efficacy of the schools that make changes in curriculum and instruction. Many educators believe that school improvement efforts will not have demonstrable effects on students for several years, but the evidence points toward quite a different conclusion. Students respond right away to changes in instruction and begin to accelerate their rates of learning provided that the educational environment is designed to do just that—teach the students to learn more effectively.

Case 5: The University City Experience

We are often asked whether the same strategies can have substantial effects in suburban schools where there are few "minority" students and where achievement has always been relatively high.

A program (Joyce, Calhoun et al., 1994; Joyce & Calhoun, 1996) in a high-achieving 11-school district—where standard test scores have ranked the district in the top 5 percent nationally—involved all the teachers and students in all nine elementary schools. The program is unusual in the wide range of support provided by its staff development program.

The district has created strong and balanced support for staff development generated by teachers as individuals, by school faculties in the action-research mode, and by the district as a unit. Individually generated staff development acknowledges the division of the workplace into units (classrooms) where individual teachers need to use their perceptions and strengths to create innovations to which they can be committed. Whole-faculty-generated action research is supported because the curricular and social climate dimensions of the school can be addressed in a way impossible through individual action alone. Further, schoolwide action research directly addresses the goals of developing shared-governance modes and increasing the capacity of the faculty to inquire into and solve problems requiring concerted, democratic action. The districtwide initiatives emphasize the importance of curricular coherence and the development of faculties that embrace professional citizenship in a community where children deserve equal educational opportunity and a common core of knowledge and skills. In this section we will deal primarily with the districtwide initiative. The others will be discussed later in the book (see especially Chapters 9 and 10) as we discuss governance and its effects on staff development programs.

The district initiatives include the study of teaching models applied to curriculum changes in the language arts that favor literature-based approaches with close connections between reading and writing. In addition, the district implemented Just Read to increase the amounts and quality of independent reading by students. (Teacher/administrator coordination and support teams were formed to articulate the curriculum and to arrange support.) The two models of teaching selected for initial study were "inductive thinking in cooperative groups" and "concept attainment," both basic approaches to teach students to build concepts—in this case, concepts that enhance reading comprehension and, through the reading-writing connection, comprehension of strategies for writing.

The focus here is on quality of writing, which was assessed by scoring sets of writing prompts given to the students in the fall and spring of the 1992–93 school year, when all dimensions of the program were in full swing. Particular attention was given to expository writing, which has proved to be so difficult to teach from a national perspective (Applebee, Langer, Jenkins, Mullis, & Foertsch, 1990). The results were compared with a baseline derived from comparisons of fall and spring writing the year before and with the average gains indicated by the National Assessment of Educational Progress (NAEP) for the nation as a whole. Here we will use part of the 4th grade assessment.

Figure 2.6 compares the means for the two periods (fall 1992 and spring 1993) for the three dimensions for which quality was assessed: Focus/Organization (F), Support (SUP), and Grammar and Mechanics (G). Altogether, the scores for 95 students were compared.

In the fall, coefficients of correlation between F and SUP and G were 0.56 and 0.61, respectively; between SUP and G, the coefficient was 0.63. In the spring, these were 0.84, 0.65, and 0.74, respectively.

Effect sizes computed between fall and spring scores were 2.18 for F, 1.53 for SUP, and 1.37 for G.

All these are several times the effect sizes of the national sample and of the baseline gains determined from the 1991–1992 analyses.

To illustrate the magnitude of the difference, Figure 2.7 compares the mean results for the spring 4th grade assessment to the 6th grade fall results.

FIGURE 2.6

Mean Grade-4 Scores on Expository Writing for Fall 1992 and Spring 1993

	Dimensions		
Period	**Focus/Organization (F)**	**Support (SUP)**	**Grammar/Mechanics (G)**
Fall			
Mean	1.6	2.2	2.11
SD	0.55	0.65	0.65
Spring			
Mean	2.8	3.2	3.0
SD	0.94	0.96	0.97

SD = Standard Deviation.

FIGURE 2.7

Mean Grade-4 Spring 1993 Scores on Expository Writing Compared with the Mean Grade 6 Scores from Fall 1992

	Dimensions		
Grade/ Period	**Focus/Organization (F)**	**Support (SUP)**	**Grammar/Mechanics (G)**
Grade 4/ Spring			
Mean	2.8	3.2	3.0
Grade 6/ Fall			
Mean	2.11	2.90	2.87

The gains here indicate that it is possible to increase writing gains per year to several times the typical average gain, even in a district with a tradition of very high achievement. One cannot parcel out the effects from any one of the three dimensions of this "full-service" staff development program, but that is not particularly important. What is important is the magnitude of the gains.

Case 6: The Schenley School Project

In Pittsburgh, Pennsylvania, a side effect of the development of an extensive districtwide staff development program was a test of what can happen if highly regarded teachers in a large district are concentrated in a high school whose lower SES population has achieved far below the national average. The Schenley School became a staff development center where outstanding teachers were brought together. Other district teachers rotated into the school, spending several weeks observing those teachers and studying instruction (Wallace, LeMahieu, & Bickel, 1990; Wallace, Young, Johnston, Bickel, & LeMahieu, 1984).

An immediate rise in achievement occurred measured with standardized tests in eight of nine curriculum areas. Students scoring at or above the national average in total language results rose from 27 percent to 61 percent; in reading from 28 percent to 45 percent; in physical science from 21 percent to 63 percent; in biology from 13 percent to 41 percent; and in algebra from 29 percent to 73 percent. The gains were maintained or increased during the second year.

As interesting as are the sizes of those improvements, it is equally interesting that they were so immediate. High schools need not feel hopeless about students with poor learning histories. The gifted Schenley teachers, working in an environment that intensified the study of instruction, immediately transformed the learning environment of their school. The students responded by focusing their intelligence on eliminating their deficits and, in the main, looking more able at graduation than many of their counterparts who had not suffered cumulative deficits in their past education.

Learning from the Cases

Making large differences in student achievement through school improvement programs is hardly routine, and the number of reports and variety of highly successful programs suggest that the technology exists for making rapid and significant change. The ones mentioned in the cases in this chapter are just a few. Others include effective implementation of "Mastery Learning" programs (Block, 1980; Bloom, 1971); Distar (Becker, 1978); teaching skills in mathematics (Good, Grouws, & Ebmeier, 1983); and broadcast television development, such as the products of the Children's Television Workshop (Ball & Bogatz, 1970). Additionally, Levine and Lezotte (1990) have discussed the effects of helping schools study demonstrably effective schools, and Calderon (1994) and her colleagues have successfully involved large groups of teachers in the improvement of bilingual teaching with a very high criterion for measuring success.

All these large-scale programs are remarkably straightforward. They focus their efforts on areas that directly affect the students; they organize everyone to achieve implementation and then study the effects. *All of them recognize the importance of providing time for staff development and making collective decisions. In a structural sense, they changed the workplace.*

Some popular large-scale innovations have had very weak or no effects; some have actually made things worse. A major reason is that they have concentrated energy on the more distal variables— ones that are a distance from the environment of the child. Perhaps the worst cases are those that provide monetary resources to schools but do not provide the technical assistance to help faculties study the knowledge base, select initiatives, and obtain the staff development that enables them to implement the initiatives and study the effects on the students.

Several studies have examined how school faculties respond to the challenge. Rosenholtz (1989) found that most faculties become what she termed "stuck" in the process, unable to agree on direction or to take action. David and Peterson (1984) studied efforts, some heavily funded, where volunteer schools were granted discretionary resources to engage in the process of self-renewal. They, too, found that most of those schools were also "stuck," in terms of effects on students, despite the grants. Most of those who were less stuck had not made initiatives in curriculum implementation or instruction but had generated changes in scheduling, parent involvement, disciplinary codes, and other areas believed to be important but which did not require changes in what is taught or how it is taught.

Calhoun's studies (Joyce & Calhoun, 1996) of school faculties learning to engage in schoolwide action research indicate that nearly all schools need facilitation and technical assistance if they are to progress to unified action that affects instruction and student learning (see also David, 1990; Sizer, 1991; Timar, 1989). For many schools, extensive technical assistance is needed if the "site-based" approach—where faculties become responsible for curriculum development—is to yield improved education for all students (Muncey & McQuillan, 1993). The reason sites need help is that the action research process depends on the development of norms of collegiality, and the process of developing collective decision making and collective action collides with the norms of privatism and autonomy that have for so long characterized the workplace (Lortie, 1975). In addition, many faculties begin by focusing on the distal—policies governing discipline, methods of reporting, assessment, and such, rather than focusing on how well students are learning and what changes are needed in curriculum, instruction, technology, and social climate. Focusing on the distal does not violate the norms of privatism (you can change discipline policy or assessment without learning to teach differently). Faculties that engage in improving education need to know from the outset that they must focus on the proximal variables sooner or later and that effects on students will not likely occur until they get to the proximal—what is taught, how it is taught, and what the school climate is like.

Yes, We Can

In the cases presented in this chapter, communities organized and made initiatives, extensive staff development made those initiatives possible, and the communities of teacher researchers studied the effects on student learning.

The staff development field is often confronted with the question (from staff developers, among others), "Does staff development positively affect student achievement?" The answer is that not all of what is called staff development will directly improve student achievement. In fact, most current offerings probably will not generate the amount of change that is necessary to affect student achievement to an appreciable extent. However, staff development can be designed that *will* affect student learning, and not a little—large changes can be made.

Such staff development is nested within the development of learning communities of teacher researchers who study curriculum and instruction and the effects of initiatives on the state of their students.

Sources of Tested Content: Inquiries on Teaching and Learning

The method of science, as stodgy and grumpy as it may seem, is far more important than the findings of science.

Carl Sagan, *The Demon-Haunted World*, p. 22

It is probably clear by now that we strongly favor creating the content of staff development from the available research on curriculum and instruction. In this chapter we will deal with some sources of content in which we have considerable confidence. We will treat the topic as an inquiry, concluding with some lingering questions and areas needing investigation.

Abraham Kaplan (1964) began his treatise on the conduct of inquiry in the social sciences by recounting the old story of a man who, returning home one night, found a somewhat inebriated neighbor crawling around under a street lamp. When asked what he was looking for, the neighbor responded, "For my house key. I dropped it." After some minutes of crawling around with his acquaintance without finding the key, our Good Samaritan thought to ask, "Where did you drop it?"

The neighbor replied, pointing down a dark alley, "Down there."

"Then why are we looking here?"

"Because there's light here, that's why."

Kaplan used his anecdote to characterize behavioral and social science research, maintaining gently that we need to look where we know how to look—in areas where we have a little light. The eventual critical questions may lie down the way in the avenues that are still dark to us. Still, we have to look where we can, lighting the candles in the dark.

Kaplan's analogy surely applies to research on teaching. For thousands of years philosophers, social scientists, and nearly all parents and teachers have conducted inquiries under their own lampposts, crawling around and using the tools at hand. Some of our seekers have been equipped with broad philosophical systems and have searched for answers to massive and profound questions. A few exceptionally bold thinkers have tried to decide what are the best kinds of teaching for entire societies—driven by the motivation to improve or even change the very society of which they are a tiny part.

Others, armed with observational and experimental tools, have focused on efficiencies, asking what kind(s) of teaching best achieve a given, relatively narrow focus, such as the quickest way to teach children how to count or how to speak a foreign language.

Some have focused on defined populations of students, seeking methods for the quick or the slow, for the deaf or the blind, for females or males, the rich or the poor. A considerable number have concentrated on subject matters and curriculum areas: reading, writing, mathematics, science, social science, and health and physical education.

All of us have conducted our own inquiries into education. Most parents have tried to learn how to rear their own children, coach the child next door, teach a Sunday school class, or teach a child to swim.

What is the cumulative yield of all these inquiries? What do we know? Are we approaching the experiential and scientific base that the medical profession enjoys? Have we discovered an array of ways of teaching that can be used for broad or narrow purpose with reasonable expectation that they will work?*

Debate: Is There a Science-Based Knowledge about Teaching?

This chapter would be easier to write if scholars generally agreed that there is or isn't a knowledge base about teaching. But there is no agreement.

Nate Gage (1979), in his presidential address to the American Educational Research Association, argued that concerns about

---

* Work, in this context, means to work well in comparison with the culturally normative methods of teaching that everyone in the society "knows"—those methods that have been transmitted to all of us, whether laymen or professionals, because we are members of this society. Researchers usually refer to the normative teaching method as the "recitation" or one of its variants. More about that subject later as we consider what is culturally normative and how the assessment of innovative educational models relies on comparison with the normative approaches to teaching.

accepting hypotheses on inadequate evidence—the Type A error—has led us to what he called "a massive Type B error," underestimating the size of the knowledge base and its firmness.

To some, Gage was persuasive, but to a large number of scholars he was not. Just a dozen years after Gage's talk, an issue of the *Review of Educational Research* was built around a large-scale meta-analysis by Wang, Haertel, & Walberg (1993). They also contended that there is considerable knowledge about teaching and presented synopses of a number of lines of inquiry to buttress their argument. However, a dozen respondents to the Wang, Haertel, and Walberg review claimed that there is no knowledge base, or not much on which we can rely. In fact, some reviewers actually contended that the manuscript should not be published because the authors had not demonstrated, despite their citation of literally hundreds of studies, that there *is* a knowledge base. Some questioned whether scientific work *can* generate a knowledge base in education; some argued that knowledge is personal and situation-specific and cannot be general in nature. However, others are more positive. A recent group examining studies of teaching in the same manner as the Wang et al. team identified a considerable number of teaching strategies that are based on varying degrees of evidence (Marzano, Pickering, & Pollock, 2001).

Can there be a knowledge base?

The programmatic, experimental paradigm, centered around experiments where teaching strategies are tried and their effects judged against control groups, is challenged from a number of points of view.

Many contemporary scholars question whether the nature of humankind doesn't actually preclude the development of prescriptive knowledge about teaching. As Bereiter (1984) and Phillips (1987) have pointed out, some argue that knowledge is so personal and ephemeral that the very search for common understanding is fruitless. In a different vein, some writers contend that the products of science are political constructions and represent the consensus of the elite, rather than unbiased representations of reality. They suggest that a rather different representation would occur were research conducted by persons of lesser status and education (Hollingsworth & Sockett, 1994). Other dissidents suggest that the empirical paradigms that have served us so well in the "hard" sciences and engineering will be relatively useless in the social arenas, including education, because clinical experience is personal and unique. They argue for the abandonment of faith in classic research and ask for a "paradigm shift" toward the accumulation of accounts of personal practitioner knowledge, rather than the conduct of traditional programmatic research. In addition, some argue that the view of experimental science as sets of inductive programs is an inaccurate stereotype—that intuition and personal vision is far more a part of scientific advancement than are structured inquiries.

A less extreme position holds that cultures, genders, and learning styles are so different that good teaching depends significantly on contextual nuances and variables. Thus, within the same learning environment common cause is made with provision for considerable variation in individual development. A drastic position is that what works for one person cannot be said to work for another because we all are so different.

So, as we assess research on teaching, we do so in an environment that is far less settled as to the value of that research than we might like. However, many people believe that there *is* science-based knowledge and that the sciences of education *have* produced general knowledge.

Regardless of the debates over epistemology, education is carried on daily; and teachers need to know whether they are on their own or whether they can rely on *any* published studies.

So what should we do? Will we tell the novice teacher—or the experienced teacher, for that matter—that we know nothing and that they must construct knowledge solely from their own experience and that what they learn is personal? Will we tell them that we know only a little and what we know has limited applicability? Or will we tell them that, while much is to be done, we know some things that are seriously worthy of their consideration? Shall we go so far as to say that they may disadvantage their students if their teaching is not informed by the knowledge base? In other words, can we build preservice or inservice knowledge on an admittedly partial but critical base?

For the past 35 years, we have been wrestling with this question, examining studies of teachers in action, reading philosophies, and, most assiduously, digging into programmatic lines of research on specific ways of designing educational environments. We have limited capability and are humble by necessity. We believe that we are, as a community, stuck with the lamps we have and the ideas that have been created under them. There is light, however, and we believe that there *is* knowledge about teaching and that it *is* communicable. We have our candles in the darkness.

Throughout the rest of this chapter we'll discuss how various pieces of the knowledge base have been found, as well as what they are. We'll build the discussion around these questions:

● What do we know? Have the inquiries into teaching generated anything more effective than generally accepted cultural knowledge about teaching?

● What is the role of the recitation in teaching both as a social norm and as a baseline against which ideas about teaching are tested? Studies of teaching have shown that the most common classroom teaching method is a question-and-answer pattern where the teacher asks the students questions about content that has been presented to them in some fashion, usually by reading or lectures (see Hoetker & Ahlbrand, 1969; Sirotnik, 1983). Bellack (1962) and his associates found that several versions of the question-and-answer pattern (inducing the students to recite what they are learning) accounted for 90 percent of the transactions in classrooms. Some studies note the efficiency of the recitation and its variants while others experiment with alternative patterns and the recitation becomes the comparison.

● Have any reliable models of teaching emerged from the inquiry? That is, have ways of designing curriculum and instruction emerged that improve on the recitation with respect to certain educational objectives?

● In comparison with normative schooling, how do gender, learning styles, socioeconomic status, and ethnicity influence the effectiveness of the developed models? In other words, are those models broadly effective or effective with certain learners more than others? Do they reduce or magnify differences in capacity to learn? Note that in the cases described in Chapter 2 the traditional effects of gender and socioeconomic differences in literacy were greatly reduced.

Caveats

We will consider these questions in terms of the social system of the United States only. Important research exists on teaching in many societies, and an international community is gradually developing. Our own collaboration has carried us to India, Egypt, England, Australia, Finland, Canada, Thailand, China, and other places. However, we know only the social and educational system of the United States well enough to carry on meaningful discussions of teaching in a social context. Even when confining our discussion to the United States, we cannot hope to cite all the research that is relevant to the questions we will explore. We provide selected bibliographic references that will enable the reader to track our path and assess our conclusions.

What Do We Know?

The lamppost under which we will look first are studies where educational models are tested in the areas of reading and writing. Why begin with reading and writing? First, they are accepted as core areas of schools in the United States. No one doubts their importance. All schools try to teach basic competence in reading and writing. Whatever the disagreements in other areas, the public has a deep interest in literacy. Second, teachers have considerable experience in these areas and thus have had plenty of opportunity to develop skill. We can assume that they are as good as they can make themselves. Third, through preservice and inservice education and the efforts of commercial publishers, American teachers have been given more help in those areas than in any others.

In Chapter 2 we began with "field research" because it speaks more sharply to the existence of an applicable research base than do studies conducted in laboratory settings only (or in classrooms that have been temporarily transformed into laboratories). We asked whether research-based school improvement programs have been able to positively influence student reading and writing in schools and school districts.

In this third edition, we find that we have concentrated on literacy during the past 10 years—and we should have begun earlier. U.S. elementary schools teach about two-thirds of the students to read and write effectively enough that they can manage the tasks of the secondary school curriculum. The picture has not changed much in the two decades of heavy emphasis on the language arts (see Santapau, 2001), which reports the National Center for Education Statistics (NCES) 2000 study and compares the results to studies conducted over the past 10 years).

The primary school years are critical, because not many students who have not learned to read competently by the end of 3rd grade ever manage to do so later on. U.S. society has been so concerned about low achievement in the cities that it has provided resources to inner-city schools (and all schools serving low SES populations) in the form of programs (called Title I or Chapter 1 or special education) to allow teachers to work intensively with small groups of children. On the whole, these "categorical programs" have not materially changed the achievement picture (see McGill-Franzen & Goatley, 2001).

Studies of teaching indicate that there is considerable variance in rates of student learning between schools and even between classrooms in the same school. In Chapter 10 we examine studies of schools and districts with extreme differences and look at differences in staff development and leadership behavior in those situations where achievement is remarkably high and low, *controlling for differences in the socioeconomic makeup of the student body*. Similarly, referrals to special education for mild and moderate learning disabilities, including referrals for presumed attention deficit hyperactivity disorder (ADHD), vary by classroom. In other words, in some classrooms the students learn effectively, reducing the diagnosis that they have learning problems.

Is there enough systematic knowledge about teaching to enable a larger percentage of children to learn to read better in those critical primary grades?

The case study districts and schools described in Chapter 2 all did quite well. Most used national and cross-national data to study literacy and provide a base against which they could compare their results. Now, let's look at the broader picture of experimental studies.

The Study of Teaching: Have Reliable Models Emerged?

Researchers have used two empirical paradigms in the attempt to generate and test teaching models that affect student learning either in new directions or to a greater degree than the dominant cultural model:

● Naturalistic studies of teachers and schools, particularly studies seeking to identify the characteristics of the most effective teachers and schools.

● Experimental studies where philosophical or psychological positions about the nature of humankind and how it learns have been operationalized and studied.

Although we have great respect for the creators of naturalistic research—what Gage called "process-product" research—we will not assess that knowledge base in this chapter. We believe the yield has been substantial and is largely being ignored at present, which is a great mistake. We refer the reader to the handbooks of research on teaching, whose chapters have given considerable attention to the naturalistic studies (see particularly the analysis by Lara and Medley, 1987 and the recent analysis by Marzano, Pickering, & Pollock, 2001).

Instead, we focus on the product of the experimental paradigm. Scanning the research we have located, we have imposed a rough sort of conceptual structure by grouping the emerging models of teaching into four families: the social, personal, information-processing, and behavioral. The bases for the classification are the emphases put on particular dimensions of humans and how they learn. The categories, of course, have overlaps. For example, scholars of cooperative learning place great emphasis on the social nature of humans and the effects of synergy on learning, but that does not mean that they are not interested in how students process academic content. Scholars of mnemonics are very much concerned with how students process information, but that emphasis does not prevent them from being interested in the self-esteem of students or whether they are self-actualizing, areas that are central in the thought of personalists.

To grasp the research, one has also to deal with the wonderful variety in the purposes of the model builders. Some create methods that are directed at objectives that are hardly touched in today's schools, while others aim directly at objectives that have been accepted for thousands of years.

Despite their differences in emphasis, all model builders must contend with an old model, the recitation. If they wish to test their model in classrooms, they must teach teachers to use their model rather than the recitation. A weak implementation will kill a study.

Inevitably, model builders have to compare the learning from their model with learning generated by the normative modes of rearing and educating children. The well-known complexities of conducting research in educational settings haunt all of them and affect the quality of their studies. Finally, when we assess the bodies of work they have produced, we must try to understand the nature and magnitude of their progress. Their first tries may produce weak effects, but they may improve their model through inquiry. Averaging the effects of all their studies may underestimate the strength they develop later.

Here, we will look at just a few of the lines of research, asking the question, "Does it appear that a knowledge base is being created under some of those lampposts?" We'll look at several models that contrast sharply with one another.

Inquiry into Information-Processing Models

Quite a number of models of teaching are designed to increase students' ability to process information more powerfully. These include

● Methods for presenting information so that students can learn and retain it more effectively by operating on it more conceptually.

● Systems that assist memorization and teach students how to organize information for mastery.

● Models to teach students to collect and organize information conceptually.

● Models to teach students to use the methods of the disciplines, to engage in causal reasoning, and to master concepts.

We'll look at a line of inquiry designed to teach students to memorize more efficiently and one designed to teach students to think scientifically.

Mnemonics

Mnemonics is a good place to start because these model-builders attempt to teach students learning skills that can be applied to a range of school subjects. Many of their studies measure outcomes of the sort that make the recitation popular.

Although research on memorization and mnemonic strategies has been conducted for more than 100 years, until a few years ago most of the yield for school practice offered few and very general guidelines, such as advice about when to "mass" practice sessions and when to "distribute" them, or spread practice out over several sessions over time. Little research had been conducted on the learning of school subjects. In the mid-1970s Atkinson at Stanford University began a productive line of work that has been greatly extended by Pressley and Levin at the Universities of Western Ontario and Wisconsin. They developed a series of systems for organizing information to promote memory and have given particular, although not exclusive, attention to the "link-word" method. Atkinson applied the method during experiments with computer-assisted instruction in which he attempted to increase students' learning of initial foreign-language vocabularies. He experimented with what he called "acoustic" and "imagery" links. The first was designed to make associations between foreign pronunciations and the sounds of known English words. The second was used to make the connection vivid (Atkinson, 1975). In one early study the link-word method produced as much learning in two trials as the conventional method did in three. The experimental group learned about half as many words more than the control group and maintained the advantage after several weeks. Atkinson also found that the method was enhanced when the students supplied their own imagery.

Further developmental work included experiments with children of various ages and across subjects. Using a link-word system in Spanish vocabulary learning, 2nd and 5th grade children learned about twice the words as did children using rote and rehearsal methods (Pressley, 1977). In later work with Levin and Miller (1981), Pressley employed a "pictured action" variant of the method with 1st and 6th grade children, who acquired three times as much vocabulary as did control groups. With Dennis-Rounds (1980), he extended the strategy to social studies information (products and cities) and learned that students could transfer the method to other learning tasks with instruction. Pressley, Levin, and McCormick (1980) found that primary school students could generate sentences to enhance memorization. The results were three times as great as for students using their own methods. Similar results were found with kindergarten and preschool children (Pressley, Levin, & Miller, 1981). With J. Levin, McCormick, Miller, and Berry (1982), Pressley's work was successfully extended to vocabulary with abstract meanings. M. Levin and J. Levin (1990) have also extended the application to abstract prose and conceptual systems from the disciplines.

It was important to learn whether better "natural" memorizers, with practice, develop their own equivalent methods. Pressley, Levin, and Ghatala (1984) found that few students, with age and practice, spontaneously developed elaborate methods for memorizing material. The better performers developed more elaborate methods than the majority, who used rote-rehearsal methods alone. However, the newly developed mnemonic methods enhanced learning for the best memorizers, as well as for the others. Hence, it appears that the method or an equivalent one can be very beneficial for most students.

The consistency of the findings is impressive. The link-word method appears to have general applicability across subject matters and ages (Pressley, Levin, & Delaney, 1982) and can be effectively taught to children. The effect sizes reached in many of the studies are quite high. The *average* for transfer tasks (where the material learned was to be applied in another setting), was 1.91. Recall of attributes of items (such as towns, cities, or minerals) was 1.5.

Foreign language acquisition was 1.3, with many studies reporting high outcomes. Delayed recall generally maintained the gains, indicating that the mnemonics strategies have a lasting effect.

The community of scholars who are studying mnemonics have developed considerable interest in the area of metacognition. Their work has given rise to the theory that helping students to inquire into themselves as learners and develop cognitive control over learning strategies can increase learning capability.

Scientific Inquiry

The clearest evidence about the potential effects of scientific inquiry on students comes from the study of the academically oriented curricula in science and mathematics (developed and used during the 20-year period from 1955 to 1975) and from the experience with elementary curricula in a variety of subject areas (Becker & Gersten, 1982; Rhine, 1981). The theory of the academic curricula was relatively straightforward. The essence of the position was stated in *The Process of Education* (Bruner, 1961) and Schwab and Brandwein's *The Teaching of Science* (1962). The teaching of science should be as much as possible a simulation of the scientific process itself. The concepts of the disciplines should be studied rigorously in relation to their knowledge base. Thus science would be learned as inquiry. Further, the information thus learned would be retained because it is embedded in a meaningful framework and the student possesses the interrelated concepts that make up the discipline's structure.

Academic reformers of the 1950s and 1960s developed and introduced entire curricula in the sciences (e.g., *BSCS Biology*), social studies (e.g., *Man, A Course of Study*), mathematics (e.g., School Mathematics Study Group), and language (e.g., the linguistic approaches). These curricula had in common their designers' beliefs that academic subjects should be studied with the tools of their respective disciplines. Most therefore required that students learn the modes of inquiry employed by the disciplines, as well as factual material. Process was valued equally with content, and many of these curricula became characterized as "inquiry oriented."

Much curriculum research resembles the experimental studies of teaching, but the unit under study is a configuration of content, teaching methods, instructional materials and technologies, and organizational forms. Any one of the curriculum elements may be studied separately or in combination with the others, and the yield is expressed in terms of whether a curriculum produces predicted effects. Research on curriculum depends heavily on training in the curriculum content and the teaching strategies needed to implement it. Following training, implementation is monitored, either by classroom observation or interviews. Effects are determined by comparing student outcomes in experimental and control classrooms. In a few studies (e.g., Almy, 1970) combinations of curricula are employed to determine effects on cognitive development and intelligence.

In reviewing the studies, El-Nemr (1979) concentrated on the teaching of biology as inquiry in high schools and colleges. He looked at the effects on information achievement, on process skills development, and on attitudes toward science. The experimentally oriented biology curricula achieved positive effects on all three outcomes. The average effect sizes were largest for process skills (0.44 at the high school level and 0.62 at the college level). For information achievement they were 0.27 and 0.11, respectively; and for attitudes toward science, 0.22 and 0.51, respectively. Bredderman's (1983) analysis included a broader range of science programs and included the elementary grades. He also reported positive effects for information (0.10), creativity (0.13), and science process (0.52). In addition, he reported effects on intelligence tests where they were included (0.50). From these and other studies we can conclude that it is possible to develop curricula that will achieve model-relevant effects and also will increase learning of information and concepts.

Vigorous curricula in one area appear to stimulate growth in other, apparently unconnected areas. For example, M. Smith's (1980) analysis of aesthetics curricula shows that the implementation of the arts-oriented curricula was accompanied by gains in basic skills. An active and effective curriculum in one area may have energizing effects on the entire school program. Hillocks's (1987) review of the teaching of writing produced similar effects. His conclusion indicated just how closely *how* we teach is connected with *what* we teach. Essentially, the inductive approaches to the teaching of reading and writing produced average effect sizes of about 0.60 compared to treatments that covered the same material but without the inductive approaches to the teaching/learning process.

Researchers have conducted more narrowly defined studies on inductive teaching and inquiry training. Since Taba's (1966) exploration of an inductive social studies curriculum, periodic small-scale studies have probed the area. In 1968, Worthen provided evidence to support one of the central theses of inductive models of teaching—that induced concepts would facilitate long-term recall. Feeley

(1972) reviewed the social science studies and reported that differences in terminology hampered the accumulation of research but that the inductive methods generally lived up to expectations, generating concept development and positive attitudes. Research on R. Suchman's (1964) model for teaching causal reasoning directly supported the proposition that inquiry training can be employed with both elementary and high school children. Schrenker (1976) reported that inquiry training resulted in increased understanding of science, greater productivity in critical thinking, and improved skills for obtaining and analyzing information. He reported that it made little difference in the mastery of information, per se, but that it was as efficient as didactic methods or the didactic cum laboratory methods generally employed to teach science.

Ivany (1969) and Collins (1969) examined variants in the kinds of confrontations and materials used. They reported that the strength of the confrontation as a stimulus to inquiry was important and that richness in instructional materials was a significant factor. Elefant (1980) successfully carried out the strategy with deaf children in an intriguing study that has implications for work with all children. Voss's (1982) general review includes an annotation of a variety of studies that are generally supportive of the approach.

Inquiry into Cooperative Learning Models

Three lines of research describe ways of helping students study and learn together, one led by David and Roger Johnson at the University of Minnesota, a second by Robert Slavin at Johns Hopkins University, and the third by Shlomo and Yael Sharan and Rachel Hertz-Lazarowitz in Israel. Grasping the research is difficult because the term "cooperative learning" refers to a considerable variety of teaching strategies, and a large body of literature on the subject varies considerably in quality. Further, various forms of cooperative learning are designed to accomplish quite different objectives. A model teaching students how to solve conflicts will be tested in relation to that objective, whereas another model may approach academic learning directly.

The Johnsons and their colleagues (1975, 1999) studied the effects of cooperative task and reward structures on academic learning. Their work on peers teaching peers has provided information about the effects of cooperative behavior on both traditional learning tasks and the effects on values and intergroup behavior and attitudes (see Johnson & Johnson, 1975; Johnson, Maruyama, Johnson, Nelson, & Skon, 1981). Their models emphasize the development of what they call "positive interdependence," or cooperation where collective action also celebrates individual differences. Slavin's extensive 1983 review includes the study of a variety of approaches where he manipulates the complexity of the social tasks and experiments with various types of groupings. He reported success with heterogeneous groups using tasks requiring coordination of group members both on academic learning and intergroup relations—and has generated a variety of strategies that employ both extrinsic and intrinsic reward structures. The Israeli team concentrated on "group investigation," the most complex of the social models of teaching.

What is the magnitude of effects that we can expect when we learn to use the cooperative learning strategies effectively? Rolheiser-Bennett (1986) compared the effects of the degrees of cooperative structure required by the various approaches. On standardized tests in the basic curriculum areas (such as reading and mathematics) the highly structured approaches to teaching students to work together generated effect sizes of an average 0.28, with some studies approaching half a standard deviation. On criterion-referenced tests, the average was 0.48, with some of the best implementations reaching an effect of about one standard deviation. The more elaborate cooperative learning models generated an average effect size of somewhat more than one standard deviation, with some exceeding two standard deviations (the average student scoring above the 90th-percentile student in the control group). The effects on higher-order thinking were even greater, with an average effect of about 1.25 standard deviations and effects in some studies as high as three standard deviations.

Taken as a whole, research on cooperative learning is overwhelmingly positive—nearly every study has had from modest to very high effects (although some have had no effects on academic learning). The cooperative approaches are effective over a range of achievement measures. The more intensely cooperative the environment, the greater the effects. And the more complex the outcomes (higher-order processing of information, problem solving), the greater the effects.

The cooperative environment engendered by these models has had substantial effects on the cooperative behavior of the students, increasing feelings of empathy for others, reducing intergroup tensions and aggressive and antisocial behavior, improving moral judgment, and building positive feelings toward others, including those of other ethnic groups. Many of these effect sizes are substantial— one or two standard deviations is not uncommon, and one effect size is as high as eight. Hertz-Lazarowitz (1993) recently used one of the models to create integrative interaction between Israeli and Arab students in the West Bank! Margarita Calderon has worked with Lazarowitz and Jusefina Tinajero to adapt a cooperative integrated reading and composition program for bilingual students with some nice results (Calderon, Hertz-Lazarowitz, & Tinajero, 1991). An adaptation in higher education that organizes students into cooperative study groups reduced a dropout rate in engineering from 40 percent to about 5 percent (Bonsangue, 1993). Conflict resolution strategies have taught students to develop integrative behavior and reduced social tension in some divided environments in inner-city schools (Johnson & Johnson, 1999).

We can predict that the cooperative learning field is ready for a "shakeout" of some type, probably a clarification of the versions that most powerfully accomplish various kinds of learning tasks.

Interpretation

We believe there is a warrant under the models developed through these lines of inquiry (and a number of others not discussed here). Note, however, that because they appear to work, there is no guarantee that something else might work as well or better. They are not final solutions, and we hope further inquiry will generate more progress and these models will become historic or survive in barely recognizable form.

The question of why the models work is complex—too much so to deal with adequately here. Our working hypothesis is that the core of each of these models is their concentration on helping students develop effective modes of learning. For example, the research on mnemonics has yielded not just tools, such as the link-word method, but ways of helping students gain control over learning strategies through the development of metacognitive concepts by which students consciously examine learning problems and select strategies for solving them. Similarly, in the study of writing, it is possible that the superiority of the inquiry methods lies in the conceptual control developed by the students—the greater awareness of writing processes and how to choose among them. Recent neurological studies lead to the hypothesis that learning capacity can be enhanced and that the richer learning environments increase the probability that learning capacity will develop (see Sylwester, 1995, and, in relation to models of teaching, the review by Joyce, Calhoun, & Weil, 2000).

Whereas the traditional instructional model of recitation questions students about what they have learned on their own (including from "stand-and-deliver" forms of teaching), the processes developed by the researchers on scientific inquiry, mnemonics, and cooperative learning have yielded important insights about teaching the students to inquire. They empower the learner, not in the political sense, but in the cognitive sense. In the rare cases where tests of intelligence and problem-solving ability have been employed, there have been gains. More work is needed in this area. For now, let's put the student into the picture.

The Student in the Equation: Gender and Socioeconomic Factors

School officials in the United States worry terribly about individual differences. Teachers using the recitation method are driven nearly crazy because students simply will not all learn at the same rate, and the atomistic, bit-by-bit approach to subject matter that characterizes recitation teaching exacerbates differences. Many teachers and school officials regard individual differences as, at best, a challenge, and, at worst, as a near-impossible burden. Schools have developed a myriad plans for grouping students in an effort to narrow student variability in instructional settings. "Special" programs are developed to remove students from the "regular" classroom to give them special attention. Last year, we studied a large California school district where two-thirds of the students were in such programs. The "regular" classroom was becoming extinct in the effort to create homogenous settings! The futility of the effort was manifest in the fact that the "cure rate" of those special programs was almost zero.

Although it is well known that socioeconomic status is a phenomenal indicator of educational progress (e.g., Coleman et al., 1966) and special programs have been developed for the children of the economically poor, those programs have mostly failed (see McGill-Franzen & Goatley, 2001). But they are continued unchanged largely because it is difficult for society to entertain the idea that its normative method of teaching might be a part of the problem.

Some negative effects of schooling affect everyone. Most U.S. citizens who were fairly successful in school regard foreign languages as difficult to master, mathematics and science as both difficult and boring, and high-quality writing as the province of a rare few. High school graduates' limited knowledge of history and geography is disturbing. Curriculum and instruction get some of the blame, but television and the properties of adolescence get more of it.

Less well known are the gender differences in achievement or that each gender suffers in different ways. Estimates differ, but the official estimate from the National Assessment of Reading Progress is that three out of four kids with "reading problems" are males. On scores indicating quality of writing, average male scores at the 4th, 8th, and 12th grade are about at the 30th percentile of the female scores. On the other hand, female self-esteem in mathematics and science drops dramatically between 4th and 8th grade, despite the fact that gender differences in mathematics and science achievement are small. As a probable consequence of their loss of self-confidence many more females opt out of advanced courses.

Inevitably, we might ask whether those models of teaching that appear to be emerging from educational science empower students regardless of gender and socioeconomic status—or at least narrow the gaps.

Many of the smaller laboratory studies do not report disaggregated data by gender, but some do. Technically speaking, all should. The larger field studies are the most intriguing to us because the sociocultural press cannot be controlled. To reduce the effects of demography, the model must be strong enough to overcome influences of parents, the textures of neighborhood life, and such.

We'll examine just a few cases, present a theory, and suggest a line of inquiry.

Let's return to the work of Slavin et al. (1996) described in Chapter 2. They concentrated their efforts on inner-city schools populated by the economically poor and where neighborhood life can be chaotic and disturbing. In general, the kids in the Success for All schools are learning to read quite well. In addition, a larger percentage of boys is learning to read than is normal in suburban schools! In addition, referrals to special education have declined substantially; if students learn to read, they are much less likely to be diagnosed as learning disabled.

Similar results occurred in a Southeastern city where the teachers of a school district studied several inductive and concept-oriented models of teaching. In one middle school serving an economically poor, entirely black community, only 30 percent of the children earned promotion each of several years before the effort. Within two years over 90 percent earned promotion by passing the same tests and standards used in the prior years. In schools serving middle-class neighborhoods, achievement measured by standard tests rose substantially. Gender differences in achievement narrowed substantially as both genders appeared to prosper (Showers, Murphy, & Joyce, 1996).

In the University City study described in Chapter 2, where quality of writing increased as the teachers implemented inquiry-oriented models of learning, the gender differences narrowed as quality of writing improved for all students. The mean male score moved from the 30th to the 45th percentile of the female distribution.

In these and other studies where curricular and instructional models appear to reduce the effects of gender and socioeconomic status, the magnitude of acceleration of student learning has been considerable. A little detail will be useful in illustrating the point.

A group of secondary school teachers in Israel, led by Sharan and Shachar (1988), demonstrated the rapid acceleration in learning when they studied and first began to use the group investigation model, a very complex form of cooperative learning. They worked with classes in which the children of the poor (referred to as "Low SES" or lower socioeconomic status) were mixed with the children of middle-class parents (referred to as "High SES" or higher socioeconomic status). In a year-long social studies course, the teachers gave pretests of knowledge to the students as well as final examinations, so that they could measure gains in academic learning and compare them with students taught by the "whole class" format most common in Israeli schools. Figure 3.1 shows the results.

Several interesting comparisons emerge as you read the figure. First, the Lower SES students scored significantly lower than their Higher SES counterparts in the pretests. Typically, socioeconomic status is related to the knowledge students bring to the instructional situation, and these students were no exception. Then, the Lower SES students taught by group investigation achieved average gains nearly two and a half times those of the Lower SES students taught by the whole class method and exceeded the scores of the Higher SES students taught with the whole class method. In other words, the "socially disadvantaged" students taught with group investigation learned at rates above those of the "socially advantaged" students taught by teachers who did not have the group investigation repertoire. Finally, the "socially advantaged" students learned more also through group investigation. Their average gain was *twice* that of their whole class counterparts. Thus the model was effective by a large margin for students from both backgrounds.

FIGURE 3.1

Effects of Complex Cooperative Learning in a History Course, by SES

	Cooperative Learning (Treatment)		Whole Class Control	
	High SES	Low SES	High SES	Low SES
Pretest				
M	20.99	14.81	21.73	12.31
SD	9.20	7.20	10.53	7.05
Post-test				
M	62.60	50.17	42.78	27.03
SD	10.85	14.44	14.40	13.73
Mean Gain	41.61	35.36	21.05	14.92

Note: SES = Socioeconomic status.
Source: Information in chart described in S. Sharan and H. Shachar, *Language and Learning in the Cooperative Classroom.* New York: Springer-Verlag, 1988. See also Joyce, Wolf, and Calhoun (1993, p. 65) for a discussion of this study's findings on the gains of cooperative learning treatment.

We cannot draw an unshakeable conclusion from the literature, and many studies do not address either gender or socioeconomic status. But there appears to be a trend in the making. Although in normative U.S. schools gender and socioeconomic status are big factors in academic progress, those models that consistently accelerate rates of learning appear to reduce gender and SES as factors. Put another way, the models appear to help both sexes from both rich and poor families. Much more work needs to be done in this particular area, but it is important that this trend runs counter to some contemporary thought about individual differences. We question the wisdom of trying to develop models specifically tailored to gender characteristics, ethnicities, and socioeconomic groups because we believe that the most effective models accommodate and actually capitalize on individual differences rather than dividing students into categories and teaching them as separate from one another.

Future Inquiry

Unless one chooses to disbelieve in social science, education has a nascent knowledge base and, as the field studies demonstrate, one that is applicable to both the traditional and progressive missions of the school. The models that were discussed here have been effective across a wide variety of subject areas and student ages. The notion that effective teaching strategies inhere in subject matter does not hold up. Cooperative learning, inquiry-oriented teaching, counseling, and other models work across subject matters.

Partly because of its wide applicability, the knowledge base can enhance the substance of both preservice and inservice study. Some powerful tools are available for teachers and, through them, for students. The existence of those tools might give food for thought to designers of curricula and preservice and inservice programs. The well-researched models provide a standard against which to judge the quality of program content. We would hope that the teaching strategies embodied in curricula and taught in programs for teachers would be at least as powerful as these models seem to be.

Let's explore some notions that might lead to avenues for further inquiry as we try to expand the knowledge base.

- The culturally normative mode of teaching is much less efficient than other models we can devise and is tremendously subject to demographic factors.
- The models that will succeed will do so by teaching students more effective ways of constructing knowledge and building skills. The learner does the learning. Creating more powerful learners is the key to generating increases in staff development.
- As students learn more about how to learn, demographic factors will be greatly reduced as barriers to learning.
- We suspect that the most effective models find places to capitalize on individual differences in personal learning styles and cultural (ethnic) patterns.
- Intelligence is problem solving, of which learning is a major component. If we learn how to learn better and how to teach others to learn better, can intelligence be seen as a major feasible outcome for education?
- Instructional models are not independent of knowledge about academics (content of the curriculum). The use of instructional models is very much dependent on knowledge about subject matter. When one learns how to use a model of teaching, one studies the substance of the curriculum and the structure of the academic disciplines.

There are lifetimes of inquiry ahead of us.

. . . . . .

Part II

The Structure of Staff Development

In these chapters we study four interlocking dimensions of staff development design that results in student achievement. The selection of content (usually curriculum and instruction) is critical, and training needs to take advantage of knowledge about how we add to our professional repertoire. Studying our use of the content in classrooms—our implementation of new repertoire—makes our progress apparent. Evaluating our process and its effects on students enables us to celebrate our accomplishments and figure out how to do even better the next time around.

Choosing Content:
Teaching Students How to
Learn

Selecting the content of staff development is one of the most critical decisions in the school improvement process. If you are to attain your student achievement goals, the content of staff development needs to be aligned with those goals. And the content needs to be robust enough to effect the types of change envisioned. Even when context (norms for continuous growth, time for learning) and process (analysis of student data, design of training) variables have been carefully tended, the selection of inappropriate or ineffectual content can sabotage the sincere efforts of groups attempting to positively influence student learning.

Contributing to the critical nature of this decision is the collective nature of school improvement initiatives. Choosing content for a collaborative change effort is a crucial step in the process because, once it is selected as a district or school focus, many people are committed to learning and implementing the new content. An individual can fairly easily change course in midstream if the content chosen is not addressing an identified need, but an entire staff abandoning a change effort can be both costly and damaging. We emphasize using the knowledge base on curriculum and instruction as a major source of content to maximize the probability that the content will pay off.

Before addressing the "what" and "how" of selecting staff development content, we'll briefly discuss the "who"—who will select the content for collective study when groups of educators share a common goal.

Who Decides the Content of Staff Development?

We have previously discussed in detail the building of a broadly representative and collaborative process for making decisions about staff development and will only briefly reprise it here.

Staff development councils need to be established at both the school and district levels. School-level councils include a representative sample of teachers, as well as the school principal; district-level councils include a representative sample of teachers and principals from the district, as well as central office staff and, in some cases, board members. In large districts, forming councils from clusters of schools is generally more practical than forming a huge council that represents a hundred or more schools. However, cluster councils need to be empowered in both the organizational and budgetary senses at the central office level of even the largest districts.

An important duty of the school or district staff development committee is to engage in the study of alternatives—the kinds of initiatives we discussed in Chapters 2 and 3—and bring information to school councils about options that appear to align with their identified needs. Final decisions about staff development content require several rounds of information gathering and negotiation, as alternatives are examined for fit with school or district achievement goals, providers are identified, costs and time requirements are determined, and the data-gathering requirements are considered. Informed decision making will be critical, for people can scarcely select options unless they know about them. Even now, many teachers, schools, and school districts are not studying alternatives that would have great promise for them simply because the information about those alternatives has not been made available during the decision-making process.

Identifying Needs for Staff Development Content

The major difference between selecting content for individuals and a schoolwide or collective effort is a heavier reliance on shared data for decision making. Also, the distinction between individuals and school needs to be clear. In the past, we have observed districts where resources have been provided to schools but used as if individual preferences were the key, generating opportunities for individuals as volunteers, rather than common direction with a commitment by all.

Content selection is dictated by the need for change that a faculty perceives. The targets for change or improvement vary tremendously among schools, depending on the process a faculty employs to identify needs and set priorities for addressing those needs. Generally, faculties use a combination of perceptions ("What do we feel are our most pressing needs?") and data ("What do our test scores tell us?") to select targets for improvement. If the process results in a list of needs in which all items have equal weight, the list may grow to 15 or 20 items and include everything from reading and math achievement to parent involvement and neighborhood gang activity. If the faculty then proceeds to select content or "treatments" to address all identified needs, the resulting plethora of change programs makes it virtually impossible to mount a coherent, facultywide approach to any single problem. A faculty is much better positioned to change something if it can focus on a top priority in a way that simultaneously acknowledges both the presence and importance of everything on the list and the near impossibility of addressing all of them effectively at one time.

In our experience, the selection of content to address identified needs frequently receives much less attention than other parts of the school improvement process. Perhaps faculties, with limited time for collaborative planning and decision making, inadvertently use most of their time in reaching a decision about what needs to be addressed and have little time left to examine their options for approaching the needs. Or perhaps, by this time in the process, people are tired of talking and eager to begin doing something.

Beliefs immediately come into play when staffs begin the process of collecting data to determine needed improvements or changes in a school's educational program. Faculties' beliefs and theories about the cause of perceived problems direct both the data collection and analysis, as well as the eventual selection of content to address problems.

Let's suppose that state reading tests at George Washington Elementary School show the mean to be below the 20th percentile of all of the state's students. Faculty concern for poor reading test performance is fueled by perceived pressure from the community and state to improve test scores. Faculty feel their competence and effectiveness are judged by these scores, and while they acknowledge that their students are reading at levels far below what they would like, they believe that the test unfairly penalizes schools with their particular demographic characteristics. The staff of George Washington elect to collect no further data at the site before choosing a program to address the identified need. The need, however, is identified as "reading test scores" rather than "reading." Consequently, the content selected is an individualized computer program in which each child spends a specified time weekly on specific skills presented and tested in the state test format. The computer lab is operated by an instructional aide who carefully keeps track of each child's progress through the battery of mini tests until he or she successfully completes and masters all the skills components of the program. Meanwhile, reading instruction in the classroom proceeds unchanged.

In the same district, Barbara Jordan Elementary School also scores poorly on the state reading tests. The faculty likewise feels community and district pressure to improve test scores but believes that, while their students certainly entered school with little reading readiness, good readers will perform well on the state reading test (or on any reading test, for that matter). Their beliefs lead them to identify their problem as "reading" rather than "test taking skills" or "test content," which leads them to seek additional information about their students' reading behavior. Individualized reading tests administered to a sample of students provide considerable diagnostic information. A study of successful programs yields useful information about processes that appear to help beginning readers become independent readers. The faculty studies recommendations about the amount of independent reading students should be doing out of school. As a result of their additional data collection and study of options, this faculty adopts content for their staff development program that includes: (1) instruction in the teaching of reading for all teachers, (2) training of tutors for an after-school program, and (3) adoption of a program to increase out-of-school reading.

In another district, secondary schools are asked to collect data on their failure rates and discipline referrals in an effort to stem the tide of dropouts. All secondary schools collect the data requested (actually, schools already had data on both discipline referrals and grade distributions but had not analyzed it as a source of information for determining directions for school improvement). Data on failure rates, discipline referrals, and dropout rates are similar for all secondary schools in the district (e.g., all had high rates of failure, discipline problems, and dropouts). Depending on each school's interpretation of these data, however, the identified needs vary dramatically. One school writes a grant proposal requesting funds for additional security apparatus and personnel; its identified problem is high crime in the surrounding neighborhood. A second school embarks upon a parent involvement program that entails notifying parents immediately if students are absent or tardy. A third school adopts a cooperative instructional strategy, reasoning that classroom practices that both decreased the isolation and pressure and increased their chances for success in the classroom would reduce discipline referrals.

Clearly, faculties can draw quite disparate conclusions from similar data about the causes of identified problems, and these collective attributions dictate the "content" that will be selected to address identified needs.

These examples illustrate some of the complexity schools face when determining content appropriate for their identified needs. Selecting content for school improvement initiatives is not a simple process of matching problems with solutions. Rather, it is a complex dynamic in which the school culture filters, or interprets, data through its norms, values, beliefs, and theories to define problems and attribute causation. Thus it determines the types of content that might appropriately address the problems as understood and agreed upon by a staff.

Examine the Options for Content

Teachers have various explanations for the source of problems— hypotheses about what causes any given problem. Our recommendations for selecting content begin with the proposal that staffs surface competing hypotheses regarding causation for identified problems (and thus alternative solutions). If a staff identifies its primary problem as "discipline" without exploring the actual occurrences of student misbehavior and possible causes for it, the choice of interventions will necessarily be narrowed.

Once data at the site have been examined, and needs identified and discussed, the search for appropriate content can begin. Again, the search for content is somewhat more heavily reliant on "objective" sources of data than when selecting content for individual needs. If an entire staff is to expend time and energy in a collective effort to address a school need, it should have some confidence that the content selected has a fairly high probability of accomplishing its objective. The district committee can serve as a resource to the school committee as they search for content and providers that align with their specific needs.

In some cases, the district committee is able to coordinate efforts among schools that have similar needs for training. The proximal principle should guide the process at this point, that is, content should be directly relevant to stated goals for change. Thus, if a school's goal is to improve the quality of student writing, its staff development content should provide opportunities to learn about the teaching and assessment of writing. Focusing on building better school-community relations in the hope of improving student achievement in academic areas is a low-probability option. (See Schmoker, 1996, for a discussion of the importance of aiming directly at the desired change.)

We have observed some of the options that follow.

Renewal Within a Curriculum Area

In elementary schools, the generalist teacher provides most of the instruction in the basic areas, and it can be argued that some area should always be in a process of renewal. Reading, language arts and literature, social studies, science, arithmetic, and the other areas are candidates. Generally, the curriculum areas are not in equally good shape; and it is not difficult to find one that could bear improvement. In secondary schools, grade levels are often convenient foci. For example, in one year, freshman courses might be considered; in another, advanced placement courses; in another, the grade-level designations of courses (articulation) within a subject. Cross-subject strategies are also feasible. Reading and writing in the content areas has been a popular staff development focus for some faculties.

Teaching and Learning Strategies

A faculty can take a strategy, such as cooperative learning, mnemonics, or one of the other models discussed in Chapter 3, and learn to use it schoolwide. Some faculties are currently studying ways of teaching every subject in such a way that the thinking ability of the students is improved (Perkins, 1984). It is feasible for teachers to add one or two strategies to their repertoire in any given year. The possibilities are great enough to provide food for instructional improvement for many years.

Technology

The use of computers, as well as videotape, broadcast television, and the Internet, are applications of technology to instruction. Some schools have positively affected their instructional programs by incorporating resource-based instruction for their students, thus enabling the study of topics and courses that cannot be offered by the faculty. In small high schools, for example, the number of offerings is necessarily limited, and resource-based courses provide many additional opportunities.

Attending to Special Populations

Population-oriented initiatives for school improvement have become popular in recent years as the states and the federal government have provided resources for students with special needs (generally known as "special" education), students of varying cultural backgrounds, students with special gifts and talents, bilingual students, and so on. Most of these initiatives are difficult to implement properly. "Pullout" programs, in which students are removed from "regular" class for special attention, have been particularly unsatisfactory, because they disrupt continuity and often generate fragmented programs for the students in question. Many of these programs need attention.

Narrowing the Focus

The school council needs to lead the faculty to narrow the list of possibilities and to select the one or two areas that will receive attention during any given year. The faculty *must* narrow the focus of school improvement. The tendency is to get too many projects going at once, with the result that none get done well.

Strangely, thinking of content simultaneously rather than sequentially can sometimes serve to narrow the options perceived to address a school's needs. For example, a school identifies its primary goal as improving the level of student literacy, but secondary goals identify a need for increased faculty cooperation in developing curriculum. The content selected for the staff development program will center on literacy, but the design of training will incorporate peer coaching teams such that teachers regularly collaborate to develop their literacy curriculum even as they integrate new learning about the teaching of literacy.

Simultaneous content can function when goals are carefully prioritized. An unexpected consequence in the sequential process of selecting content is becoming mired in what Schmoker (1996) calls "perpetual preparation," the condition in which schools can spend years in planning, building a positive school culture, and other activities that actually postpone addressing the identified problem.

Identifying Potential Providers

Each school forwards its candidates for improvement efforts to the district committee, which then has the task of trying to find staff development support for the initiatives. Perhaps teachers from some of the schools can obtain training that they can bring back to their faculties. Or maybe the district cadre needs to consider some of the suggested areas. The committee also needs to assess costs and decide how much assistance can be given to particular schools. The eventual decisions need to be a result of negotiation.

This procedure centers on identifying potential providers of service—teaching and administrative personnel and persons from local universities, teacher centers, intermediate agencies, and professional organizations. The district committee asks if they are prepared to offer service to others and what it might be. It asks personnel to recommend others who might offer service. The committee asks university departments, not only in education but in academic areas, if they would like to provide service. Finally, it asks school councils to canvass their personnel and approaches the other agencies and departments in the district for their ideas.

Once providers have been identified, an additional negotiation is needed before the content decision can be finalized. A potential provider and the school faculty need to discuss specifics of the projected staff development. Most providers have preferred ways of working with schools, and schools also have expectations that should be made explicit before final arrangements are made. The provider needs to probe faculty members about their desires for increased student learning and in what content areas, to understand competing initiatives currently vying for faculty time and energy, and to determine if what he or she has to offer is actually a match with the school's agenda. The school needs to learn how the provider intends to proceed and, if necessary, to negotiate modifications before any contracts are signed. It is far better to discover during preliminary negotiations that a specific provider and a school's goals for increased student learning do not mesh—rather than months into an initiative when the work of an entire faculty can be derailed by misunderstandings.

District-Selected Content

Most districts are not organized to accompany staff development with systemwide initiatives in curriculum, instruction, or technology to ensure a healthy implementation (Crandall et al., 1982; Fullan & Park, 1981; Fullan & Pomfret, 1977; Hall, 1986; Joyce, Calhoun, & Hopkins, 1999; Huberman & Miles, 1984). For example, even though district committees can produce great curriculum guides and order and deliver textbooks and other materials to classrooms, implementation—including the use of new textbooks, in many cases—often doesn't occur because the staff development component has not been extensive enough.

There are two reasons for this state of affairs. The first is that educators have simply not understood the amounts and types of study that are necessary for people to learn how to employ new procedures—and often new content—in the classroom. The second is that many educators find it difficult to make the hard decisions to narrow the district focus in any given period. Ideas for school improvement abound, and many districts have a dozen initiatives going at the same time, none of them supported substantially enough for a systemic implementation. Coordination is a problem. We have observed all too many districts where a large number of departments or other organizational units generate initiatives without the knowledge that groups on the other side of town—or the far side of the building—are generating similar ones. Thus the curriculum units; departments of elementary, secondary, and special education; staff development offices; departments serving the gifted and talented; and many others generate initiatives and communicate them to schools and teachers willy-nilly.

The answer we propose is to replicate the process we have described for identifying the focus of school-based initiatives but with the purpose of identifying one or two important initiatives that will have center stage in the district for a year or two (as in the case examples in Chapter 2). Teachers, study groups, schools, and committee members need to put forth their wish lists of initiatives. Lists need to be developed and culled. The committee needs to ask whether the district has unfinished business with past initiatives or has committed to expenditures for facilities and equipment that will not be used well without staff development. Have videocameras and players been purchased for schools? How is the computer initiative doing? Have additions been made to the library, or has it acquired access to electronic libraries or become stocked with self-instructional programs? It is even possible that the district initiative for a given year will be the same as that selected by one or more schools in the district.

The list we generated when thinking about the possibilities for schools can serve the same purpose when thinking about the district. Curriculum, technology, and teaching skills and strategies can all become a focus in the larger organization.

It is within the schools, however, that the district initiatives will be implemented, so communication is essential during the decision-making and planning process. For example, if a teaching strategy like cooperative learning is a district focus, the result will be training for a large number of people in many sites and much hard work in every school to implement the strategy. Or if school social climate becomes the focus, than all school faculties will have to learn to examine their social climates and make plans for improvements. It may be that many districts would be wise to plan their initiatives no less than a year in advance so that they can develop the strong cadres necessary to support the training.

○ ○ ○

The selection of content for staff development programs is a critical decision, especially at the school and district levels where student-achievement concerns drive the decisions for groups of professionals. Representative councils of teachers and administrators need to engage in a reasoned process before selecting content, studying alternatives, and aligning new initiatives with district or school goals. Schools may be better served by thinking about prioritized goals, selecting content that aligns with their primary goal, and embedding secondary goals within the staff development process. A necessary part of the process is identifying staff developers equipped to provide the desired service and negotiating with those providers clear understandings about the content and processes of the proposed staff development. Individuals will be evaluating personal needs, whereas schools and districts will determine needs for groups of students. Adequate training will be the key to the success of all three components. Hence let us turn our attention, in the next chapter, to the design of training and to the research that now enables us to plan staff development programs that have a high probability of succeeding.

5 Designing Training and Peer Coaching: Our Needs for Learning

In the early 1980s, we published a review of research on training design and a set of hypotheses relating to transfer of new learning to classroom practice (Joyce & Showers, 1980). In the 20 years since, two notable changes have occurred in the field of staff development. First, the duration and intensity of many training events have greatly increased, including various forms of follow-up and continuing technical support; and second, one-shot events tend to be carefully prefaced with, "This session is for awareness only." In other words, we've achieved greater clarity between objectives that entail the acquisition of information and those that include changes in educational practice.

Gradually, we have made substantial changes in our framework for thinking about staff development in the years since this book first appeared. We've been influenced by the work of organizational and change theorists (Fullan, 1990, 2001; Huberman, 1992; Miles, 1992; Seashore-Louis & Miles, 1990). Our own numerous attempts to work with districts, schools, teams of teachers, and individuals to increase student growth in all its manifestations have ripened some of our concepts and altered others. The school/school district complex is clearer to us. The learning environment that students experience is located in schools. The school is the organizational unit where curricular and instructional changes take place, and the challenge is for them to become self-renewing organizations where the faculties continually seek to improve the educational environment. The school district greatly affects what will happen in the school. The district creates the overall structure for staff development (including provisions for time), helps schools locate promising options, and generates initiatives across curriculum areas that schools cannot mount by themselves.

We have also continued to refine a training design that enables teachers to learn and use new knowledge and behaviors that translate into success for more students. Our collaborations with many gifted teachers have been invaluable in this pursuit as we have studied and experimented together to make training more productive. We have also evolved in our thinking about the role and function of collaboration in the service of school improvement. At this point, training and peer coaching have become so inseparable in our minds and our practice that we have treated them together in a single chapter in this edition.

Providing the Conditions for Learning

Our first goal is to design training that enables people to learn knowledge and skills new to them and to transfer that knowledge and skill to active classroom practice—and thus identify principles for designing programs that will result in a high level of skill and its implementation. Our second goal is to search for ways of conducting training that increases the aptitude of faculties to learn skills more easily and effectively. In other words, we want to design training that allows people to learn to be more effective learners. This chapter is oriented around those two goals. During the discussion we will often use effect sizes (standard deviation units) to make comparisons between treatments more clear.

Training Design

Design involves identifying types of outcomes or content to be pursued and selecting training components or strategies likely to bring about success in achieving those outcomes. Let's first look at outcomes, then at the available components of training, and finally at the relationship between types of outcomes and combinations of components.

What do we expect good training to accomplish? Aside from the content—academic knowledge, approaches to curriculum and instruction, how students develop and learn, use of technologies, and so forth—what is the nature of the behaviors necessary to put that content into work in the classroom? Let's begin with the categories of behavior—the kinds of things we need to learn to make a particular initiative in curriculum and instruction come alive in the workplace. We see these categories as types of outcomes as a staff development strand evolves (as in the cases described in Chapter 2 and the models of curriculum and instruction discussed in Chapter 3).

Types of Outcomes

Potential outcomes are as follows:

● Knowledge or awareness of educational theories and practices, new curricula, or academic content. The outcome has been fulfilled when the knowledge (or awareness) has been achieved.

● Positive changes in attitudes toward self (role perception changes), children (minorities, handicapped, gifted), and academic content (science, English as a second language, math). The outcome has been accomplished when we have greater understanding of our attitudes, greater empathy toward particular groups, and better understanding of curriculum areas.

● Development of skill (the ability to perform discrete behaviors, such as designing and delivering questions of various cognitive levels, or the ability to perform clusters of skills in specific patterns, as in a synectics exercise). When we can produce these behaviors, the outcome has been achieved.

● Transfer of training and "executive control" (the level of knowledge that generates consistent and appropriate use of new skills and strategies for classroom instruction). This type of outcome is achieved when we can implement a new curricular or instructional procedure and study the effects on student learning. We want to emphasize: *This is the place where the interface between staff development and student achievement exists. The learning environment of the students changes, and those changes are of a quality and amount that enable increased learning to take place.*

The outcomes differ in their relationship to the repertoire of teaching strategies and skills we possess and also in their complexity.

Relation to Existing Repertoire. Are the outcomes within or adjacent to our existing repertoire or are they additions to our regular practice? This is an important question because learning things that are close to our regular practice is much easier than learning new repertoire. For example, the use of particular concrete aids or manipulatives in mathematics may be a desired outcome of a series of workshops. Achieving that objective is much easier for someone who comes to the workshop with a history of regular use of concrete materials than for someone for whom such practice is new.

Complexity. There is no hard-and-fast rule for what is complex, but certainly some repertoire is made up of relatively simple skills that fit easily into the flow of classroom activities. Examples abound in the field of cooperative learning. Asking students to "confer with their partner" and make sure that they understand a set of directions is relatively simple. Asking those same students to cooperate in the development and testing of hypotheses, however, involves integrating a new set of skills.

	Content			
	Redefining of Existing Knowledge and Skills		**Addition to Repertoire**	
Training Outcomes	**Simple**	**Complex**	**Simple**	**Complex**
Awareness/Knowledge: Theories, Practices, Curricula				
Attitude Change: Self, Children, Academic Content				
Skill Development: Discrete Behaviors, Strategies				
Transfer of Training: Consistent Use, Appropriate Use				

FIGURE 5.1
Decision-Making Matrix: Selecting Objectives

The left side of the matrix defines characteristics of the content. If the substance is knowledge and skill that teachers generally possess but that need refinement for optimal classroom use, decision makers will work in the top left sector of the matrix. For example, training that focuses on teacher praise and encouragement of student work, or even the amount of "wait time" allowed students to respond to questions, would be classified as "refining of existing skill." Presumably, teachers already provide verbal encouragement to students for their efforts and ask questions during classroom recitations. The object of training becomes a more appropriate use of existing behaviors.

If, on the other hand, the content represents an addition to teachers' repertoire, the right half of the matrix is used. Obviously, "new repertoire" must be defined in relation to the knowledge and skills of individuals—what is new to one person may exist in the repertoire of another.

Research on classroom teaching, however, has fairly well described how most teachers teach. We can be fairly certain that few teachers use the curricular and instructional models described in Chapter 3, for example, the more complex varieties of cooperative learning and group investigation, key-word and link-word memory strategies, synectics, and inductive thinking. (e.g., Good, Grouws, & Ebmeier, 1983; Goodlad & Klein, 1970; Medley, 1977; Sirotnik, 1983). On the other hand, most teachers praise students, correct them, orient them to lessons, and provide practice in class and as homework. Therefore, training that concentrates on those practices is for most teachers an elaboration and strengthening of existing practices.

In addition to deciding whether content will be a refining of existing knowledge and skill or an addition to repertoire, designers should also estimate the difficulty level of knowledge and skills to be learned. Placing content on a simple-to-complex continuum will clarify later decisions about the intensity and duration of training experiences.

Given the objectives of any element of a program, the next task is to design training that is highly likely to achieve the desired effects.

Training Components

Several elements are at our disposal. The first component focuses on *knowledge* and consists of exploration of *theory* or *rationale* through discussions, readings, and lectures; this is necessary for an understanding of the concepts behind a skill or strategy and the principles that govern its use. Study of theory facilitates skill acquisition by increasing one's understanding of demonstrations, by providing a mental image to guide practice and clarify feedback, and by promoting the attainment of executive control.

The *demonstration* or *modeling* of skill is the second component; it greatly facilitates learning. Skills can be demonstrated in settings that simulate the workplace, mediated through film or videotape, or conducted live in the training setting. Demonstrations can be mixed with explanation; the theory and modeling components need not be conducted separately. In fact, they have reciprocal effects. Mastery of the rationale of the skill facilitates discrimination, and modeling facilitates the understanding of underlying theories by illustrating them in action.

The third component is the *practice* of skill under simulated conditions. The more closely the training setting approximates the workplace, the more transfer is facilitated. Considerable amounts of skill can be developed, however, in settings far removed from and different from the workplace. "Peer teaching" (practice with other teachers) even has advantages. It provides experience as a "student," enables trainees to profit from one another's ideas and skills, and brings mistakes to the surface. Peer teaching sessions, as well as practice with small groups of children, are safer settings for exploration than a full classroom of real students. How much practice is needed depends, of course, on the complexity of the skill. To bring a teaching model of medium complexity under control requires 20 or 25 trials in the classroom over a period of about 8–10 weeks. Simpler skills, or those more similar to previously developed ones, will require less practice to develop and consolidate than those that are more complex or different from the teacher's current repertoire.

Peer coaching, the fourth component, is the collaborative work of teachers to solve the problems or questions that arise during implementation. It begins during training and continues in the workplace. Peer coaching provides support for the community of teachers attempting to master new skills and to plan and develop lessons. This planning time is essential to changes in curriculum and instruction.

Logically, we can theorize that where awareness or knowledge is the desired outcome, the simpler the content, and the more it is adjacent to repertoire, the more one can rely on presentations, discussions, and the occasional demonstration. But the more transfer is desired and the more complex and newer the content, the more all the training components will have to be employed. Let's see whether research on staff development confirms that supposition.

Research on Training

Before looking at the research, let's look at the general context within which staff development is designed. As described in previous chapters, a process must be in place to decide the substance of the training, who will provide it, when and where it will be held, and for what duration. The norms of the workplace impinge on the receptivity of participants to various configurations of training experiences, as do labor-relations histories and interpersonal relationships among participants. We have less data on the effect of many of these environmental and governance variables on training effectiveness than we have on actual training components. However, we recommend participatory governance modes to increase understanding of both the content and reasons for selecting it.

Cohesiveness and strong school leadership are critical to the success of training. The best trainers, working with the most relevant and powerful content, will find little success or receptivity in poor organizational climates. However, good climates and high motivation will not substitute for well-designed training. Fortunately, research and experience have reached the point where we can state that for specific training outcomes certain training components or combinations of components provide optimal conditions for learning. Nearly all teachers can master a very wide range of teaching skills and strategies provided that the training is well designed (outcomes and components are well matched) and the school climate facilitates and promotes cooperative study and practice.

Hence, training designers must answer several questions before planning any training experience. For whom is the training intended and what is expected to result from the training? Is follow-up built into schools as a permanent structure or must follow-up be planned and delivered during training? Does the training content represent new learning or is it an attempt to refine existing knowledge and skills?

Also, designers need to decide which training components will be used and how they will be combined, including the presentation of information or theory about the topic, live and mediated demonstration or modeling of new skills and teaching models, and opportunities for practice of new skills and strategies in the training setting, as well as in the workplace. Peer coaching of new skills and strategies, which largely occurs in the workplace, ideally is taught and practiced in the training setting as well, unless its use is routine in the school or district.

Research on training provides some interesting insights into the efficacy of various training components and, particularly, combinations of them (Bennett, 1987; Showers, Joyce, & Bennett, 1987).

First, let's look at knowledge as an outcome and the effects of various components on acquisition of knowledge.

Information or theory-only treatments (lectures, discussions, readings) increase knowledge by an effect size of about 0.50 (one-half of a standard deviation on a normal curve). In other words, where tests of particular knowledge were given before and after the informational treatments, the mean following the workshop was about at the 67th percentile of the distribution on the pretests.

When the informational component is combined with demonstrations, practice, and feedback during practice, the effect size averages 1.31. The post-test means were close to the 90th percentile of the distribution of scores on the pretests.

The importance here is that when knowledge is an objective, the use of demonstrations and practice increases knowledge considerably over information-giving treatments alone (Bennett, 1987). The increase in understanding is so large when demonstration and practice are incorporated that, even when knowledge is the primary objective, presentation-only treatments should be avoided in most settings. The multidimensional approach is much more effective. We have found that many staff development organizers where knowledge of, for example, special needs students is the objective, will design presentation-only events or even presentation-with-reading-and-discussion treatments and have much less effect than had other components been included.

Now let's consider skill from the same perspective.

The advantage of the combinations is equally clear when skill is the desired outcome of training. In most studies, skill is measured by asking participants to exhibit those skills during simulations in the workshop settings. Theory or demonstration alone results in effect sizes for skill of around 0.5 of a standard deviation for refining existing skills and even lower for new skills. When demonstrations and practice are added, the effect size rises to about 1.18 in the average study. When coaching is added to the theory, demonstration, and practice treatment, skill continues to rise.

What about transfer into the classroom?

Traditionally the question of transfer of training has been asked much less frequently in research on staff development than has the question of skill acquisition. Consequently, fewer studies of training have measured transfer effects than have measured skill acquisition, and transfer is vital to the changes in the learning environment that can affect student learning. Perhaps the assumption has been that skill, once developed, would automatically be used in classroom instruction. Recent analyses of the literature on training confirm what many trainers, teacher educators, and supervisors have long suspected—transfer of learned knowledge and skill is by no means a sure bet. Several findings emerge in studies that have asked the transfer question (e.g., Did participants use new skills in the classroom, did they use them appropriately, did they integrate new skills with existing repertoire, was there long-term retention of the products of training?).

First, the gradual addition of the informational, demonstration, and practice training elements does not appear to noticeably affect transfer (effect size of 0.00 for information or theory; theory plus demonstration; and theory, demonstration, and feedback).

In other words, transfer to the workplace is minimal for what would often be considered a high-powered series of training sessions where presentations and discussions, demonstrations, and practice sessions are included and various degrees of skill development are ascertained.

However—and this is an important finding—a large and dramatic increase in transfer of training—effect size of 1.42—occurs when coaching is added to an initial training experience comprised of theory explanation, demonstrations, and practice. In our own work with the Second Chance program (described in Chapter 2), we expect that 90 percent or more of the participants will reach a good level of skill if training includes theory presentation, demonstration, and practice—and the workplace enables regular peer coaching to take place.

We have concluded from these data that teachers can acquire new knowledge and skill and use it in their instructional practice when provided with adequate opportunities to learn. We have hypothesized further that effective training systems develop a "learning to learn" aptitude; that, in fact, individuals learn more efficiently over the long term by developing the metacognitions that enable self-teaching in settings where essential training elements are missing.

We've derived a few principles from the combination of research and experience:

● Where knowledge is the desired outcome, a multiple component design gives the best results.

● Where skill is an objective, a multiple component design gives the best effects.

● Where transfer to the classroom is the objective, the full array is needed—theory, demonstration, practice, and peer coaching. (Coaching by trainers will give the same effects, but is not practical in most settings.)

When student learning is desired, transfer is necessary. And that means both organizing the peer coaching process and developing the multidimensional training that provides skills that can be transferred into instructional settings in the form of changes in student learning environments.

Staff development design that increases student learning must include curricular training content and instructional models that change the learning environment sufficiently to allow students to learn more. (A fine curriculum that is at the same level as the existing one will probably not increase student learning much when it is implemented.) Then the design needs to ensure the development of knowledge and skill. And the workplace needs to change so that peer coaching can take place.

By extrapolating from the research and making judgments from our experience, we can depict the relationship between types of training outcomes (knowledge, skill, transfer) in terms of the percentage of participants likely to attain them when the combinations of components are employed (see Figure 5.2). Note that these estimates are very rough, but they give rules of thumb for estimating the product of training.

FIGURE 5.2

Training Components and Attainment of Outcomes in Terms of Percent of Participants

	Outcomes		
Components	**Knowledge (thorough)**	**Skill (strong)**	**Transfer (executive implementation)**
Study of Theory	10	5	0
Demonstrations	30	20	0
Practice	60	60	5
Peer Coaching	95	95	95

By attainment we mean a real and strong transfer—solid knowledge, good skills, consistent implementation. We also assume a new and fairly complex repertoire.

Notice how knowledge and skill continue to improve as components are added and continue to grow as implementation occurs (extensive practice in the workplace). But that implementation depends both on the development of knowledge and skill and the companionship provided by peers as the new knowledge and skills are used to change the students' learning environment and as the effects on those students are studied.

To reiterate, the content must be good. In one of our recent studies of a large state's staff development offerings, we estimated that only about 5 percent of the offerings were curricular, instructional, or social climate models different enough from common practice that student effects could be expected, even if they were implemented beautifully (Joyce & Belitzky, 1999).

Skills Teachers Need, as Learners, to Master New Knowledge and Skills

As research on effective teaching yields more data, it becomes increasingly urgent that teachers be able to use the products of that research. Designing training that maximizes opportunities for mastery of new information and skills is an important task. Are there learning-to-learn skills that some teachers develop in or bring to the training setting, and if so, can they be developed in others? And what do we know about conditions that nurture and develop learning-to-learn skills?

Ripple and Drinkwater (1982), in their review of research on transfer of learning, noted the following about learning to learn:

> The concept of learning-to-learn implies the development of strategies or learning sets as a result of such experience (practice with a variety of problems). Preliminary practice on tasks that will transfer positively to performance on different criterion tasks is required for the development of learning to learn strategies. (p. 1949)

From research on training and curriculum implementation, school improvement and change, and our personal training experiences, we have identified several practices, attitudes, and skills that appear to facilitate learning aptitude.

Persistence

Practice of new skills and behaviors increases both skill and comfort with the unfamiliar. The benefits of practice are well known to educators and are often reiterated in training settings. Yet many trainees try a new skill or practice only once or else never try it at all. In learning a new skill, pushing oneself through the awkward first trials is essential. In initial trials (when performance is awkward and effectiveness appears to decrease rather than increase), "driving through," or persistence, seems to differentiate successful from unsuccessful learners. Avoidance of the difficult and awkward is not unique to teachers—or to golfers, skiers, and tennis players, for that matter. Changing one's own behavior is difficult, especially when one has fairly dependable strategies already fully developed.

Acknowledgment of the Transfer Problem

Mastery of new skills, especially when they differ substantially from existing skills, is rarely sufficient for implementation in classroom practice. Introducing a new procedure or teaching strategy into an existing repertoire of instructional behaviors generally creates dislocation and discomfort. Yet, considerable practice of new behaviors is required if teachers are not only to become technically proficient with them but also to integrate them sensibly and appropriately with existing behaviors. Teachers who understand the need for and expend the extra effort to identify where the new behaviors fit and how they can be effective are much more likely to implement an innovation. Understanding that transfer of training is a separate learning task is a metacognitive condition that appears to increase efficiency in skill acquisition, as well as eventual transfer of learning. Both trainers and teachers tend to underestimate the cognitive aspects of implementation—teachers have assumed they have only to see something to use it skillfully and appropriately, and trainers have devoted little or no time during training to attacking the transfer problem.

Teaching New Behaviors to Students

Part of the difficulty in introducing new curricula or teaching processes into the classroom is student discomfort with change. Students quickly learn the rules of the classroom game and how to respond to the demands of the learning environment. Those who are successful with existing conditions may be particularly reluctant to have the rules changed. When new procedures are introduced, students may exert pressure on the teacher to return to the familiar patterns of behavior with which they are comfortable, or at least which they understand well. Consequently, a teacher who typically runs a brisk recitation followed by rapid-fire recall questions has students who have learned how to signal they know the answers, how to avoid being called on when they don't know the answers, and what to expect in terms of feedback (e.g., the message that there is a "right" answer).

If this teacher then introduces an inquiry process in which knowledge is viewed as emergent and tentative and which shifts responsibility to students, student discomfort with the new demands may encourage the teacher to abandon the new strategy after one or two trials. When this happens, neither teacher nor students develop sufficient expertise with the new strategy to evaluate potential benefits and uses.

Teachers who directly teach the requisite skills to students, including both the cognitive and social tasks required by specific innovations, are much more likely to integrate successfully the new behaviors with existing instructional repertoire.

Meeting the Cognitive Demands of Innovations

Teachers frequently have complained that their training has over-emphasized "theory" and neglected the practical aspects of teaching. It is probable, however, that without a thorough grounding in the theory of an innovation, or what Fullan (1990) calls "deep understanding," teachers will be unable to use new skills and strategies in any but the most superficial manner. Understanding of the theory underlying specific behaviors enables flexible and appropriate use of the behaviors in multiple situations and prevents the often ludicrous following of "recipes" for teaching. Thus, a teacher who wishes to organize presentations or entire courses with advance organizers must understand the conceptual framework of the material to be so organized and be able to extract and organize concepts into a hierarchy of ideas. The teacher who wishes to apply the link-word method to the acquisition of foreign language vocabulary must understand the research from cognitive psychology regarding the role of association in memory. And the teacher who wishes to implement a contingency management system must completely understand the nature of reinforcers and how they operate.

Teachers who master the theory underlying new behaviors will implement those behaviors in greater congruence with the researched and tested ideal and are more likely to replicate results obtained in research settings with their own students.

Productive Use of Peers

During the past few years, research on training has documented the benefits of peers helping peers in the implementation of innovations. Regular, structured interaction between or among peers over substantive content is one of the hallmarks of a profession and is viewed by other professionals as essential professional nourishment rather than a threat to autonomy. A family dentist does not hesitate to consult a root canal specialist in the midst of an examination if he or she feels the need for consultation, nor does a hairdresser feel constrained in getting a second opinion regarding the type of permanent needed for a particular head of hair. This propensity to seek the advice and assistance of other professionals was vividly illustrated when one of the leading cardiologists in the world explained to us his decision-making process in the operating room. Fifteen medical personnel (surgeons, anesthesiologists, and cardiologists) discussed the pros and cons of reopening a patient's chest versus using drug therapy following bypass surgery in which the patient's heart was fibrillating. Rather than feeling embarrassment that he had asked for other opinions, the cardiologist seemed to assume we would find comfort in the fact that he had consulted the other professionals on the spot.

Educators also have begun to appreciate the benefits of mutual study and problem solving in relation to professional competence. In our staff development programs, we must build in collegial work on the mastery and use of innovative practices and content; and we must ensure that training and follow-up include collaborative opportunities. Such collegial programs contribute not only to the individual competence of participating educators, but also build their sense of membership in a profession. Further, teachers, in particular, who assume a proactive stance in relation to self-help peer relationships, appear to gain much more from such programs than do teachers who merely "submit" to them.

Observing other professionals work is a valuable learning experience in itself, and collaborative analysis of teaching and planning for appropriate use of an innovation usually results in more—and more focused—practice. Finally, the proactive teachers who can and will state what they need—what they understand and what they don't—rather than relying on their peers' mind reading—are likely to benefit more from professional collegial study than teachers who are passive in the relationship.

Flexibility

Flexibility appears to be a highly functional attribute. We may have to reorient our traditional thinking about curriculum and instruction. For example, how do we traditionally introduce new content and processes to students in the first stage of learning? Do we "provide" content through lecture and summaries of our own? If the new content consists of learning an inductive thinking strategy, for example, we may need to reorganize our instructional materials and strategies and supplement them with data for the students to use to come up with their own conclusions and generalizations.

Teachers may even have to rethink their roles as instructors in the classroom. For those who have conceived their roles as information givers, instructional processes that transfer greater responsibility to students for their own learning may require rethinking of educational goals, ways, and means. In the transfer stage of learning, when teachers are attempting to use new content and processes appropriately in the instructional setting, a reorientation to students may be necessary. When new and different expectations are held for students, teachers must figure out what learning skills students possess and which must be directly taught in order for students to operate within different frameworks. Flexibility in the learning process can be summed up as a spirit of inquiry, a willingness to experiment with one's own behavior, and an openness to evidence that alternatives have something to offer.

Coaching

In general, training is expected to result in sufficient skill that practice can be sustained in the classroom and transferred into the working repertoire. As we continue to experiment with the design of coaching, *the major purpose of peer coaching remains the implementation of innovations to the extent that determination of effects on students is possible.*

In the past few years, we have become increasingly convinced that creating the conditions that nurture learning and growth requires a much greater organizational innovation than we originally thought. The organization cannot remain passive in relation to the study teams it shelters but rather must actively support the norms of experimentation, collaborative planning and development, and implementation of content aimed at collective goals.

In the following pages we will revisit the structure and function of peer coaching teams; compare and contrast them with other forms of "coaching"; and share what we believe are the next steps most likely to increase the power of school improvement efforts.

The Evolution of Coaching

Our understanding of how education personnel can help each other has come from a variety of sources. Only within the last 25 years, however, have the processes of training and implementation come under close scrutiny. By the early 1970s, educators recognized that a great many efforts to improve schools, even when they very well funded and approved by the public, encountered great difficulty and achieved very low levels of implementation. Since that time, innovators, organizational specialists, curriculum development personnel, and technologists have behaved much less naively. The nature of training, organizational climate, curriculum implementation, teacher learning processes, and the organization of the school district itself have been attended to with much greater care. We draw on all of these for our knowledge about how all personnel can work together to ensure that skill development and content mastery result from training and that personnel are skillful in the collaborative effort to transfer those products into active educational practice.

History, Pre-1980

We acknowledge the work of many of our colleagues. The concept of teachers as trainers has been explored by Sharan and Hertz-Lazarowitz (1980), among others. Berman and McLaughlin (1975) noted the importance of in-class assistance and teachers observing other teachers for effective educational change programs. Fullan and Pomfret (1977) cited the importance of training and administrative support in the implementation of curricula.

The work most similar to ours is that of Sharan and Hertz-Lazarowitz (1980). They provided extensive initial training (52 hours) to teachers learning a complex new teaching strategy and supported the initial training with consultant-assisted self-help teams composed of three or four teachers. The teams engaged in cooperative planning of teaching processes and content, mutual observation of teaching, and feedback by teammates. Their teacher self-help teams were developed on the basis of earlier work by Roper, Deal, and Dornbusch (1976). In the second year of their project, 65 percent of the participating classroom teachers were using small-group teaching (group investigation) regularly and appropriately.

As we studied the work of Sharan and his associates, we were struck by the thoroughness and duration of training, the consistency of in-class follow-up, and particularly by the help provided by peers as they attempted to implement a teaching process quite different from their normal practice. Also, their implementation, although not perfect, was so much higher than the level of most reported studies.

History, 1980–Present

During the past 20 years, our understanding of how we learn new behaviors and put them into practice has continuously evolved, both as a result of work by colleagues in schools and universities and our own efforts with teachers and schools.

When we first advanced the notion of "coaching" (Joyce & Showers, 1980), we had just completed an exhaustive review of literature on training and presented our findings as a set of hypotheses about types of training likely to result in various levels of impact. The training components discussed in that early work were guided by what was then present in the literature, for example, presentation of theory, modeling or demonstration, practice, structured and open-ended feedback, and in-class assistance with transfer. Given the state of knowledge about training in 1980, we believed that when educators were attempting to think about and refine their current practice, "modeling, practice under simulated conditions, and practice in the classroom, combined with feedback" would be the most productive training design. When teachers were attempting to master new curricula and approaches to teaching, we hypothesized that continued technical assistance of some form at the classroom level would be essential for adding new practices to existing repertoires.

In the early 1980s, we formally investigated the latter hypothesis in studies designed to explore the impact of coaching on long-term implementation, following initial training in *new* content (Showers, 1982, a and b, 1984, a and b). We found that continuing technical assistance, whether provided by an outside expert or by peer experts, resulted in much greater classroom implementation than was achieved by teachers who shared initial training but did not have the long-term support of coaching. These early studies structured the coaching process by pairing teachers with an outside consultant or an expert peer, with the assumption that the "coach" would have to have greater expertise in the new content if the relationship were to be productive. We were heavily influenced by the literature on supervisory practices and struggled to create the kind of structured feedback that appeared to facilitate skill development. We were wrong about that. A highly skilled trainer can provide technical feedback, but persons just learning a new model of teaching or curriculum are not in a position to offer technical advice to other novices with the procedure.

We can divide the results of our early studies of coaching into two categories: facilitation of transfer of training and development of norms of collegiality and experimentation.

Coaching appeared to contribute to transfer of training in five ways.

● Coached teachers and principals generally practiced new strategies more frequently and developed greater skill in the actual moves of a new teaching strategy than did uncoached educators who had experienced identical initial training (Showers, 1982, a and b). Apparently, the support and encouragement provided by peers while attempting new teaching strategies help to sustain practice through the often awkward stages of implementing different teaching practices and teaching students how to respond to them. Even though uncoached teachers had shared 30 hours of training with coached teachers, they tended to practice the strategies little or not at all following training, despite their stated intentions to use the new models of teaching for classroom instruction.

● Coached teachers used their newly learned strategies more appropriately than uncoached teachers in terms of their own instructional objectives and the theories of specific models of teaching (Showers, 1982, a and b; 1984, a and b). Coached teachers had opportunities to discuss instructional objectives, the strategies that theoretically were best designed to accomplish those objectives, and the types of curricular materials needed for specific strategies. Consequently, they experimented with new instructional strategies in their own curriculum areas more quickly than uncoached teachers and shared lessons and materials with each other early in the coaching process. Uncoached teachers, on the other hand, tended to practice in their classrooms using lessons they had seen as demonstrations or in peer practice during initial training sessions. Once they had exhausted those possibilities, they had difficulty finding appropriate occasions for use in their own curriculum areas and tended to quit practicing. Interestingly, however, regular interviews revealed their continuing intention to use the strategies as soon as they had time to think through their potential applications.

● Coached teachers exhibited greater long-term retention of knowledge about and skill with strategies in which they had been coached and, as a group, increased the appropriateness of use of new teaching models over time (Baker & Showers, 1984). Six to nine months after training in several new models of teaching, coached teachers had retained and, in several instances, increased their technical mastery of the teaching strategies. Uncoached teachers, however, were in many cases unable to even demonstrate the new strategies after that period of time had elapsed. They were as surprised as we were by the loss of skill, although in retrospect we all should have realized that disuse over a spring, summer, and fall would lead to skill loss.

● In our study of peer coaching (Showers, 1984, a and b), coached teachers were much more likely than uncoached teachers to explain new models of teaching to their students, ensuring that students understood the purpose of the strategy and the behaviors expected of them when using the strategy. For example, students of coached teachers were more likely to understand the nature and definition of concepts, metaphors, and analogies and were therefore more able to operate independently with concept attainment and synectics teaching strategies. These students not only had more experience (practice) with the strategies but had been provided direct instruction in component model skills. Students of uncoached teachers, on the other hand, had insufficient practice with the strategies to develop skill and confidence with them. Therefore, when their teachers occasionally attempted one of the new strategies, the more outspoken students were likely to suggest that they not waste time with the new strategy but rather conduct the lesson in ways with which they were all familiar and, by implication, "competent."

● Finally, coached teachers in our studies exhibited clearer cognitions with regard to the purposes and uses of the new strategies, as revealed through interviews, lesson plans, and classroom performance (Showers, 1982, a and b; 1984, a and b). The frequent peer discussions regarding appropriate use of strategies, suitable objectives, experiments with new uses of strategies, lesson and materials design, and so forth seemed to enable coached teachers to "think" with the new strategies in ways that the uncoached teachers never exhibited. Uncoached teachers who did occasionally use the "trained" models of teaching tended not to depart, at least consciously, from the exact forms and applications they had experienced in training. Therefore, if the synectics strategy was demonstrated in training as a pre-writing activity and organizer for writing, uncoached teachers were unlikely to apply synectics to problem-solving situations. Or, if an inquiry strategy was demonstrated with science content, uncoached teachers were less likely to apply the strategy to investigation of social policies or questions in anthropology and literature.

Current Practice

In the mid-1980s, our attention turned to school improvement and the application of training and coaching technologies to schoolwide initiatives for change. These efforts presented quite different circumstances than work with groups of volunteer teachers pursuing their individual interests in curriculum and instruction. Working with entire schools necessitated collaboration with staffs to determine their students' most pressing needs, to select content appropriate to their needs and design training to enable the staff to learn the new content, and to study implementation and impact of new content. Increasingly we find it necessary to discuss at length with staffs how we might work together and to request democratic decision making by faculties to determine if, indeed, the school wants to work with us.

First, when we work with entire faculties, *all teachers and administrators agree to be members of peer coaching teams.* The collective agreements governing the teams are

● Commitment to practice/use whatever change the faculty has decided to implement.

● Assistance and support of each other in the change process, including shared planning of instructional objectives and development of materials and lessons.

● Collection of data, both on the implementation of their planned change and on student effects relevant to the school's identified target for student growth.

Second, *we have omitted feedback as a coaching component.* The primary activity of peer coaching study teams is the collaborative planning and development of curriculum and instruction in pursuit of their shared goals. Teachers, especially when learning teaching strategies designed for higher-order outcomes, need time to think through their overarching objectives as well as the specific objectives leading to them. Given the time required to plan sequences of lessons and units, collaborative planning is essential if teachers are to divide the labor of new development and use each other's products.

Omitting feedback in the coaching process has not depressed implementation or student growth (Joyce, Calhoun, & Hopkins, 1999; Showers, 1989), and the omission has greatly simplified the organization of peer coaching teams in school settings. In retrospect, it is not difficult to understand this finding. Learning to provide technical feedback required extensive training (and time that might better have been used in planning and development) and was unnecessary after new behaviors were mastered. Peer coaches told us they found themselves slipping into "supervisory, evaluative comments" despite all their intentions to avoid them. Teachers shared with us their expectation that feedback provide "first the good news, then the bad" because of their shared histories with various forms of clinical supervision. They admitted they often pressured their coaches to go beyond technical feedback and give them "the real scoop." To the extent that feedback actually was evaluative or was perceived to be evaluative, it was not meeting our original intention in any case.

Third, *we have redefined the meaning of "coach"; when teachers observe each other, the one teaching is the "coach" and the one observing is the "coached."* Teachers who observe other teachers who are attempting to implement new behaviors do so in order to learn from their colleague's efforts with the innovation. There is no discussion of the observation in the "technical feedback" sense that we used in our early studies. Generally, brief conversations on the order of "Thanks for letting me watch you work. I picked up some good ideas on how to work with the students on . . ." follow these observations.

Coaching appears to facilitate the professional and collegial relationships discussed by Little (1982, 1990), for example, development of a shared language and norms of experimentation. Our data about this process are somewhat less formal than that on skill acquisition and transfer. However, both anecdotal and interview data indicate that the effects of coaching are much more far reaching than the mastery and integration of new knowledge and skills by individual teachers. The development of school norms that support the continuous study and improvement of teaching apparently build capability for other kinds of change, whether it is adoption of a new curriculum, a schoolwide discipline policy, or the building of teaching repertoire.

By building permanent structures for collegial relationships, schools organize themselves for improvement in multiple areas. We suspect that the practice of public teaching; focus on the clinical acts of teaching; development of common language and understanding; and sharing of lesson plans, materials, and problems contribute to school norms of collegiality and experimentation. In the course of long-term relationships with school districts, we conducted a number of informal studies on the "learning to learn" effect by asking successful coaching teams to teach themselves new (to them) models of teaching through print and video media alone—without the assistance of formal training. They have been able to do so, which we attribute partly to their growing ability to learn and partly to the cohesion that has developed during the peer coaching process.

Other Forms of Coaching

The term "coaching" has been used in multiple contexts in the past 15 years. We will briefly discuss some of them in order to identify similarities and differences with the practice of coaching we now employ.

In our research, we have observed the terms "technical coaching," "collegial coaching," "challenge coaching," "team coaching," "cognitive coaching," and "peer coaching" (as practiced in the traditional supervisory mode of pre-conference/observation/post-conference). All seem to convey that they not be confused with or used for evaluation of teachers. Technical coaching, team coaching, and peer coaching have in common with our practice a concern for learning and implementing innovations in curriculum and instruction (e.g., Showers, 1985), whereas collegial coaching and cognitive coaching appear to aim more at the improving of existing practice and repertoire. With the exception of our current version of coaching, all use feedback procedures as a vehicle for improving or changing classroom practice but have not developed research to test the efficacy of feedback.

Since the first edition of this book was printed, peer coaching appears to have turned sharply to peer supervision in many applications, which does pull those forms of coaching toward an evaluative stance. Peer supervision and evaluation, as well as principal and supervisor evaluation seem to be normative in the literature (see, for example, Garmston, 1987). We have puzzled over this phenomenon—why would so many schools and districts spend rare resources of time and money on training teachers, principals, and supervisors to provide nonoffensive feedback rather than organizing teachers in school settings to work collaboratively on new learning? We don't know the answer to this question but will share several possible explanations.

One possible explanation for the narrowed focus of peer coaching might be the lack of intensive training targeted at schoolwide learning goals in many schools. Since many schools and districts still run staff development programs aimed at individuals, teachers in a given school could be engaged in different learning activities (or none at all) and thus organizing the teachers into teams to work on the implementation of shared learning would be difficult. To the extent that peer coaching is expected to improve classroom practice, peers, principals, or supervisors would necessarily be thrown into one-on-one sessions working on existing repertoire or individual agendas.

Related to the first possibility is the fact that many schools have staff development programs unrelated to their school improvement plans. For example, we recently visited a school in which the school improvement plan focused on literacy while the staff development program consisted of a series of seminars on recent brain research.

We also considered the persistence of existing schedules and the difficulty of finding time in the school day for groups of teachers to meet. This explanation seems the easiest to remedy, although teachers and administrators must first acknowledge the need for collaborative work.

Finally, we have wondered if the emphasis of many states on test scores has thrown the field of teacher evaluation into some disarray. When the primary judgment of a school's effectiveness is its score on a statewide test, it may be that traditional forms of teacher evaluation have been abandoned and the seemingly more benign forms of coaching (under the rubrics of cognitive coaching and mentoring and reflective coaching) adopted.

Whatever the reasons for the apparently wholesale move to supervision and evaluation as coaching modes, we regret the development. Despite the difficulty of setting schoolwide goals for improvement, engaging collectively in training, and working collaboratively in teams to implement new learning and evaluate its effect, it is well worth the effort, both in terms of faculty cohesion and student learning.

Next Steps in the Evolution of Training and Coaching

A perennial question drives our work—how to best help teachers in their efforts to teach students in ways that build intellectual independence, reasoning and problem-solving capability, competence in handling the explosion of information and data, and, with the help of technology, the ability to navigate the Information Age. We believe there are specific behaviors that staff developers can incorporate in training settings and in continuing technical assistance to assist educators in their efforts.

First, we can help schools and teams of teachers in the *redesign of their workplaces during training settings*. Rather than simply advocating that workplaces provide time for collaborative planning and problem solving related to a school's specific plans for change, we can provide time during training to begin to solve the problem of finding time for the analysis, discussion, and decision making necessary for collective change efforts.

Second, *peer coaching study teams can be formed on the first day of training* if they are not already in place so that teams have opportunities to experiment with productive ways of working together. When entire school faculties are engaged in training together, they have many options for forming teams, and staff developers can facilitate discussion of those options. When training continues over a period of days, teachers can try alternative formats in order to experience the relative costs and benefits of alternative plans. Schools that are trying to develop an integrated curriculum as part of their improvement plan may want to experiment with cross-subject or cross-grade teams. Schools with a focus on multicultural curriculum may want to balance teams by ensuring that faculty expertise on various cultures is spread among them. However teams are formed, it is useful for them to have immediate practice in working together toward shared goals.

Third, we can *provide examples of formats or structures for collaborative planning*. Many teachers have shared with us the difficulty they experience in jointly performing an activity that traditionally they have done individually. A structured "walk-through" of a planning activity that allows teams to respond to questions within specific time frames provides practice in thinking aloud the things individuals want to accomplish and in identifying the overlap with the agendas of colleagues. For example, a sequence might include

- Think about your year's "course." What are your big, overarching goals for your students this year?
- Now think about the first six weeks of school. What objectives will you need to accomplish during the first six weeks if you are to meet your year's goals? How much time can you spend in review and still meet your objectives?
- What instructional strategies are most appropriate for the various objectives you have set for the first six weeks? Are they consistent with your year-end goals?

● Given the overlap of objectives in your group, are there ways you can divide the labor and develop materials that others can use?

Fourth, peer coaching study teams need time to plan how they will *monitor their implementation* of whatever initiative they have agreed to adopt, and how they will *determine the effect of that initiative on their students*. When whole schools have agreed on a specific change agenda (e.g., to learn and use cooperative strategies in conjunction with constructivist approaches to teaching), study teams may want to first address these issues in small groups and then combine their ideas in a whole-school session. Then the faculty can devise a plan for monitoring both their implementation and their effect on students, schoolwide. Measuring the impact of planned changes in the educational program is of critical importance to any school improvement and change effort. The training setting is an optimal time to plan the "mini studies" that teams can conduct throughout the year in order to know if all their efforts are having the desired effects.

We are aware that including these types of activities in training sessions increases the time, and thus the cost, of staff development activities. We are convinced that, to the extent such activities result in greater clarity about means and ends, more thorough implementation of planned changes, and more immediate information about student effects, the additional effort will be well worth the investment.

○ ○ ○

From the research on training and studies of transfer of training, as well as clinical experience over the past 35 years, we have identified teacher skills, understandings, and characteristics that appear to facilitate learning. The concern for identification of "learning to learn" skills stems from the contradictions that exist between skill learning and use of those skills in classroom settings. It is well documented that teachers can learn a wide variety of skills, strategies, and practices. It is also well documented that behaviors learned in training settings are less often implemented in classroom practice, even though more intensive training programs that include follow-up training and employ peer self-help groups have much better implementation records than the field as a whole.

R. Snow (1982), commenting on three papers prepared for a symposium on "The Student's Role in Learning," noted that "learning is a function of the amount of active mental effort invested in the exercise of intelligence to accomplish cognitive work" (p. 5). He further asserted that "it is possible to train directly the cognitive and metacognitive processing skills involved in intelligent learning and it is possible to prompt intrinsically motivated learning by intelligent arrangement of educational conditions" (p. 10). If the skills and characteristics identified in this chapter do indeed help teachers become better able to master and implement new content and instructional practices, we are a step closer to developing the conditions that enable teachers to master the "cognitive and metacognitive processing skills involved in intelligent learning."

From a career perspective, it may be that learning how to acquire good practices should be equally as important as the good practices themselves. The effectiveness of preservice teacher training programs may well depend on the skill of the teacher to navigate the consolidation phase in many kinds of settings. The creation of effective inservice training programs may equally depend on the skills of teachers to acquire ever-increasing knowledge and practices and to learn how to consolidate them.

The addition of peer coaching to school improvement efforts is a substantial departure from the way schools often embark on change efforts. On the surface, it should be simple to implement—what could be more natural than teams of professional teachers working on content and skills? It is a complex innovation only because it requires a radical change in relationships between teachers and between teachers and administrative personnel.

Many educators believe that the essence of the coaching transaction is in the offering of advice to teachers following observations. It is not. Teachers learn from each other in the process of planning instruction, developing the materials to support it, watching each other work with students, and thinking together about the effect of their behavior on student learning. The collaborative work of peer coaching is much broader than observations and conferences.

Implementation: Moving from Workshops to the Classroom

Implementation is where productive change in curriculum and instruction happens or falls apart. We have to keep growth by educators and students central as we think about implementation. We don't want anyone to fail! And we care whether kids will have the chance to learn from powerful models of learning as schools strive to become better.

In the previous two chapters we have examined change and improvement processes in the contexts of individuals, schools, and districts attempting to change. We have focused greater attention on the school in our discussion of needs identification and content selection, and the design of training and peer coaching study teams, arguing that the district and school are the units with the greatest potential for producing substantial student growth. In this chapter we will again focus on whole school improvement and change efforts as we discuss the importance of implementation and the means for monitoring it. Once again, we illustrate with a case study, focusing on implementation and its effects when teachers are studying several models of teaching.

Assessing Impact

The failure to monitor implementation of curriculums, instructional strategies, and other innovations has cost school improvement efforts dearly in the past, resulting in both inability to interpret student learning outcomes and spurious conclusions regarding the impact of change programs. *The primary reason to monitor implementation of innovations is to interpret their effect on students.* This is true whether a single teacher is experimenting with changes in his instructional program or an entire school or district is attempting changes to accomplish a collective goal.

A second reason to monitor implementation of planned changes, whether for individuals, schools, or districts, is to determine objectively at what level of intensity or frequency students are experiencing a planned change. It is important for an individual teacher to determine if new content or practices are actually implemented in the classroom, given the initial purpose for the change.

For schools, data on implementation serve as a gauge of the organizational capacity of the school to make a decision and act upon it. Districts vary considerably in their abilities to implement a change, whether in curriculum or technology. We suspect in some cases that the absence of implementation data screens the need for an implementation strategy from district personnel. For example, we have observed several districts in which, following adoption of new reading texts and a three-hour teacher orientation session, it was assumed that the new curriculum was in place. The districts lacked the capacity to implement a new curriculum but nonetheless proceeded with a strategy that could not possibly succeed. Our experience is that many districts engage in similar "adoption cycles" without a design that makes a difference. The teachers feel (and are) buffeted by initiatives that ask them to change without adequate support.

Monitoring Implementation

Setting a Target. Whether for individuals, schools, or districts, the first step in implementing anything is defining what it will look like. If a school has decided to use cooperative learning strategies to address academic and social needs and arranged for staff training, how will they know when they have the new processes in place? If every teacher uses a cooperative strategy once a week, can the school expect students to benefit? Will they need to use their new cooperative strategies heavily in the initial weeks of implementation in order to teach students how to function productively in cooperative groups? These are questions that need to be discussed openly and revisited frequently.

Data Collection. Once targets have been set for use of whatever innovation has been selected, a process is needed for collecting information on actual use. This type of data collection represents both new behavior and a departure from norms for many school faculties. Assuming that the process and structure described in Chapters 2, 3, and 6 are in place, the school or district committees can design procedures for collecting the necessary data and communicating to staffs its purpose and use (e.g., these are *our* data and we need them for our own decision-making process). However, leaders should not assume that there will not be negative fallout from the public use of data—it violates the traditional norms of privatism that have pervaded the culture of educators.

The type of change implemented determines the nature of the data collected. For example, if a school, as part of its writing program, has decided to increase the number of computers available and teach all students a word processing program, faculty will want a variety of data. First, they need to set a target—how often do they want students to write on their computers and why? How many students currently compose at the computer? How often do they write at a computer? Do some students write on computers at home? How long does it take for students to become proficient with at least rudimentary word processing skills? Once frequency targets are set and word processing instruction has begun, teachers will want information on actual computer use for word processing. They will also have questions about the impact of word processing on the quality of their students' writing (see Chapter 9 for a discussion of formative evaluation projects).

Let's look at another example: the adoption of science kits by an elementary school. This may appear to be a simple implementation problem. But focusing the effort requires a series of clarifying questions. As in all change efforts, the adoption of a new curriculum usually results from dissatisfaction with existing programs. Why was the new curriculum selected? What knowledge and skills do faculty want their students to acquire as a result of using the science kits, and how often will they need to experience the new curriculum if these objectives are to be accomplished? Are there sufficient materials/equipment for all classrooms to meet the implementation targets? Will the faculty simply monitor the number of units "used" by each classroom, or are they actually interested in the frequency of student behaviors like hypothesis setting, conducting of experiments, observation and data collection, analysis of findings, and drawing of conclusions? These questions must be answered before the faculty can set its targets for implementation and design a system for determining when they will have their new science curriculum in place.

Once schools are clear on their questions regarding implementation, the nature of the data to be collected is clear. If the target is thrice-weekly composition on a computer, students can simply file all writing assignments in a folder or write their names and dates on a chart that lists writing prompts. If the object of implementation of a science curriculum is "hands-on" science—to engage students in systematic observation and analysis of phenomena, teachers can tally student experiences on a chart or collect students' written reports of science experiences.

Using the Data. Individuals, faculties, and districts use implementation data for several purposes. The first is the fairly straightforward issue of accomplishing what was planned ("After extensive analysis of our students' needs, selection of content, training and practice, have we put in place what we set out to do?"). The ability to follow through on plans builds both individual and collective senses of efficacy and the confidence to explore future alternatives to current practice.

Second, in nearly all change efforts, obstacles to implementation arise. Good implementation data provide the basis for analysis of obstacles as well as their potential solutions. Is the implementation faltering because of insufficient equipment or materials? Are teachers discovering they need additional or different training to accomplish a thorough implementation? Is specific assistance or cooperation from parents necessary before targets can be realized? When data reveal that targets for implementation are not being met, immediate problem solving should address why and generate whatever assistance is needed. Discovering at the end of the year that a change was never put in place leaves everyone feeling discouraged and ineffectual.

Finally, information about the implementation of any change makes it possible to interpret student outcomes. Whenever we change current practice, we expect specific student benefits in behavior (fewer suspensions, greater involvement in learning opportunities), achievement (higher grades, improved test scores, increased reading comprehension), thinking skills (the ability to identify categories in large amounts of unorganized information, to hypothesize and synthesize), self-esteem, or whatever perceived need impelled us to change in the first place. Solid use of a planned change, as well as variations in implementation, enables us to understand the impact of our behavior of students and to plan next steps in the use of innovations.

Studying an Implementation: The Richmond County, Georgia, Models of Teaching Project

The following in-depth case illustrates some of the dimensions of implementation discussed to this point.

The implementation study reported here was part of a districtwide school improvement project aimed at increasing student achievement and restructuring the workplace of teachers (see Joyce, Murphy, Showers, & Murphy, 1989, the *precis* in Chapter 2, and

Showers, Murphy, & Joyce, 1996). The study examined the implementation of several alternative models of teaching by faculties engaged in schoolwide school improvement programs. The functioning of study teams was also observed because entire faculties were organized into peer coaching study teams designed to facilitate the appropriate and consistent use of alternative teaching strategies.

Specific implementation questions were as follows:

● Did the faculties implement the content of the training? (For example, what levels of use and what degrees of transfer of training were achieved with the models of teaching in which teachers were trained?)

● What factors affected variation in faculties' use of the models of teaching? (For example, did cohesiveness of faculties and peer coaching study teams, individual growth states, grade level, age, and experience affect implementation?)

● Did changes in the workplace occur as a result of whole faculty participation in the project, specifically the development of faculty and administration ability to set specific goals for school improvement?

Sample

One hundred and sixteen teachers and administrators—the faculties from the first three target schools—were involved in the project. Although data were collected on all of them, this report deals with case studies of a subset of 18 teachers—6 from each of the three target schools—who were selected on a stratified random basis. The case study sample for each of the two elementary schools included 1 teacher from each grade level (K–5); at the middle school, it included 2 teachers from each of grades 6, 7, and 8. A 2nd grade teacher was dropped from the sample because of an extended illness that required her early retirement.

Training

The content for the first summer's workshop included four models of teaching—cooperative learning (Johnson et al., 1981), inductive thinking and concept attainment (Bredderman, 1983; El-Nemr, 1979), and mnemonic strategies (Pressley, Levin, & Delaney, 1982)—selected because of their research-based impact on student learning (Joyce, Calhoun, & Weil, 2000). Instruction followed the theory/demonstration/practice mode during the summer workshop.

Participants planned lessons they would teach and then shared the plans—and their skepticism about whether the plans were practical —with colleagues. When school opened, all participants were urged to practice their new strategies frequently during the first few weeks.

In September, administrators scheduled specific times for study teams to meet. Together with counselors and supervisors, the teams practiced in classrooms with students. The trainers asked the teachers to concentrate on teaching their students how to respond to the models of teaching they were learning. Although the students could respond immediately to the new cognitive and social tasks presented by those models, it would take about 20 trials before *the teachers* would become really proficient.

Procedures

Six times during the 1987–88 academic year, the consultants observed the "sample" teachers in their classrooms and informally interviewed them regarding their use of models. Teachers were asked to maintain monthly logs detailing their use of the teaching models over which they had received training during the summer of 1987 and were videotaped near the end of the first project year to determine skill levels with various models of teaching. Videotapes were completed for fourteen of the seventeen sample teachers.

All teachers completed formal interviews regarding their use and attitudes toward the teaching strategies that were the object of this implementation effort. Interviews were completed with all sample teachers in April 1988 and again in January 1989.

Sixteen of the sample teachers attended a second two-week training session during the summer of 1988 and were studied during their second year of implementation. The procedures for examining implementation were identical to the first year of the project.

Data Collection: Practice

Amount of practice was simply a tabulation of the number of teacher-logged trials per month. Teachers varied somewhat in their response to the expectation that they turn in a monthly log recording their practice with the new strategies. Some teachers recorded every lesson while others recorded only examples of different types of lessons. Six informal interviews recorded during the year—as well as the formal interviews—helped validate the information recorded on logs.

Data Collection: Levels of Transfer

We analyzed teachers' use of the strategies through a rating system that places each person's implementation on a scale from 1 (low) to 5 (high). This scale, which we call "Levels of Transfer," is shown in Figure 6.1.

We analyzed lesson plans, interviews, logs, and observations to determine levels of transfer. For each of the teachers, all lessons reported on logs and six systematic observations during each year of the project provided data for determining transfer level. Interview data supplemented lesson plans and observations with self-reports on teachers' use of the teaching models in their classrooms. Each lesson analyzed was assigned a score of 1 (imitative use) to 5 (executive control) and means were computed for each teacher.

Factors Affecting Variation in Implementation

To examine factors that we hypothesized may affect variation in teachers' use of the models of teaching, we calculated "States of Growth" (an orientation to the external environment with respect to both the formal and informal opportunities for professional development) for each teacher. States of growth data were derived from interviews and observations of study teams. Data on teachers' grade level, age, and experience were available from employment records housed both at the school and at the central office. Let's explain what we mean by the concept and then proceed to the results of the study.

McKibbin & Joyce (1980) (see Chapter 9) derived the states of growth measure in their study of staff development in California. Through a structured interview process, they examined teachers' and administrators' responses to opportunities for professional development through formal staff development offered by universities, counties, state-sponsored agencies and districts; informal opportunities provided by peers; and participation in non-professional but personal growth opportunities available in the general environment (books, film, theater, etc.). McKibbin and Joyce reported that teachers who participated fully in both formal and informal professional development activities also tended to have well-developed interests in the personal domain; that is, teachers who actively reached out for growth opportunities in their professional lives were generally engaged in growth. Furthermore, teachers characterized by high growth states were more likely to implement innovations for which

FIGURE 6.1

Levels of Transfer

Level 1 represents *imitative use*, that is, exact replication of lessons demonstrated in training settings. Furthermore, the types of lessons selected for imitation often represent only the most simple and concrete examples of a class of demonstrations. For example, if a cooperative "numbered heads" activity were demonstrated with a list of spelling words during training, and teachers were subsequently observed to use numbered heads only with their spelling lists, their level of transfer would be judged to be imitative, although appropriate. Likewise, the fact that various forms of more complex cooperative activity had been demonstrated during training (but were absent from early teacher practice) would tend to place a teacher at a Level 1 level of transfer.

Level 2 indicates *mechanical use* (or horizontal transfer) in that the same teacher who was using "numbered heads" activities only for spelling begins to use numbered heads for drills in reading vocabulary, addition and multiplication facts, etc. Practice increases at this level but there is little variation in types of implementation. More complex examples of the models of teaching learned during training continue to be missing from teacher practice.

Level 3 is *routine* use, in that certain activities, types of lessons, and objectives become identified with specific models of teaching. For example, as students learn the states and capitals of the United States, geographic features of regions of the country, and major land forms and oceans of the world, teachers routinely select mnemonic strategies to accomplish their objectives. Use of the strategies is frequent at this stage; but alternative strategies are not considered at this point, nor are curriculum objectives thought of in other than a lower-order, concrete fashion.

Level 4 is called *integrated use* and generally occurs for different models at different rates. For example, a teacher who has frequently used mnemonics strategies for learning concrete bits of information in multiple subjects begins to understand that sequences of events in history, major points in a philosophy, and policy issues faced by presidents and governors are also areas for application of mnemonic strategies. The proportion of imitative to innovative, subject-specific use has become quite small.

Finally, **Level 5** is designated as *executive use* of the content of training. Executive control is characterized by complete understanding of the theories underlying the various models learned, a comfortable level of appropriate use for varieties of models of teaching, and consequently the ability to select specific models and combinations of models for objectives within a unit as well as across subject areas. Integrated curriculum objectives as well as higher-order objectives are frequently observable at this level. Thus a teacher introducing a piece of literature to 5th grade students might begin with objectives relating to understanding of the relationships that evolve between certain characters in the book. Although the teacher may employ inductive thinking, concept attainment, and mnemonic and cooperative strategies to teach the necessary vocabulary and word attack skills to enable the students to read the story with comfort, major emphases will be on analysis of the relationships between characters through categorization and interpretation of key passages from the piece and writing with analogies to examine the changing nature of evolving relationships.

they received training and to achieve transfer of those innovations into their active teaching repertoires.

In a recent study in which both growth states of individual teachers and climate ratings of their schools were examined for their influence on teacher implementation of training, Hopkins (1990) found growth states to be a more powerful predictor of implementation than was school climate (although the latter was not without effect).

The growth states hierarchy is described in full in several sources (Joyce, Bush, & McKibbin, 1982; Joyce & Showers, 1988; McKibbin & Joyce, 1980). Briefly, people are characterized as the following:

● *Gourmet Omnivores* are individuals who not only reach out for opportunities in their environments but who generate or initiate those opportunities for themselves and others. These individuals are active participants in many growth opportunities but are discriminating about their choice of activities. They are knowledgeable about the range of options available to them. According to Joyce and Showers (1988), gourmet omnivores are "mature high-activity people who have learned to canvass the environment and exploit it successfully" (p. 134).

● *Active Consumers* are similar to gourmet omnivores in that they continually scan their environments for growth opportunities and take advantage of those opportunities in both the professional and personal domains. They differ from gourmet omnivores in that they are less initiating and less likely to create opportunities and options where none exist.

● *Passive Consumers* comprised about 70 percent of the initial sample in the California Staff Development Study (Joyce, Bush, & McKibbin, 1982). They are characterized as amiable, conforming, and highly dependent on their immediate social context. They attended required staff development programs but seldom did anything with the content, and the activities engaged in outside the work setting depended very much on whether their families and friends initiated such activities.

● *Reticents* actually "expend energy pushing away opportunities for growth . . . they have developed an orientation of reluctance to interact positively with their cultural environment" (Joyce & Showers, 1988, p. 136). Consequently, reticents resist opportunities for growth and in fact often perceive efforts by peers or administrators to effect change as forms of conspiracy designed to leave them less powerful and less efficacious.

Results

What, then, was the degree of implementation in the Richmond County project, and what were the factors contributing to it?

Practice

Knowing that skill development requires a certain amount of practice before fluid and appropriate use is possible, we encouraged teachers at the three project schools to practice their newly learned models of teaching frequently, especially at the beginning of the school year immediately following training. In earlier studies, teachers who had postponed practice found it difficult or impossible to use the content of training. We urged teachers to implement the simpler forms of cooperative learning immediately and pervasively during the first month of school in order to teach students how to work in cooperative groups and to ease the implementation of other models of teaching. Teachers were so successful in this effort that, by the end of the first month, most of the elementary teachers were reporting a minimum of two cooperative sessions per day and the middle school teachers at least four per week. In fact, one elementary teacher reported 80 trials with cooperative learning during the four weeks of September! Teachers found it much more difficult to implement the Concept Attainment, Mnemonics, and Inductive Thinking strategies. Figure 6.2 displays the results.

Analysis of teacher logs for the 1987–88 academic year shows that for our random sample of teachers, the new models of teaching were practiced 14.48 times per month (for School A, 16.8; for School B, 11.1; and for School C, 14.98). During the second project year, the average monthly use of models was 22.73 (for School A, 14.8; for School B, 24.4; and for School C, 29).

Teachers on the whole practiced their new strategies fairly frequently. The question of greater concern to us, however, was the level of transfer of training to teachers' active repertoires—how appropriately were the new strategies being used? If teachers did not develop at least a routine level of transfer during the first year, would they ultimately develop integrated use and executive control with the models of teaching?

Figure 6.3 summarizes the levels of transfer achieved by our sample during the project. Again, data on cooperative learning lessons were not included in transfer scores, as they artificially inflated the levels of transfer achieved in Concept Attainment, Mnemonics, and Inductive Thinking.

FIGURE **6.2**

Average Monthly Practice by Teacher with Three Models of Teaching for Two Years*

School	Teacher	Average Monthly Practice*	
		1987–88	1988–89
A	A**	19.6	20
	B**	13.0	20
	C	11.0	8
	D**	23.0	—
	E	15.6	14
	F	18.6	12
B	A**	18.0	40
	B**	20.0	38
	C**	10.1	20
	D	3.6	10
	E	3.7	14
C	A**	14.3	36
	B**	12.0	28
	C**	12.8	24
	D**	13.6	28
	E	17.2	—
	F**	20.0	29
		X = 14.5	X = 22.73
		SD = 5.4	SD = 10.3

X = Mean
SD = Standard Deviation

* Excluding cooperative learning lessons.
** Teachers who used cooperative learning one or more times per day.

For year one, the mean transfer of training score for our sample was 3.3 (routine use). Of the 17 teachers, 3 were still largely operating at the imitative stage of transfer (level 1), 3 had reached a mechanical level (level 2), and the remaining 11 had developed routine or integrative use levels of transfer. Thus, while 15 of the 17 teachers were practicing frequently enough to develop skill in the

FIGURE 6.3

Transfer of Training by Teachers with Three Models of Teaching for Two Years

School	Teacher	Transfer of Training	
		1987–88	1988–89
A	A	3.1	3.0
	B	4.0	4.5
	C	1.8	1.0
	D	4.7	—
	E	3.1	2.5
	F	3.8	3.0
B	A	4.3	4.5
	B	4.6	5.0
	C	3.5	3.5
	D	2.0	1.5
	E	1.9	2.5
C	A	3.6	3.5
	B	4.4	4.0
	C	2.5	3.0
	D	2.0	2.0
	E	1.9	—
	F	4.9	5.0

Levels of Transfer: 1 = imitative use; 2 = mechanical use; 3 = routine use; 4 = integrated use; 5 = executive use.

new models of teaching, only 11 (65 percent) were using the strategies appropriately enough to predict that their students would derive the intellectual, social, and personal benefits promised by research underlying the models.

In the second year of the project, 10 (67 percent) of the 15 remaining sample teachers had developed a routine or higher level of transfer with the models. Two of the three schools had increased both their practice and levels of transfer with models of teaching, while the third school (School A) actually suffered losses in both areas. Possible school-level causes for both gains and losses will be discussed later.

Frequency of practice with the models was correlated with level of transfer at $r = 0.62$ (Spearman Rank Correlation Coefficient) during year one of the project and at $r = 0.75$ during the second year. Clearly, no one reached high levels of transfer without frequent and consistent practice. However, several teachers continued practice of the new strategies without apparently developing greater understanding of their use. They continued to imitate lessons they had observed with trainers or peers and found it difficult to depart from their teacher's manuals to experiment with alternative strategies for achieving similar instructional objectives.

Factors Affecting Variation in Use and Transfer

This project involved the entire faculties of three schools in the training and implementation of an innovation for school improvement. We hypothesized that individual characteristics (states of growth, years of teaching experience), small group characteristics (functioning of study groups) and school variables (principal leadership, faculty cohesion) might all affect teachers' rates of implementation. Figure 6.4 presents data on states of growth and implementation.

Individual Factors. Growth states scores were computed for all teachers in our sample near the end of the first project year. The mean growth state for our sample was 3.1 (SD = 0.96, range 1–5), with the mean for School A at 2.67, School B at 3.0, and School C at 3.5. As reported by McKibbin and Joyce (1980) and by Hopkins (1990), states of growth has proved to be a powerful predictor of implementation of innovations, both in projects involving whole schools and those involving only volunteers. In this project, in which entire faculties participated if 80 percent or greater of their teachers requested the program, states of growth correlated 0.87 with transfer levels during year one and 0.88 during year two (Spearman Rank Correlation Coefficients).

A common belief among both professional educators and the general public is that young teachers (e.g., teachers just entering the profession) are more open to innovation than older, more experienced teachers who have presumably become tired and set in their ways. The Joyce, Bush, and McKibbin (1982) study found no relationship between years of teaching experience and the willingness and ability to engage in professional growth. The good news from their study was that mature, experienced teachers are often at the height of their professional powers, while the bad news was that some young teachers just entering the profession are actively pushing away growth opportunities—in effect, they quit learning at age 22.

FIGURE 6.4

**Teacher Growth States and Transfer of Training
of Three Models of Teaching**

School	Teacher	Growth States	Transfer of Training	
			1987–88	1988–89
A	A	3	3.1	3.0
	B	3	4.0	4.5
	C	1	1.8	1.0
	D	4	4.7	0.7
	E	2	3.1	2.5
	F	3	3.8	3.0
B	A	4	4.3	4.5
	B	4	4.6	5.0
	C	3	3.5	3.5
	D	2	2.0	1.5
	E	2	1.9	2.5
C	A	3	3.6	3.5
	B	4	4.4	4.0
	C	3	2.5	3.0
	D	3	2.0	2.0
	E	3	1.9	—
	F	5	4.9	5.0

Growth States: 1 = Reticent (satisfaction of basic needs); 2 = Withdrawn (psychological safety); 3 = Passive Consumer (concerns for belonging and security); 4 = Active Consumer (achievement orientation); 5 = Gourmet Omnivore (self-actualizing).

Levels of Transfer: 1 = imitative use; 2 = mechanical use; 3 = routine use; 4 = integrated use; 5 = executive use.

We examined the relationship between years of teaching experience and transfer of training for our sample and found a low correlation between "experience" and "transfer" ($r = 0.13$ for the first year of the project, and $r = 0.10$ for the second year). (A high positive correlation would have favored mature teachers, whereas a high negative correlation would have favored beginning teachers.) Thus, for our sample, years of teaching experience was not associated with ability to transfer training into regular classroom practice.

Peer Group Influences. All teachers in the three project schools were members of peer coaching study teams that were organized during the initial two-week workshop to facilitate the implementation of models of teaching. Study teams met weekly at the school sites on schedules worked out by the members of the team in conjunction with their administrators. The charge to study teams was threefold. It emphasized only activities that were believed to increase practice with and implementation of the newly learned teaching strategies. Teachers were to share lessons and materials already used in case others could use the plans/materials and thus cut down on preparation time They were to observe each other trying the new strategies—to learn from each other and study student responses to the strategies. And they were to plan future applications of the strategies within their curriculum areas in an attempt to integrate a model's use with existing repertoire and instructional objectives.

Study group functioning was conceived on a continuum from the merely pro forma (teachers meet as scheduled, verbally share experiences, and observe each other as scheduled) to enthusiastic participation (teachers share lessons and materials and observe each other easily and frequently) to fully collegial groups (teachers move beyond enthusiastic participation to setting common goals and developing lessons and units that all or part of the group will use in the future).

In the first year, none of our sample teachers belonged to a fully collegial study group, although some of the groups occasionally worked in a fully collegial fashion for several weeks at a time. Twelve of our 17 sample teachers, however, belonged to "enthusiastic" groups that shared past lessons and materials freely and increasingly observed each other at unscheduled times because they enjoyed seeing each other try out lessons. The remaining five teachers belonged to pro forma groups and were passive members of those groups, neither complaining about the static nature of their meetings nor initiating more dynamic activities.

One is tempted to view the study group functioning as a glass half-empty, given the shortfall between what was possible and what occurred. However, we view the glass as half-full, given that, prior to the project, teachers in the project schools never saw each other work and rarely met to discuss matters of curriculum and instruction (unless one counts monthly faculty meetings). With three exceptions, they shared no lesson planning or materials development, even though five or six teachers in a school might be teaching the same grade level or subject and using exactly the same texts. The implementation of study teams in the project schools did, in fact, greatly reduce the isolation in which most teachers formerly worked. Further, the level of study team functioning correlated 0.61 with transfer of training during the first year of the project.

Study team functioning during the second year was much more mixed. The organization and facilitation of study teams requires active administrative support, not only for scheduling but for maintaining focus and purpose. One of the schools (School A) lost a very active administrator and gained a new (first-time) administrator. The same school, halfway though the second year, was "raided" by an administrator who was assembling faculty for a new school. Thus the School A teachers knew that nine of their number would be leaving at the end of the year. This combination of factors was reflected in less practice for School A, declining rates of transfer, and lowering study team functioning during year two of the project. In the other two schools, two of the teams achieved fully collegial status, two alternated between enthusiastic and fully collegial functioning, four functioned at an enthusiastic level, and two functioned at a pro forma level.

Study team functioning was influenced by the states of growth of individual members. Teams were generally composed of four to six teachers. The four most successful study teams all had leadership from active consumers or gourmet omnivores. The presence of an active, growth-oriented individual, however, was not sufficient to ensure fully collegial functioning if one or more members were reticent or withdrawn. Study teams comprised of passive consumers were often enthusiastic but needed occasional structure. For example, they would approach the project consultants and ask for ideas or development projects to work on. They would then work enjoyably on a new idea or unit or materials development scheme until it was finished.

On balance, we believe the study teams functioned to boost implementation of an innovation for our project schools, to increase teacher interaction about curriculum and instruction, and to reduce the norms of privacy and isolation. We do not believe, however, that the organization and functioning of study teams alone can change the climate of a school and create fully collegial interactions where few or none existed before—at least not in two years. Perhaps, given our history of school cultures in which teachers have had so little opportunity to work in collegial fashions and make collective decisions, time will be required to develop truly collegial patterns of work. Whether this means more years or more intensive time together is not clear to us at this point. We are convinced, however, that collegiality will develop only in conjunction with meaningful and challenging reasons for collaborative work, such as efforts to improve curriculum and instruction for increased student learning.

School-Level Factors. We have already discussed the role of administrative leadership in the organization and the functioning of study teams. Principals and assistant principals performed several other roles as well. First, they were instrumental in their school's participation in the project, since schools were not considered for inclusion unless 80 percent or more of the staff were interested and principals wrote letters of application. Second, they provided varying amounts of pressure and support with respect to practice of the new strategies. During the first year, administrators at Schools A and B not only regularly observed (separate from "formal evaluation" observations) and encouraged teachers as they tried the new strategies but also borrowed classes and practiced the new strategies themselves. Administrators at Schools A and B met with study groups, and administrators at School C designated two lead teachers to meet with study groups and assist them during the first few months of the project. At Schools A and B, administrators generated schoolwide implementation projects for specific models of teaching during the first year. During the second year, this activity was continued and increased in Schools B and C. Since project consultants met regularly with administrators and encouraged their active leadership and participation, we cannot predict what the absence of administrative support would have meant to the project. However, the lessening of administrative support at School A during the second year, and the concomitant losses there, suggest that the support of administrators was crucial to project success.

Changes in the Workplace

Structural changes in the ways teachers worked with each other have already been discussed. Possible increases (or decreases) in general cohesion and problem-solving ability can best be illustrated by what happened at the end of the project. Schools B and C retained their study group formats; selected curriculum areas to focus on (schoolwide) and set goals for student achievement in those areas; secured additional training from consultants in their respective curriculum areas foci; and began working on the integration of teaching models with new training in content and materials. School A, at the close of the project, was struggling to retain its study group format and to incorporate 11 new staff members who had not had training in models of teaching. The principal was considering retiring. The new assistant principal was gamely trying to coordinate some sort of school improvement focus for the year but had no consensus from the staff two months into the school year.

It is difficult to determine how enduring even large structural and attitudinal changes will be at specific school sites. Clearly, stability of staff and administration are important, as are shared experiences in decision making and training. Norms of continual renewal for individuals and groups probably must extend beyond specific schools to entire districts and the profession at large before even large-scale change efforts can have long-range prospects for durability.

Implementation of the content of training was achieved at all three sites, although individual differences occurred. Given the history of implementation of curricular and instructional innovations (Fullan & Pomfret, 1977, Joyce & Showers, 1983, 1988), the implementation of teaching models by three school faculties (for whom the models represented additions to repertoire) was a considerable achievement. Sufficient training allowed all teachers to practice their newly acquired skills, and teachers and administrators were able to restructure the workplace to the extent that teachers could regularly work together on implementation questions. At the end of the first project year, 88 percent of the teachers were using the new strategies regularly and skillfully enough (a mechanical level of transfer or higher) that students had developed the requisite skills for learning within the models' frameworks. Sixty-seven percent of the teachers had achieved a routine or better level of transfer and thus had good prospects for integrating the new models into their regular teaching repertoires.

We were heartened by the overall success of the implementation effort and the benefits to students as a result of the project (for details of impact on students, see Joyce et al., 1989; Joyce & Calhoun, 1996).

○ ○ ○

The implementation of planned changes is crucial to the success of school improvement efforts if increased student growth is the intended outcome. Monitoring of an implementation—including setting a target, collecting data on an ongoing basis, and using that data to identify obstacles—empowers staffs and builds confidence in their collective ability to accomplish what they set out to do.

As can be seen from the Richmond County example, monitoring an implementation can include any variables staff believe will influence use of innovations. Studying implementation is not technically difficult but represents a change in norms and behavior for many staffs. With the help of a consultant or facilitator, individuals, teams, and schools are quite capable of studying their implementation, and, as we will see in the next chapter, the impact of changes on their students.

The study of implementation should be an inclusive process—everyone can use it as the basis for an ongoing inquiry into their practices and effects. If the study of implementation becomes a normal part of the operation, individual teachers, peer coaching teams, schools, and the district as a whole (rather than just a few persons or outside consultants) should spawn little "action research" projects as described in Chapters 2 and 7. Again, subject matter is important. You simply can't design the study of teaching without the study of academic content.

Inquiry and Evaluation: Learning What Our Students Are Learning

The only real evaluation is whether students learn more. And the only real issue in evaluation is whether we study student learning as a consequence of what we learn in curriculum, instruction, and the social climate of the school.

Evaluation is an inquiry, a process of asking questions and seeking answers so that the program can be gradually improved. Many educators conceive of evaluation as an end point, a judgment—"This program is successful; that teacher is effective." We view evaluation as a way the system or a community of action researchers can provide information for itself about its efforts on an ongoing basis. We emphasize the "formative" aspect of evaluation because we believe in the importance of ensuring that educators use the data emerging from their efforts to improve their programs.

In the context of a staff development system, formative evaluation is a critical element that maintains focus, linking a vision of what schooling can be for students and progress toward that vision. And because we imagine a system in which governance is shared, each person has a role in designing and executing the evaluation process, interpreting the results, and acting to improve things.

Determining the extent to which new content and processes are implemented needs to occur before questions about student outcomes can be addressed. Assuming the change that was planned is implemented, however, the questions of greatest interest to most teachers, administrators, and parents can be asked: How are the changes we have put in place affecting our students?

We acknowledge the difficulties inherent in evaluating staff development programs. We recognize that the implementation of each event and program is heavily influenced by its context. The energy and interest of the schools and teachers amplify or diminish the effects of training events. Also, staff development influences its ultimate goal, student learning, through a chain of events. Content of high potential needs good training design if it is to come to life in the classroom and achieve its potential. Measuring response to a series of training events by, for example, determining how participants liked them or whether initial skill and knowledge were developed provides only a beginning. If the skills are not employed (skillfully enough that student learning is affected), the chain is broken.

Additionally, the measurement of many of the important variables is technically difficult. Frequently, tests of student behavior and learning have to be constructed—some of the most used commercially available instruments are not appropriate for all the objectives that we may have.

Finally, cost limitations almost always result in designs where a sample rather than the entire population is studied. (We definitely favor the thorough study of a sample rather than a more superficial study of the entire population because the chain of events and moderating variables can be tracked only by the collection and analysis of high-quality data.)

Having acknowledged the difficulties, we believe (and that belief is supported by ample evidence from reports of action research) that individuals, schools, and districts are perfectly capable of conducting evaluations of the effect of changes on students as a consequence of staff development programs.

A Framework for Evaluating Staff Development Programs

Because it is not universally agreed that the purpose of staff development is ultimately student achievement, we reiterate our position here: Student achievement is the intended outcome of staff development. Consequently, the evaluation of staff development programs turns on the study of student growth.

In the next few pages we suggest a simple framework for evaluating staff development programs and provide examples of individuals, schools, and districts that have employed it.

Formulating Clear Questions

Once an individual, faculty, or district has determined primary needs or concerns with respect to student performance, selected a course of action to address those needs, engaged in training, and studied the implementation of the planned change, educators must ask clear questions about the intended student outcomes. What propelled the move to change or improve something about the instructional program, curriculum, climate, or policies of the class/school/district? Was the concern for reading comprehension, the quality of writing, or what? Was the problem the number of failures and retentions experienced by students? Whatever the initial problem or concern, the first step in designing an evaluation is revisiting that beginning point and stating the problem in measurable terms. Ask questions like these: "Has students' reading comprehension increased?" and "Has the number of student suspensions decreased?" These queries serve to maintain focus on the purpose of the entire enterprise and provide direction for the kinds of data to be collected.

To Sample or Not to Sample

Once a question or questions have been formulated that clearly reflect a teacher's or faculty's intentions with respect to student outcomes, the teacher or faculty must decide about the number of students to be observed or measured to answer the questions. If a school asks the question, "Has the frequency of student suspensions decreased?" there is no need to select a sample of students for study. Most schools already keep accurate records of the incidence and cause of student suspensions, and the faculty need only compile and summarize the data. If, on the other hand, a faculty asks the question, "Has reading comprehension increased?" it will almost certainly want to select a sample of students to study in depth. The nature of the question governs the type of information needed as well as the cost of collecting it and, thus, the choices about sampling.

Data Collection

The type of data to be collected is again affected by the questions asked. Questions about reading comprehension indicate a need for tests of reading comprehension. In elementary schools, staffs will probably want to administer individualized tests to a stratified random sample of students, given their greater reliability for young children and their greater yield of diagnostic information. Questions about quality of student writing will require the use of a rubric to score the organization and coherence of compositions, the use of detail to support major points, and the mastery of the mechanics of writing (spelling, punctuation, and capitalization). The type of data collected must align with the intended outcomes. When the primary target of an intervention is increased student self-esteem, evaluation of the effort must measure changes in self-esteem.

Studies of implementation are not surrogates for studies of student learning. If the original impetus for an intensive program of word processing was the quality of student writing, implementation data would likely monitor the frequency with which students composed at the computer and the types of writing prompts to which they responded. On the other hand, evaluation data would examine the quality of compositions composed at the computer and perhaps the frequency with which students produced compositions, as compared with a baseline measure.

A second issue of concern to evaluators is the quality of data collected. Are the data valid and reliable? Have we measured what we set out to measure, and do our data accurately reflect students' knowledge and skill? We recommend, whenever possible, that evaluators use developed measures with established track records for validity and reliability. For example, the variable of self-esteem or academic self-concept is frequently measured in school improvement projects. Creating a measure of self-esteem and testing it are costly and time-consuming activities; and excellent measures already exist (e.g., for young children, see Harter's [1982] "Perceived Competence Scale for Children" and for adolescents, see March and O'Neil's [1984] "Self-Description Questionnaire").

Teacher-made tests are certainly defensible sources of data. No one knows better what academic content students were asked to master, and thus no one is better positioned to construct tests over that material. We suggest, however, that teacher-made tests be extensive rather than brief. Teachers are not interested (as are, by necessity, the makers of standardized tests) in *sampling* the information their students have mastered. They want students to know all addition and multiplication facts; knowing only certain facts is not productive, given the teacher's initial reason for wanting students to master such material.

In addition to determining the type of data to be collected, evaluators must decide how frequently and at what intervals they will gather data. If grade distributions are the indicators selected to evaluate program effects, data will be "collected" four to six times during an academic year. If written compositions are to be collected and scored for a sample of students during a year, a teacher or staff may want feedback on progress every six to nine weeks. In the case of suspension data, information is collected continuously, or with every instance monitored. And if reading comprehension is being studied, data might reasonably be collected three times during an academic year. Student learning of sight words might be measured on a monthly or even a weekly basis, as illustrated in the examples described later in this chapter.

The primary tasks for evaluators are to ensure that the types of data collected relate to the intended outcomes; that the measures are appropriate (valid, reliable, and accurate) for the outcomes of interest; and that data are collected at appropriate intervals. Once evaluators make these decisions, they can use many resources to help them identify measures and their appropriate use (e.g., see Calhoun's 1994 *How to Use Action Research in the Self-Renewing School*). Obvious categories of data collection tools include observations, interviews, questionnaires, document analysis, and tests.

Data Analysis

Fortunately, a degree in statistics is not required to sensibly analyze data. The purpose for collecting the data and the need to communicate findings to all interested parties, however, necessitate organizing the data collected into usable forms.

The first step is to return to the questions that motivated the staff development focus; they will usually provide clues to the most useful ways of organizing information. Second, think about the audience(s) for the information and the uses to which it will be put. If, for example, the change being implemented is intended to improve student behavior and reduce referrals and suspensions, data may be summarized in a weekly form that includes the number of and reasons for referrals and suspensions. When the audience is teachers, results might be graphed and updated on a weekly basis so that all can see that their behavior makes a difference. When the audience is parents, a graph for a four- to six-week period might be inserted in an article describing the school's concern and the action it has taken with respect to student referrals and suspensions.

A major purpose of formative evaluation is to provide information that enables individuals and groups to adjust their behavior. Data are meant to be communicated, and the form data analysis takes needs to be governed primarily by its relevance to the questions asked and its clarity in communicating results.

Nothing is more satisfying professionally than determining that effort and energy, whether individually or collectively expended, has resulted in positive outcomes for students. Such information justifies the effort and builds both individual and group efficacy, a sense of confidence, and competence. On the other hand, if ongoing evaluation data suggest that the desired outcomes are not being accomplished, it's better to know before enormous amounts of energy and resources have been expended. We would warn evaluators, however, to be cautious about eliminating programs before they have had a chance to work. Negative results can just as easily generate re-examination of the implementation or adjustments to the program. Beware of disposing of new programs too quickly, especially when new content and processes have been selected because of their successful track records in other settings.

Let's put all this together and see what it looks like with respect to the evaluation of the system and each of its components.

The Study of the System

We need to create a parsimonious, embedded program of evaluation tied to a continuous effort to make the staff development system work better. The study is an active inquiry into how people use the system and what is done with the content of the program, with the purpose of learning how to improve the system.

The dynamics of each of the three components that make up a complete staff development system—one that serves individuals, faculties, and district initiatives—differ sufficiently that each deserves special consideration. Let us assume a fully functioning three-component system and explore some of the questions we might ask of each.

The Individual Component

1. Who is served and what affects participation? Assuming that the component possesses a good variety of offerings, an easy task is to count participants and their characteristics by type of offering. An intermediate agency we are familiar with used data in some interesting ways. Its offerings for teachers (developed through a democratic process similar to the one we have been describing but with representatives from the 40 districts they serve) were categorized as follows:

● Content addressing personal needs—items containing content such as "stress management," "time management," and "personal finances."
● Various approaches to classroom management.
● Various teaching strategies.
● Basic teaching skills.

● Curriculum area studies—approaches to the teaching of reading and writing, multicultural education, and the teaching of mathematics and other subjects.

The agency discovered that workshops with "personal need" content and "classroom management" topics drew several times more participants than did the workshops in any of the other categories, such as the curriculum and instruction topics. However, the participants in curriculum and instruction categories tended to be "repeaters" who were likely to attend multiple events. And this small, loyal band reported great satisfaction and found the content useful in their professional work.

The planners observed that the workshops on teaching and curriculum were much longer than the others and were scheduled so that sessions followed one another closely—sometimes as often as three evenings per week. Friendship groups or teams from schools often attended those workshops.

Now—what to do next? The agency could have decided to offer more workshops of the more popular types and reduced the less well-attended ones, but the planners decided to experiment with ways of increasing the popularity of those dealing with the study of curriculum and instruction. They scheduled them differently, spacing the sessions farther apart. And they began to advertise for teams from schools. Within a year, those workshops were attended to capacity. However, the increases were not at the expense of the other categories. The agency had increased its clientele.

The agency planners also worked to increase the effectiveness of all the categories. One example was in the area of classroom management. They noticed that the highly structured behavior modification approaches drew more participants than the approaches derived from individual and group-centered therapies, such as the Classroom Meeting Model. They conducted a small interview study with the teachers of a nearby school and discovered that most of the teachers saw management from a highly structured perspective. The finding resulted in an introductory offering called "alternative models of classroom management" that turned out to be popular and generated an increase in participants for the group dynamics–centered workshops.

The agency modified its program on the basis of simple, thoughtfully analyzed, and carefully interpreted "head count" data.

2. What happens to the content? How much of the content finds its way into practice, does the use persist, and what are the perceptions of its effects? Here the evaluation approaches the transfer question that is so vital to the effectiveness of the system. Sampling will become very important, because studying transfer by all the teachers attending a large smorgasbord of offerings would entail enormous effort.

Using the previous example, suppose our agency begins by analyzing the objectives of the workshops, selects the ones that have content and skill objectives that are pertinent to instruction, and categories them. Then, suppose the agency randomly selects one workshop from each category and, further, randomly selects six participants from each workshop for follow-up studies. Those persons are interviewed at intervals following the workshop, seeking information about use and types of use and perceptions of effects on students. The results are likely to resemble those obtained in the Ames study, where teacher reviews about the effectiveness of several initiatives were reported (see Study 3 in Chapter 10; see also Joyce & Calhoun, 1996).

Because we know that it is possible, with good design, to have consistent levels of transfer of 90 percent or better, the question is how closely the results of the interviews approach that figure. If the use of content is low, then improving training design needs to be considered. For example, a district we know offered 10 days of instruction in various forms of cooperative learning to several hundred of its teachers, providing substitutes for participants or paying them for summer and Saturday study. Interviews revealed findings of particular interest. First, only about 25 percent of the teachers used any of the varieties of cooperative learning following the 10 days of training; second, nearly all of those who did used the simpler, highly structured forms. Hardly anyone used the more complex forms that had occupied most of the workshop time. The planning group faced a number of issues. One was whether to go to a "bring a friend" format and organize participants into peer coaching teams and see if that would help. A second was whether the workshop was adequately designed. (It turned out that there were very few demonstrations!) A third was whether too much was being attempted in one package, leading them to consider having an introductory offering of the simpler, highly structured forms, working on implementation, and following with other offerings of the more complex forms.

A simple evaluation design provided plenty of information on which to improve their system. Note how the interview phase depended on sampling both staff development offerings and people, making the process feasible in terms of cost and effort. The process would have broken down if they tried to interview all the participants in all their offerings.

In our own work, we ask teachers to provide us with simple usage logs that include information about how the students are responding and what kinds of help the teachers feel they need We select a sample for more in-depth study to help us plan staff development events tailored (as best we can) to their perceptions of their needs.

3. Are the participants studying the effects on their students? We now turn to a major "process objective" of staff development, which is to support reflective teaching and facilitate the "teacher as researcher." We assume now that the workshops include provisions for discussing how participants will study the responses of their students and will provide them, when necessary, with classroom-relevant tools for doing so. Our search is for economical ways of helping people conduct studies in the context of teaching—and learning what kinds of help they may need to do so.

One direct way is to schedule sessions where people share their studies, which helps build community and gives us a chance to see what they produce. In our own work, we have found that helping people study student responses is one of our most technically demanding tasks because of the wide range of preparation people have for this aspect of teaching.

An example comes from a workshop where we worked with upper-elementary teachers on mnemonic devices to help students learn and retain number facts. Some teachers developed a pretest to ascertain what facts the students knew, then taught them how to use the mnemonics, and then gave a post-test to find out how much they had learned. They were also interested in retention and gave additional tests at two-week intervals for a month, following each with study sessions. By that time all the students knew just about all the facts. Teachers then scheduled a test two months later so they could study whether the information had transferred into long-term memory.

Some of the other teachers left out the pretest, so learning could not be ascertained, but gave delayed recall tests. Several teachers reported they would not use pretests because "that was cheating. The kids would know what would be on the final test." Nonetheless, the sharing process helped all the teachers get a sense of how effective the mnemonics teaching had been, and the discussions over the "pretest" problem was useful to all. The amount of information gained by the first group of teachers was impressive and helped prepare people for similar studies on the effects of other models of teaching.

4. What do people think about their experiences? When and how to sample opinion is the question. We want to move from an evaluation system that depends, as most staff development programs currently do, on questionnaires about sessions. Opinions are important, to be sure, but their measurement is trickier than is sometimes assumed, and the overreliance on satisfaction surveys is what we question.

One simple way to sample opinion is to incorporate it into the type of interview study discussed previously. On the whole, interviews give more information than do questionnaires (especially about how to improve events) and tie the study of opinion to the study of use. If people like a staff development program but don't use the content, we need to know why. As Huberman and Miles (1984) state, initial attitudes do not necessarily predict use, but as people become good at something, their attitude toward it improves dramatically. Thus we recommend studying attitudes along with use. In the River City project described in Chapter 2, people who developed "executive control" most rapidly became the most positive, even if they started with lukewarm attitudes toward the content. Those who were stuck for long periods of time at the level of routine use tended to become discouraged until they "broke through" and their learning curve went up.

Studying initial reactions to staff development is tricky to say the least. Unless tied to the study of use, first opinions can be deceptive. In Hopkins's (1990) study, the participants in a lengthy workshop were positive toward the process and the content; but subsequent use, even supported by periodic workshops and get-togethers, was low for most teachers. Huberman and Miles's (1984) extensive long-term studies found initial attitudes a poor predictor of subsequent use, which is the bottom line of attitudes. We will make just a few technical comments on the use of questionnaires:

● *On the Nature of Items.* Closed-ended items need to be few and not redundant. Asking opinions of the service provider (the "presenter'" in common argot), the content, and the process generally produce highly correlated responses. If one item will do, why use three? Mixing items on different aspects of events tends to confuse respondents. Asking opinions about room arrangements, refreshments, audio-visual aids, materials, providers, content, and process all at once can generate deceiving results. If the room is uncomfortable and opinion is asked about that, there is likely to be an effect on opinions expressed about the people and content. We favor sticking with a few items about content and process and asking people directly what they think about the nuts-and-bolts aspects.

● *One Size Fits All?* We strongly resist the use of "omnibus" questionnaires that seem to proclaim: "This questionnaire can be used to evaluate any event." "One size fits all" questionnaires are almost impossible to design. For example, consider the results of opinion surveys at an organization's recent national conference. For a simple example, a one-hour talk that was applauded repeatedly by an audience of nearly 1,000 people was accompanied by a form asking "Was adequate time provided for interaction among the participants?" (none) and "What was the quality of the handouts?" (there were none). Even though such a form may provide a place for "not applicable," the fact that such questions are asked implies some degree of appropriateness and can confuse responses. If we want to find out how people feel, we can take the time to tailor our instrument to the event.

● *Charming the Response.* "Charming the response" is real. When we're asked our opinions, can we sort out our reactions to the content and process from a strand of the event designed to get us to produce favorable responses? In other words, can service providers lead us to "want" to give their events high marks?

You bet they can. An excellent review of the literature on the subject (Abrams, 1984) includes studies where responses were spectacularly manipulated. It stands to reason that most experienced service providers have, perhaps unconsciously, "learned" to get good if not excellent ratings, which makes interpretation difficult. We don't worry much about this except that inexperienced providers sometimes show up badly, and we don't want a situation where young and new talent is not nourished. A major task in building the "cadres" we mention so frequently is helping talented teachers transition to the role of giving service to their peers. The job is not technically difficult, but many teachers fear that their peers will not respond positively to them in the new role. We believe much of the fear comes because they know intuitively that, without experience, they will not yet have learned how to ensure positive response. We are uncomfortable when novice teachers are submitted to a questionnaire "evaluation" right after their first workshop—and their responses are compared to those of "the old smoothies."

Evaluating the Individual Component: The Basics

We have suggested that evaluation address four questions:

- Who participates in what?
- What happens to the content?
- Are participants studying the effects on their students?
- What do people think about their experiences?

The evaluation is run as an inquiry into how to improve the system, where participants in decision making, service providers, and participants join together to improve the component. Evaluation needs to be embedded and economical, with sampling used when possible, and the "working together to improve the system" mode is shared by everyone. We avoid collecting data that are not needed or will not be used (those heaps of files of questionnaires) and implementation becomes the fulcrum of the process.

The Collective Component

In previous publications we divided staff development efforts into three categories based on who is addressed. Some components are directed toward individuals; some are directed toward collectives, such as school faculties; and some support district initiatives. The collective component serves schools in two ways. One is by providing facilitation to schools as they analyze what they teach, how they teach, and the social climate of the school and, consequently, to make initiatives to improve it. The second is staff development in support of the schoolwide initiatives in curriculum, instruction, and technology. We will concentrate on the assessment of facilitation first and discuss the effects of staff development when we discuss the study of the district initiatives.

Studying the Effects of Facilitation

Studying process effects is not easy and can be very time-consuming if the questions are not sharply defined. Essentially, the questions center around the faculty's ability to organize itself, engage in focused study, and generate initiatives and, most important for the system, to determine whether facilitation needs to be modified, which it almost always does.

Let us imagine a district with a dozen schools. (More or less will not affect what we recommend here. Size would affect organization but not the process of evaluation itself.) The district has organized an action research facilitation team with members from each school faculty. The team has studied approaches for transforming the school into a self-renewing organization. Their job is to help the schools move forward and to facilitate the development of the organization more or less along the lines we described in Chapters 1 to 3. The first questions are asked of all the schools.

What is the condition of the structure for collective action? As in the case of the individual component, we begin with counting and seek to know:

● Are the schools organized into peer coaching partnerships in preparation for learning new things?
● Has time been provided for team and faculty meetings?
● Are data being collected on the "vital signs" of the school: grades, other indicators of achievement, disciplinary action, connection of the school with parents and other community members?
● Has a process for collective decision making been established?

The facilitators can collect and share these data by organizing the faculties to periodically prepare summaries of progress. Thus the pictures they paint for one another are products of the faculties they are facilitating.

If progress is being made, all to the good. If it is not, the facilitators and committee, including the principals, need to think about how to change their handling of the facilitation. Generally speaking, schools who cannot establish these or equivalent structures will have a difficult time proceeding to develop initiatives (Joyce, Wolf, & Calhoun, 1993). If there are signs of sticking at this level, the facilitators can interview teachers to obtain their perceptions about what is wrong and how to fix it. The results can be shared and further decisions made about how to change the facilitation process.

What kinds of initiatives are the schools developing? The initiatives the schools develop are the fulcrum of the site-based school renewal process. What is being selected and why? What are the student learning objectives? What kinds of staff development are planned? How will implementation be studied? How will effects on students be studied? What is the level of commitment to the initiatives?

Again, the facilitators can lead the schools to respond to these questions and the answers can be shared with an eye to improving the process and the initiatives themselves.

What is the product of the initiatives in terms of implementation and effects? The same questions can be asked and types of data collected as in the discussion of the individual component, but data are now collected and shared by the faculties. The facilitators share the information, again plan how to improve facilitation, and get ready to continue the cycle.

Next Time Around

After completing the foregoing process, the cycle is repeated. The process should be easier the second time around. The facilitators should become more expert.

The need to continue to study and improve will continue. This is the most difficult of all the components. The goal is that every school will be able to enter and complete the process as a part of normal operations.

The District Component

Now we turn to districtwide initiatives in curriculum, instruction, and technology, governed as we describe in Chapter 2. These have substantial student learning goals and designs to track implementation and effects on students so that the initiatives can be improved and the ones that follow them can be planned better. In other chapters, we have described the way the University City and River City districts went about the process of evaluating their districtwide initiatives. Here we will illustrate the process by turning to another districtwide initiative that was studied carefully. In this case, an interesting aspect of student achievement-oriented staff development surfaces; frequently a degree of controversy ensues when substantial rises in student achievement are sought. In the case below, not only are there persons who do not believe the objectives can be achieved, but some do not believe that those objectives are desirable or that the avenue of approach will be up to the task. Thus the evaluation system has to deal with a substantial array of issues.

A Community of Kindergarten Teachers Study Literacy

We have stressed throughout this book that the evaluation of staff development where curricular and instructional changes are the content needs to be formative, embedded in the implementation process, and internal, that is, carried out by the participants. In the following pages we will describe a particularly complex undertaking in the Northern Lights, Alberta, School Division #69.*

Our focus is on eight kindergarten classes in three schools in the Cold Lake area of the school division. Responding to a school improvement initiative by the province whereby schools were provided with the resources to engage in various school improvement efforts, the principals of the three schools approached their kindergarten teachers and parents. Together, they proposed two changes. One was to move from a two-day schedule to a four-day schedule. The second was to incorporate the teaching of reading and writing into the curriculum. It fell to the curriculum director of the district to contact consultants who could help the schools generate the literacy components of the curriculum and provide the needed staff development. None of the eight teachers had previously taught a reading/writing curriculum to kindergarten students and several had not had a course on the teaching of reading during their preparation. Two were first-year teachers and two others were in their third year of teaching. Another was an experienced French Immersion teacher who now agreed to teach listening, speaking, reading, and writing simultaneously to children who ranged in age from 4 1/2 to 5 1/2 or a little more. The district provided staff development sessions of four initial days in September; it provided further sessions about every three weeks throughout the year.

The curriculum was designed after a thorough search of the literature on early literacy (see Calhoun, 1997). The central component is the Picture Word Inductive Model (Calhoun, 1999; Joyce & Calhoun, 1998), but a series of other components are incorporated, making a multidimensional curriculum, as follows:

● *The Picture Word Inductive Model.* The Picture Word Inductive Model is employed in cycles of three to four weeks built around large photographs that are mounted in the room surrounded by sheets of blank paper. The students identify objects and actions, "shaking the words out of the picture," using their naturally developed vocabularies. As the words are shaken out, the teacher draws

---

* Bruce Joyce, Emily Calhoun, and Marilyn Hrycauk developed the curriculum and organized the staff development described here, aided by a group of gifted teachers from the Northern Lights, Alberta, School Division #69: Bev Gariepy, Christine Michaud, Elaine Blades, Melanie Malayney, Carol Kruger, Jennifer Lawton-Godziuk, Christine Cairns, Andrea Fama, and Gloria Lane.

lines from the relevant items in the picture to words that are spelled for and by the children, generating a picture dictionary that the students can use to study the words. Then, the teacher gives each student cards with the words on them. Students study the words, going to the picture dictionary to identify words they don't recognize immediately. Teachers also lead students to study the words by using their cards to classify them. The teachers model classifications based on the phonetic and structural features of the words. Then, the students develop titles for the picture, also modeled by the teacher, and those are written down and new words spelled and studied. Next the teachers model the sentences, and the students dictate sentences using the words in the picture. Thus high-frequency "useful little words" are added to their word banks.

Finally, the teachers generate a paragraph using those sentences and discuss how they constructed the paragraph (composing while thinking aloud). Each week the teachers study the word recognition by a sample of the students, how many they can recognize out of context. Throughout the cycle, the students continue to classify the words (and eventually the sentences) and practice reading words, sentences, and the paragraph. Teachers send all of these products home with the students to be read to the parents.

● *The alphabet.* D'Nealian printing is used. The students, in addition to studying the alphabet on the picture word chart, use manipulables—sets of letters—to classify their work and to share their classifications with others. Periodically, students study letter recognition—teachers and students know how many letters students can recognize out of context and how many they need to master.

● *Reading to and with the students.* A balance of fiction and nonfiction is read to the students. Teachers explain how authors structure text and illustrations and how titles and the covers of books make promises to readers and how to take advantage of that.

● *Writing.* The students write from the beginning, when they scribble and draw pictures. They can also paste the words from the pictures into their writing. The teachers model sentences and the students follow along. Eventually they are structuring paragraphs.

Study of Student Learning

Throughout the year the teachers study emergent literacy using the Emergent Literacy Inventory (Pikulski & Taylor, 1999), recognition of letters, words learned, categories developed by the students, and the generation of titles, sentences, and paragraphs. Parent and teacher perceptions of students' comfort are also included.

Their study of student learning was designed to take into account the knowledge base on literacy during the kindergarten years. We need, therefore, to pay attention to the areas of agreement and disagreement in the literature before discussing some of the specific findings in the Northern Lights inquiry.

Debates about Kindergarten Curriculums

The Northern Lights Inquiry into Literacy in Kindergarten takes place in a period where there is considerable international interest in how to shape the kindergarten curriculum. There are areas of general agreement among scholars, practicing educators, and laymen and areas where there are differences in opinion. Information from research and cultural norms play mixed and alternating roles as issues are discussed. Interestingly, scholars, practicing educators, and laymen agree and differ on much the same grounds. We will try to sort out the issues and the bases for various positions beginning with areas of agreement and proceeding to those where differing opinions, often strongly held, create lively controversy as policies are made.

Apparent Agreements. Areas of general agreement include whether there should be kindergarten at all, the role of kindergarten in developing interpersonal skills, and whether kindergarten eases the transition from home to school. Questions include the following:

● *Should there be kindergarten?* Nearly everyone agrees that kindergarten transitions children from home to the institutional setting of the school and that the transition is a "good thing." The society can afford it, so why not have it? Most people believe that it is beneficial for all children. Does normative practice in kindergarten have later benefits in academic achievement? The research (remember this is normative practice) indicates modest effects and suggests that normative (referring to the range of customary practices most often used in the past 20 years or so) attendance in kindergarten somewhat levels the playing field for low socioeconomic status (SES) students, although poor elementary school curriculum and instruction can wipe out those benefits.

● *Can kindergarten develop the interpersonal skills that help children transition from the family setting to the institutional setting?* Most agree that kindergarten can have this effect. However, in this area, scholarship from the 1930s to the present indicates that the effect varies, depending on the nature of instruction (Anderson, H., & Brewer, 1939). Normative kindergarten classrooms differ in the extent to which they are set up to be cooperative or competitive. Authoritarian and integrative practices by the teacher are apparently transmitted to the students. Integrative classrooms generate integrative behavior when students are in unsupervised situations; authoritarian classrooms generate aggressive behavior when the students are in unsupervised interactive settings. Research on cooperative learning bears on this question (e.g., Johnson & Johnson, 1999).

The style of instruction in both more and less academically oriented kindergartens can have substantial influence on the behavior of the students. Just having kindergarten does not guarantee effective and desirable socialization.

● *Can kindergarten ease the transition from home to school?* Most people believe so and would like the warm, cooperative climate that generates integrative behavior. Scholars agree on this, and current studies indicate that kindergarten has socialization and academic benefits, albeit relatively modest ones, which may be a function of the curricular and instructional emphases.

Apparent Disagreements. Educators hold differing opinions about issues like the following (see Natale, 2001): the length of the kindergarten day, the place of formal literacy instruction in the curriculum, and the model of instruction teachers should use.

These are complex issues, and some are argued with considerable heat, which makes sorting out the positions difficult. On the other hand, we *should* passionately care about our students, so heat comes with the territory. The following questions are in contention:

● *How long should the kindergarten day be?* The issue is usually joined in terms of whether the best transition is on a half-day or full-day basis. There are two types of arguments, one having to do with the general cognitive and physiological energy that students around age 5 bring to kindergarten. The other has to do with the changes in society that pull opinion toward the full-day option.

Some have argued that students are simply not mentally and physically ready for a full day in an institutional setting. Others argue that they are. In the United States, more than half of kindergarten students are in full-day settings, and few teachers or parents manifest much concern. In the United Kingdom, students enter 1st grade at age 5, and few argue that they are not ready. The issue may again be one of the curricular/instructional patterns used and whether pace and type of activity can be modulated when students tire. Most scholars, practitioners, and parents probably object to a "boot camp" modality but would be pleased with a warm, flexible environment.

Some people argue that most parents are going to arrange some sort of care on a full-time basis because they work. Some respond that the social need is not a sufficient reason school systems should generate child care for the whole day. Others point out that it is better to have the children in one setting all day rather than have them transition to other caretakers twice and perhaps three times during a day. Also, full-day kindergarten can ensure that the children are under the care of trained and nurturing people organized by school personnel rather than day care entrepreneurs whose training and supervision may be indifferent.

In terms of a general policy, there is considerable evidence that most 5-year-old children manage just fine in a full-day school experience, but there are individual differences. The real issue is whether the curricular/instructional framework has the modulating capability to respond if a student needs rest and nurturance. A hard-driving, relentless curriculum is not desirable regardless of whether the academic content is substantial. As long as there is controversy, however, districts need to study how the students are responding, pay close attention to the curricular/instructional situation, and provide needed staff development. For any given child, the issue should not be regarded as settled.

● *What is the place of formal literacy instruction in the curriculum?* The normative kindergarten curriculum emphasizes the general development of listening-speaking skill and a gentle nudge toward print literacy through recognition of the letters of the alphabet. Emergent literacy—as children develop their listening-speaking vocabulary and knowledge about the existence of print representations of spoken language—is the watchword, with the kindergarten year oriented toward building general competence in language and, by doing so, preparing students for the first academic grade of school. The major issue to be debated is whether to generate a curriculum with the actual objective of teaching the students to read and where language competence is developed in the act of learning to read rather than as a precondition to the reading/writing curriculum.

Again, some of the arguments surround the issue of developmental readiness. Others surround the extent to which literacy research has laid a sufficient base that curricular/instructional modes can be developed that are developmentally appropriate *and* that provide the gifts of literacy to kindergarten students.

At one extreme, some psychologists maintain that print literacy is simply beyond the capability of kindergarten students. On the other hand, there is evidence that literacy-oriented kindergarten curriculums have benefits that are seen in academic advantage on high school graduation (see, for example, the longitudinal study by Ralph Hanson and his associates; Hanson & Farrell, 1995). And some classrooms and curriculums appear to bring students into literacy without apparent developmental damage (see, for example, Bereiter & Englemann, 1966). Which hypothesis will be acted on in policy—that students are not developmentally ready or that there are curriculums that make literacy available to students at their developmental stage?

Further, when cultural transmission is seen as a goal, print literacy provides major access to the culture—reading and writing are major dimensions of the culture. *Early literacy is not just a matter of getting ready for the primary grade curriculum in reading.* Learning to read and to write are major channels to the culture; when one is able to read, enormous cultural resources are available—the worlds of fiction and nonfiction are opened. Opportunities for development abound.

● *What modes of instruction should be used?* The overriding issue is whether we know enough to build appropriate curriculums. And curriculum development has not stood still since the arguments began. Have we learned more than we knew when the issue was first formulated? The Northern Lights teachers organized to test the proposition that a fully modern curriculum, one based on a broad view of the field as a whole, permits the development of a multidimensional modulating curriculum that has a good chance of success without grinding students against unreasonable demands.

A Multidimensional Approach

We are not the only ones who have looked to multidimensional channels of literacy acquisition to create a curriculum. We believe in the spirit of the approach at the Benchmark School (Gaskins, 1999). It has tried to leapfrog over the "reading wars" and study whether general research on literacy has brought us to the point where we can create a new generation of approaches to literacy—ones that generate cognitive activity and bring students to print literacy in delightful and rigorous ways.

Direct instruction in phonics—to targeted needs—always waits in the wings to help those who need it.

For now, let's look at the results of the multidimensional approach in the kindergarten classes in Northern Lights School District #69.

Given the controversies in the field, researchers designed the inquiry to include

● Students' phonemic awareness and alphabet knowledge as they entered kindergarten and how they developed as the year progressed.

● Students learning to acquire sight vocabulary.

● Students learning to develop phonetic and structural concepts through classification.

● Students learning to express themselves through the development of titles, sentences, and paragraphs.

● Students' transition to trade books.

Implementation: Eight Kindergarten Classes

Logs at three-week intervals enabled the teachers to report the implementation of components of the curriculum and information on student learning. The logs were structured to facilitate action research by each teacher, particularly on the student learning that resulted from the phases. Because the central element of the curriculum (the Picture Word Inductive Model) takes place in several variable-length cycles, some logs reported progress during a cycle and others at the end of the cycle. In both cases, the logs provided information about the phases or dimensions of the model. The number and length of cycles were ascertained from the logs as well as the thoroughness of implementation by phase or dimension.

Researchers accumulated data by section (or kindergarten class) and made estimates of the degree of implementation.

By the end of January (about halfway through the school year), all eight teachers had either completed three cycles with their students or were in the fourth cycle. They were using, at least partially, all phases of the model and collecting student learning data. Some teachers had developed appropriate spin-off activities. The consultants and district coordinator judged all the teachers to have generated an adequate implementation, and six were judged to be very high.

Studying Student Learning

Data collection was embedded in the implementation process. Teachers first estimated the status of formal literacy on entrance to kindergarten. They estimated that, of the 140 students who entered the eight sections in September, 3 had reached some degree of proficiency in reading and 10 were able to correctly recognize most of the letters of the alphabet.

Throughout the year, the teachers included the study of the following variables. (See Chapter 10, Study 3, the Models of Teaching Language Arts Program results.)

● *Emergent literacy, particularly phonemic concepts.* Teachers looked at this variable in the fall and again in early May, by means of the Emergent Literacy Inventory (Pikulski & Taylor, 1999).

● *Children's knowledge of the alphabet* (out-of-context recognition of the letters and their names) and phonemic development. Teachers measured this early in the year for diagnostic purposes and later to determine progress. Both are widely recognized as predictors of progress in reading.

● *Mastery of sight words.* During each of the early cycles, teachers studied student acquisition of sight words, in the form of the words "shaken out" or interpreted from pictures, at regular intervals during the cycles. They examined retention during the winter and spring.

● *Ability to read sentences and paragraphs related to the picture word cycles.*

● *Reading level.* Beginning in November and again in late February and early June, teachers used the Gunning process (Gunning, 1997) to determine the approximate grade level of trade books the students could read with comprehension.

Learning to Recognize Letters

The first formal assessment of out-of-context alphabet recognition (presenting the letters to the students and asking them to name them) occurred during the last week of September and again in December. Both upper- and lower-case letters were included. Of the 140 students, just 15 identified all or virtually all (48 or more) of the letters correctly in September (see Figure 7.1; note that this figure shows "section" results, not individual student results).

Gender differences were very small (an average difference of just three letters). The finding was important to the teachers because gender differences are often fairly large in the early years. The genders were learning to recognize letters at about even rates.

The September/October data were also useful to the teachers because they drew attention to the need to concentrate on the learning of the alphabet in the context of the Picture Word

FIGURE **7.1**

Letters Recognized by Section in September and December/January

Section	Sept. Mean	Dec./Jan. Mean
A	34	52
B	32	41
C	26	44
D	24	42
E	28	48
F	34	44
G	38	50
H	34	46

Note: See Chapter 10, Study #3, the Models of Teaching Language Arts Program results. Sections A–H represent eight kindergarten classes. Mean refers to the mean number of letters recognized by each section.

Inductive Model and through classification. All students needed their alphabet. Alphabet learning seemed to be under control as teachers assessed again in late December and early January. Most of the students had reached 50 or more, and all but one recognized two-thirds. That student recognized only 11 letters. Nearly all students recognized almost all the letters when they appeared in the context of words and sentences—another important finding for the instructors.

Importantly, nearly all the students learned that they could learn to recognize the letters out of context. The teachers concentrated on helping students complete their mastery of the letters and succeeded in doing so. By April, all the students could recognize all the letters out of the context of words.

Learning Sight Words

At the beginning of each cycle using the Picture Word Inductive Model, students were able to "shake out" information in the form of words from each picture. The teachers studied the students' recognition of the words as the students studied and classified them. Here we will look at the results and the relationship between the acquisition of the words and the development of alphabet recognition. We will concentrate on the words directly shaken out of the picture rather than words. Three cycles are typical.

● *Cycle One.* Twenty-two words were shaken out. At the end of week one, the average number of words identified out of context was 5. By the end of week four, the average was 16; one student knew all 22.
● *Cycle Two.* Twenty-two words were shaken out. At the end of week one, the average number of words identified out of context was 12; by the end of week three, the average was 20.
● *Cycle Three.* Twenty-eight words were shaken out. At the end of week one, the average number of words identified out of context was 20; at the end of week two, the average was 26, with just three students recognizing 24 and none recognizing fewer.

The progression can be interpreted in a number of ways. The students appear to be more efficient. By the end of January, all the students appeared to be able to add to their sight vocabularies; within the first week or two, just about all the words were shaken out of the picture. Aggregating the data from all the sections, the students correctly identified about 30 percent of the words after two weeks in the first cycle; they identified 90 percent after two weeks in the later cycles. The teachers could see a real "learning to learn" effect in these data.

Aside from the words shaken out (not including words learned as titles and sentences and paragraphs generated), the average student had developed 64 words as sight vocabulary by December. As the students learned to learn, the sense that they were entering the world of print literacy was palpable. By June, nearly all the students could recognize well over 100 words just from the "picture shake out" activity, plus a quantity of other words encountered from the titling, sentence-making, and paragraph-making activities. The students learn to transform the words through structural properties (such as making plurals out of singulars and combining words to create compounds), and they create new words by combining onsets and rhymes (and attacking new words by substituting known phonemic and structural elements).

Classification

The primary purpose of the inductive activity is to introduce the students to the study of word structures, both structural and phonetic, through classification. The students are asked to classify data sets of words, sentences, and eventually paragraphs, looking for common attributes and building generalizations about structures.

Let's look at the efforts of the students in the three cycles we described.

In the first cycle, the students classified words according to the presence of letters and initial consonants ("these all have 'b' in them" or "these all begin with 'b'"). Students noticed the first structural feature—plurals containing "s" at the end—and some were able to make plurals by adding "s."

In the second cycle, students noticed onsets and rhymes and meaning categories such as "these all are parts of the teddy bear." Multiple syllable and compound words were also placed together. As the teacher modeled categories (such as "beginning with 'ch'"), the students were able to identify those and add other blends.

Simple declaratives were most common in the first cycle, such as "A teddy bear is in the picture." The students were able to identify these sentence structures as teachers modeled and classified them.

The teacher modeled building paragraphs about the pictures and led the students to basic structures. The students illustrated them and took printouts home to read. By the fourth cycle nearly all the students were able to dictate simple paragraphs.

Throughout the year data like these indicated progress and identified needs that could be addressed. For example, if students were struggling with several words, the teachers made data sets emphasizing those letters and organized the students to concentrate on them. Teachers provided caption books to students who needed them.

Transition to Trade Books

Teachers assessed the Gunning levels in December, March, and June by having students read books at the following levels and answer questions to test comprehension of the major ideas. Fluent reading with comprehension marks the level the student has reached. Testing is discontinued when deviations from print become excessive or comprehension is poor. The inventory levels are

- *Picture Level.* Single words on a page are illustrated.
- *Caption Level.* Phrases or sentences, most but not all illustrated.
- *Easy Sight Level.* Longer and more complex, mostly high-frequency words.
- *Beginning.* Four levels, A–F, progressively longer passages, less repetition and predictability.

● *Grade 2A*. Require sizable sight vocabulary and well-developed word attack skills.

By December, all students were judged to be at Picture Level. They could read sentences and paragraphs generated within the Picture Word cycles and were just beginning to transition to simple, well-illustrated books. By February, half appeared to be at Beginning A Level, one at Caption Level, and two at Picture Level. They were transitioning to trade books, nonfiction, and fiction.

The May assessment indicated continued development. Of the 46 students for whom complete data are available (out of the original sample of 48), all but 1 appeared able to read at Caption Level or above. That student was able to successfully read Picture Level books. Figure 7.2 portrays the findings, by percentage of students attaining various reading levels, including emergent levels.

FIGURE 7.2

End-of-Year Reading Levels by Percent of Students (Gunning Scale)

Below Caption	Caption	Sight	Emer A	Emer B	Emer C	Emer C+	Total
2	26	28	11	9	4	20	100

Note: See Chapter 10, Study #3, the Models of Teaching Language Arts Program results. Caption = *Caption Level:* Phrases or sentences, most but not all illustrated. Sight = *Easy Sight Level:* Longer and more complex, mostly high-frequency words. Emer = *Emergent Reading Levels.*

All eight kindergarten sections apparently succeeded in bringing all the students to some level of print literacy. There were small differences in degrees of success by cohorts, but they are minor in terms of the overall success across the eight sections.

Because of this level of success, variables such as gender, SES, and prior language development did not appear as factors predicting success. Males and females and students differing in socioeconomic background appeared to progress equally in terms of learning the alphabet, sight vocabulary, progress in phonemic awareness, levels of reading, and parent and student estimates of satisfaction.

Phonemic Awareness Measures

Teachers administered the Emergent Literacy Inventory in October and May. Two findings are of interest. The first is that differences in entry levels did not relate to later progress. The second is the level of progress in the students manifesting the greatest problems on the initial administrations of the Emergent Literacy Inventory. Of the 15 students manifesting problems in October, 13 of the 15 made considerable progress, indicating few problems with the Inventory (the phonemic awareness problem appeared to be compensated for). The other 2 students made progress but still manifested problems, although they could read at Caption Level.

Comfort and Satisfaction

No student or parent manifested discomfort or dissatisfaction.

Altogether, Northern Lights illustrates a student learning-oriented evaluation where the teachers studied their own implementation and the student learning that was taking place. On the basis of the study of student learning, teachers could adjust or change the teaching-learning strategies based upon what was being learned. Importantly, the teachers and school administrators regularly interviewed the students and surveyed the parents to determine the students' levels of comfort with the literacy process. The results were overwhelmingly positive; but the data collection will continue, and if it appears that a student is particularly uncomfortable, the approach will be adjusted.

○   ○   ○

The evaluation of staff development programs is an inquiry involving all personnel in an analysis of the fruits of their labors. Evaluations should serve as mirrors as individuals and groups reflect on their behavior and plan next steps in the cycle of growth and improvement.

Evaluation requires a clear question as a beginning point, a question that plainly investigates the intended student outcomes of any change effort. Whether it is necessary to select a sample of students in order to answer the question adequately varies from setting to setting, as was evident from the examples in this chapter. The types of data collected will be determined by the nature of the question asked, as will the analysis of the measurements taken. Data should be summarized in simple and direct forms that clearly relate to the question addressed and are easily communicated to all interested parties.

The examples of evaluations provided in this and other chapters illustrate simple and direct designs for inquiring into the links between teaching and learning. While the information yielded in each case was invaluable to the individuals and groups conducting the studies, the benefits of such activity go far beyond the obvious advantages to students. A major benefit to teachers and administrators is the increased sense of efficacy that results from planning changes in what is taught and how it is taught and seeing the results of those efforts. And again, we can't assess what we don't possess. Knowledge of subject matter is critical.

. . . . . .

Part III

People, Organization, and Leadership

The rich variety of human beings that populate our profession makes school renewal both wonderfully interesting and challenging. As we interact we create little professional cultures that act on us to make change easy or difficult. These chapters present research on us and the social systems we create. Chapter 8 looks at our individual differences and how those differences affect our participation in staff development. Chapter 9 looks at leadership from the perspective of personality and professional orientation. Chapter 10 presents three studies comparing not only staff development and leadership in high- and low-achieving settings but also responses to three types of governance—individual, school, and district. We close in Chapter 11 by discussing the development of standards by the National Council for Staff Development.

People and Initiatives: Studying States of Growth

8

We teach not only what we know but who we are. And who we are also affects what we learn and how we handle information.

For many years we have known that personality—the structure of our minds—affects our teaching style and how we understand and interact with our students (see Joyce, Peck, & Brown, 1981).

We have also known that we have individual differences in how we react to learning experiences that are designed for us. We know that what appeals to one person may not appeal to another. Although frequently the match of experience to our preferences is attributed to substantive matches and mismatches (some of us like the content better; some of us like the process better), the other side of the coin is that our personalities react to other people and the nature of the environment differently. We can find ourselves comfortable with people who disagree with us in particular issues but who process information similarly, and yet we can be uncomfortable with people we agree with on these issues but who process information differently from us.

In this chapter we talk about personality. The purpose is to help us gain conceptual understanding of why we behave as we do and why people react differently to many well-intentioned efforts to improve schooling and teaching.

We draw on a line of research that we have conducted with our colleagues for forty years. That line of work has taken us from studying personalities interacting in groups to studying individual personality as an influence on teaching. In the case of the work at hand, we try to understand why teachers and administrators respond as they do to their jobs and to each other.

Celebrating Individual Differences

This chapter celebrates individual differences. We expect individual differences and rejoice in the mix of personalities that people our profession. With Stevenson and Stigler (1992), we are puzzled when educators worry that we as people don't respond identically to experiences. And we worry that our common characteristics are not more celebrated and capitalized on. As we begin a chapter that is built around a long line of research into individual differences—one that reveals dramatic variety—we need to discuss some of the things that we have in common. We believe it is possible to establish a democratically operated staff development system that brings us together and yet respects our personalities.

First of all, the training research affirms that teachers are capable learners and are able to master a wide range of curricular and instructional strategies and to use them effectively in the classroom. Education personnel are so often maligned as "burned out," "aging," or academically impoverished (Vance & Schlecty, 1982) and are described as working under intolerable conditions. Although we are in favor of recruiting the best possible talent into education and providing them with the conditions under which they will flourish, we are very pleased with the capability of present personnel, especially because the time of initial preparation is so meager and its quality is so suspect. Teachers have lots of learning ability.

Second, it appears that staff development programs can be designed to help educators increase their learning capability. The more skills people develop and the more they widen their repertoire, the greater is their ability to master an even greater range of skills and strategies. Learning how to solve problems increases the ability to learn how to solve problems. However, programs that increase learning capacity involve participants openly and comfortably in the shaping of the process.

Third, educators have the very human tendency to respond affirmatively to a positive social and organizational climate; and, given a chance, they know how to create one. Faculties that are organized into study and coaching teams and that work together for the improvement of the school are more cohesive, have higher morale, and are more responsive to initiatives from one another and from administrative leadership than faculties whose members work in isolation (see Joyce & Calhoun, eds., 1996).

It is essential that the definition of teaching responsibilities includes the role as faculty member much more prominently than it has in the past. Teachers who have worked in relative isolation naturally concentrate on their roles as organizer of the classroom and as instructor. However, both school improvement and systemic initiatives require collective action. And the study of teaching, even for individuals working on their personal/professional skills and knowledge, is greatly facilitated by contact with others.

Creating a collective environment requires *time* as much as anything else. If we build in time for interaction while studying and thinking about practice, it is not difficult to move from the norms of autonomy that were generated by the isolating structure into norms of collaborative activity.

Individual Differences

We need a frame of reference that will enable us to think about individual differences in personnel and to take those differences into account.

A number of ways of thinking about individual differences are candidates for our use at the present time. Some of these have been developed to help us think about the learning styles of children and can be applied to adults, as well. Some are developed to distinguish various styles of thinking (e.g., Joyce, Calhoun, & Weil, 2000) and examine how those styles affect problem solving. At least one current theory attempts to describe differences between children and adults as learners (Knowles, 1978).

A number of broad conceptualizations of personality can be applied to the behavior of teachers as instructors and as learners (Erikson, 1950; Harvey, Hunt, & Schroeder, 1961; Maslow, 1962). One heavily studied construct, Conceptual Systems Theory (Hunt, D., 1971), has been a useful predictor of teacher-student interaction; the breadth of styles employed by teachers, sensitivity to students and responsiveness to them; and, most pertinent here, aptitude to acquire the competence to use teaching skills and strategies (for example, see Joyce, Peck, & Brown, eds., 1981).

In this chapter we will discuss a framework that was developed from the study of the professional and personal lives of teachers in the California Staff Development Study (Joyce, Bush, & McKibbin, 1982; Joyce, McKibbin, & Bush, 1984). Its purpose was to guide practice in the organization of human resource development programs and school improvement efforts (Joyce, Hersh, & McKibbin, 1983; McKibbin & Joyce, 1980). Although it was developed from a strictly practical orientation, the findings are correlated with the theories of personality growth and take conceptual development, self-concept, and psychological maturity into account.

The Concept of States of Growth

As we indicated, the concept of States of Growth was developed during a large-scale longitudinal study of staff development and school improvement practices in California. The objective was to obtain a detailed picture of teachers' growth opportunities from their school setting, the district, universities, intermediate agencies (county offices of education and professional development centers), and other institutions. Researchers made case studies of more than 300 educators from 21 districts in seven counties; they surveyed more than 2000 others through questionnaires. In addition to information about participation in the formal systems of support (courses, workshops, and the services of administrators and supervisors), interaction with peers was examined, as were those aspects of personal life that might have implications for professional growth. Thus data were collected on what came to be termed the "formal," the "peer-generated," and the "personal" domains, depending on the origins of the activities that people engaged in.

The focus was the dynamic of individual interaction with the environment. The thesis was that within any given environment (say, a school in the San Francisco Bay area), opportunities for productive interaction leading to growth would be theoretically about equal. That is, formal staff development systems, colleague interaction, and opportunities to read, attend films and events in the performing arts, engage in athletic activity, and so forth would be available to all personnel in profusion. *Thus differences in activity would be a function of the individual's disposition to interact productively with the environment.* If we discovered differences, we could proceed to try to understand their origins and develop ideas for capitalizing on them.

The Formal, Peer-Generated, and Personal Domains

The amount of interaction in all three domains varied greatly. The differences were vast in both urban and rural areas and among elementary and secondary educators. They are easily illustrated in regions like the San Francisco Bay Area and the Los Angeles Basin. In these areas, literally thousands of courses and workshops are available, and most principals and supervisors have been trained to provide active clinical support. Many professional development centers in county offices and other agencies involve teachers in the selection of staff development opportunities, and organizations of teachers in writing, science, and other curriculum areas are active. In addition, of course, the opportunities for personal activity of all sorts abound in these great metropolitan areas, which also are close to mountain ranges, waterways, and oceans. The nature of the differences in each domain is interesting.

Formal Staff Development Opportunities

Participation ranged from people who were aware of and experienced only the activities sponsored and required by the district (possibly only one or two workshops or presentations and one or two visits by supervisors or consultants) to very active, aware people with definite plans of professional enhancement. A small number effectively exploited the opportunities in universities and the larger teacher centers.

Peer-Generated Opportunities for Growth

The range here was from people who had virtually no professional discussions with any other teachers to people who had close and frequent interaction, who experienced mentoring relationships (on the giving or receiving end or both), and who gathered with others to instigate the introduction of innovations or initiatives for the improvement of the school.

The Personal Domain

Some educators were extremely active in their personal lives, with one or two well-developed areas of participation. Some others made virtually no use of the rich environments in which they lived. We found some very active readers and others who barely skim the headlines of the daily paper; some Sierra Club activists and others who had never visited nearby Yosemite; some members of performing arts groups and others who have not seen a film or a live performance in 10 years or more.

Consistency

Somewhat to our surprise, the levels of activity were correlated across domains. That is, those who were more active professionally were also more active personally. Looking for reasons, we concluded that the differences in levels of activity were produced by the individuals' orientations toward their environments, moderated by social influence.

Orientations Toward the Environment

The essence of the concept is the degree to which the environment is viewed as an opportunity for satisfying growth. Thus the more active people view the environment as a set of possibilities for satisfying interaction. They initiate contact and exploit the possibilities. Less active people are less aware of the possibilities or are more indifferent to them. The least active people expend energy protecting themselves from what they see as a threatening or unpleasant environment, avoiding contact and fending off the initiatives of others. Also, the people who are more active and more initiating are also more *proactive*. That is, they *draw* more attention from the environment, bringing more possibilities within their reach. This phenomenon multiplies the opportunities for many people. It was not unusual for us to discover that certain schools that were characterized by a cluster of active people (and generally by an active principal) were regularly approached by central office personnel, teacher centers, and universities to be the "trial" sites for everything from computer technology to community involvement programs. Those people and their schools receive more resources and training while some schools, characterized by a cluster of resistant people, were approached last, and many initiatives passed them by.

Social Influence

Close friends and colleagues, and the social climate of the workplace and the neighborhood, moderate the general dispositions toward growth. Affirmative and active friends and colleagues and positive social climates induce people to engage in greater activity than they would if left to themselves. This finding provides another dimension to the general theme of Chapter 3. The synergistic environment is not only essential for collective action but to generate the kind of colleagueship that will be productive for individual states of growth.

Also, as we will emphasize later, a major goal of a human resource development system is to increase the states of growth of the personnel in the system, potentially benefiting the individuals as well as the organization and ensuring that the children are in contact with active, seeking personalities.

Levels of Activity

Although the orientations toward growth are best represented on a continuum, over time people gradually develop patterns that have more clearly discernible edges, and it is not unreasonable to categorize them, provided we recognize that the categories blend into one another. With that caveat, the following prototypes are presented because they can be useful in explaining behavior and in planning staff development programs and organizing faculties to vigorously exploit them.

Gourmet Omnivores

These prototypes are mature, high-activity people who have learned to canvass the environment and successfully exploit it. In the formal domain, they keep aware of the possibilities for growth, identify high-probability events, and work hard at squeezing them for their growth potential.

They constitute the hard-core clientele for teacher centers and arrays of district and intermediate agency offerings for volunteers. They initiate ideas for offerings and find ways of influencing the policymakers. However, they are not negative toward system initiatives. They have the complexity to balance their personal interests with the awareness that they belong to an organization.

Our Gourmet Omnivores find kindred souls with whom to interact professionally. They learn from informal interaction with their peers. A group of omnivores may work together and generate initiatives or attend workshops or courses together. It was often groups of omnivores who learned to use computers and developed computer centers in their schools.

It is in their personal lives that Gourmet Omnivores become most clearly defined. Characterized by a general high level of awareness, their distinguishing feature is one or two areas in which they are enthusiastically involved. These areas vary quite a bit from person to person. One may be an omnivorous reader; another a theatergoer; a third an avid backpacker or skier; a fourth a maker of ceramics. Some run businesses. They generate activities in close consort with others. The spouses of omnivore tennis players are likely to find themselves with rackets in their hands, and the close friends of moviegoers will be importuned to share films. Because of their proactivity, our mature Gourmet Omnivores have learned to fend off opportunities and protect time for their chosen avocations.

What is striking is their habit of both exploiting and enriching whatever environment they find themselves in. In the workplace, they strive to learn all they can about their craft and give and take energy from their peers. In their private lives, they find opportunities for development.

They are also distinguished by their persistence. McKibbin and Joyce (1980) found that they both sought training with a high likelihood for transfer and, once back in the workplace, they practiced and created the conditions of peer support that enabled them to implement a remarkably high proportion of their new skills. They are also more likely than others to bring the ideas they gain in their personal lives into the workplace and to use them in their teaching.

About 10 percent of the people we studied fit the profile of our "Gourmet Omnivores," and another 10 percent were somewhat less active, although still quite engaged with aspects of their environment.

Passive Consumers

By far the largest number of those we studied (about 70 percent) resembled the prototype we term the Passive Consumer.

The distinguishing characteristics of our Passive Consumers, as opposed to Active Consumers, are a more or less amiable conformity to the environment and a high degree of dependence on the immediate social context. In other words, their degree of activity depends greatly on who they are with. In the company of other Passive Consumers, our prototype is relatively inactive. We studied one school in which all of the personnel in one wing of the building were passive; their interchange with others was amiable but involved few serious discussions about teaching and learning. They rarely visited one another's classrooms. None attended staff development activities that were not required by the administration. They had no objections to being required to attend those workshops— one day in the fall and one in the spring. They enjoyed them, but they did nothing with the content.

In another wing of the school, two Passive Consumers found themselves in the company of two Gourmet Omnivores and an Active Consumer and were drawn into many of the activities generated by their more enterprising colleagues. They found themselves helping to set up computer workstations for the students, cooperating in scheduling and the selection of software, learning word processing, and learning how to teach their students to use self-instructional programs. They attended workshops on the teaching of writing with the study group instigated by the Gourmet Omnivores and began revamping their writing programs.

In personal life, our prototype Passive Consumer is also dependent on a consort. If Passive Consumers have relatively inactive spouses and extended families, they will be relatively inactive. If they are with relatives, friends, and neighbors who initiate activity, their levels of activity will increase.

Reticent Consumers

Whereas our Passive Consumer has a relatively amiable, if rather unenterprising, view of the world, about 10 percent of the people we studied expend energy actually pushing away opportunities for growth. We speak of these persons as Reticent Consumers because they have developed an orientation of reluctance to interact positively with their cultural environment. We can observe this dynamic in both professional and domestic settings.

Our prototype Reticent Consumer attends only the staff development that is required and is often angry about having to be there, deprecates the content (whatever it is), and tries to avoid follow-up activities. Our Reticent Consumer treats administrative and peer initiatives with equal suspicion and tends to believe that negative attitudes are justified because "the system" is inherently oppressive and unfeeling. Thus even peers who make initiatives are deprecated "because they are naive" if they believe that they will gain administrative support for their "idealistic" notions. Hence our Reticent Consumer tends to view our Gourmet Omnivores as negatively as they do the hated administration. The hard-core Reticent Consumer even rejects opportunities for involvement in decision making, regarding them as co-opting moves by basically malign forces.

The structure of attitudes was similar in discussion about personal lives. Our Reticent Consumers tend to emphasize what they see as defects in people, institutions, services, and opportunities in a range of fields. Film, theater, athletic activity, state and national parks, books, and newspapers all are suffering rapid decay. ("Only trash gets published these days. . . . Movies are full of sex and violence.") In the richness of an urban environment they tend to emphasize crowding as an obstacle to participation to events. ("If I could get tickets. . . . If you didn't have to wait for a court . . . You can never get in to the good movies. . . . ") In the rural environments, lack of facilities gets the blame.

Even so, our Reticent Consumer is not unaffected by the immediate social context. They do not "act out" their negative views as much in affirmative school climates. In the company of Gourmet Omnivores, they can be carried along in school improvement efforts. Affirmative spouses who tolerate their jaundiced opinions good-naturedly involve them in a surprising number of activities. In the right circumstances, they learn to take advantage of the opportunities in their lives. With respect to staff development, people who are normally quite reticent can respond positively to well-designed events and can practice well in the company of their "peer coaching" colleagues.

Conceptual Structure, Self-Concept, and States of Growth

We turned to a number of developmental theories in an attempt to seek reasons for the differences in states of growth manifested by the teachers we were studying. Two of them are of particular interest to us here because their descriptions of development appear to correlate with the states of growth we found (Joyce, McKibbin, & Bush, 1984). One is conceptual systems theory (Harvey, Hunt, & Schroeder, 1961; Hunt, D., 1971), and the other is self-concept theory (Maslow, 1962).

Conceptual Systems Theory

Conceptual systems theory describes persons in terms of the structure of concepts they use to organize information about the world. In the lowest developmental stages, people use relatively few concepts for organizing their world, tend to have dichotomous views with few "shades of gray," and attach much emotion to their views. They tend to reject information that does not fit into their concepts or to distort it to make it fit. Thus people and events are viewed as "right" or "wrong."

At higher stages of development people develop greater ability to integrate new information, are more de-centered, and can tolerate alternative views better. Their conceptual structure is modified as old concepts become obsolete and new ones are developed. New experiences are tolerated and bring new information and ideas, rather than being rejected or distorted to preserve the existing state.

For an example, let us consider people at the lower and higher developmental stages on a first visit to a country with a culture different from their own. Persons characterized by the lower conceptual levels are suspicious of the "different" and tend to find fault with it. ("You can't *believe* what they eat there.") They peer through the windows of the tour buses with increasing gratitude that they will soon be returning to their own country. They speak loudly to the "stupid" hotel personnel who don't speak their language. They clutch their wallets to keep them away from the conniving, dishonest "natives" and their "unclean" hands.

Their higher-conceptual-level companions are fascinated by the new sights, sounds, and smells. Gingerly they order the local dishes, comparing them with the familiar, finding some new and pleasing tastes, and bargaining for a recipe. They prefer to walk, avoiding the bus unless time forbids. They ask shopkeepers to pronounce the names of things. They brush off the grime to get a better look at the interesting vase in the corner. They speak quietly and wait for the hotel personnel to indicate the local custom.

There is a substantial correlation between conceptual development and the states of growth of the teachers and administrators we studied. The Gourmet Omnivores are in a continual search for more productive ways of organizing information and have more complex conceptual structures as a result. Their openness to new experience requires an affirmative view of the world and the conceptual sophistication to deal with the new ideas they encounter. Our Passive Consumers have more limited structures and less ability to figure out how to reach for new experience and deal with it. Our Reticent Consumers are busy protecting their present concepts and act offended by the presence of the unfamiliar. They can be as negative toward children they do not understand as they are toward the facilitators who try to bring new ideas and techniques into their orbit. Conceptual development is correlated with variety and flexibility in teaching styles, with ease in learning new approaches to teaching, and with ability to understand students and modulate to them (Joyce, Peck, & Brown, 1981).

A change to a more productive orientation involves change to a more complex structure capable of analyzing people and events from multiple points of view and the ability to assimilate new information and accommodate to it.

Self-Concept Theory

Several decades ago Abraham Maslow (1962) and Carl Rogers (1961) developed formulations of personal growth and functioning that have guided attempts since then to understand and deal with individual differences in response to the physical and social environment. Rather than concentrating on intellectual aptitude and development, their theories focused on individuals' views of self or self-concepts. They took the position that our competence to relate to the environment is greatly affected by the stances we take toward ourselves.

Strong self-concepts are accompanied by "self-actualizing" behavior, a reaching out toward the environment with confidence that the interaction will be productive. The self-actualizing person interacts richly with the milieu, finding opportunities for growth and enhancement and, inevitably, contributing to the development of others.

Some people feel competent to deal with the environment but accept it for what it is and are less likely to develop growth-producing relationships from their own initiatives. They work within the environment and what it brings to them rather than generating opportunities from and with it.

Others bear a more precarious relationship with their surroundings. They are less sure of their ability to cope. Much of their energy is spent in efforts to ensure that they survive in a less than generous world.

It is not surprising that we found a relationship between the states of growth of the people we studied and their concepts of self. Our Gourment Omnivores are self-actualizing. They feel good about themselves and their surroundings. Our Passive Consumers feel competent but are dependent on the environment for growth-producing opportunities. Our Reticent Consumers feel that they live in a precarious and threatening world. The faults that they find in their surroundings are products not of being well developed and able to discern problems the rest of us cannot see but of an attempt to rationalize their need to protect themselves from a world of which they are afraid.

Recent Research

Hopkins (1990) and his colleagues, measuring states of growth and self-esteem independently, found them to be nearly congruent. In the implementation of a complex arts curriculum, scores indicating levels of use were matched with four "psychological states" levels with the following results:

Psychological State	Implementation
Group One (Highest)	71.8
Group Two	50.7
Group Three	44.7
Group Four	18.1

Hopkins also found that the organizational climate of the faculties where the teachers worked influenced implementation, but not to the extent of the psychological states.

In Chapter 6 we discussed the extensive study of implementation in the Richmond County program. Researchers measured states of growth using the interview procedure from the California Staff Development study. Coefficients of correlation computed with two measures of implementation were 0.87 and 0.88.

In the Ames study (Joyce, Calhoun et al., 1994; Joyce & Calhoun, 1996) discussed in Chapter 10, the responses to the Individual Growth Fund, which provided the individual teachers throughout the district with funds for their personal staff development, varied widely. About one in six teachers did not use the fund, and another sixth made minor use of it, while some of the teachers generated extensive and satisfying inquiries. Although the psychological measures we've described were not employed, clearly individual differences influenced both use and satisfaction to a great extent.

The Ames study confirmed again an observation about the relationship between age and experience and the response to growth opportunities. The correlation between age and response was zero and there was no curvilinear relation. In 30 years of our work in this area, we have found age to be an insignificant variable. The rhetoric about "burnout" does not stand the test of formal investigations. In studies of response to Models of Teaching (Joyce, Calhoun, & Weil, 2000), age correlates, if anything, with increasing power as a learner and problem solver.

The Potential for Growth

The theories of conceptual growth and self-concept both help us understand the states of growth and ways of thinking about education personnel as growth-oriented programs are planned and carried out. They help us understand why people respond as they do and provide us with a basis for creating environments that are likely to be productive both in terms of the content of the programs and the people for whom they are intended.

Information about states of growth helps us to understand why people respond as they do to initiatives of various kinds and to capitalize productively on individual differences. It also helps us to try to help people grow in their ability to grow, not only in the technical senses that we have stressed in the previous chapters, but also in their orientations toward the world and what it offers them.

The success of initiatives will depend partly on whether the central administration personnel, principals and other school site leaders, and committee and council members behave like "Gourmet Omnivores" and "Active Consumers." The behavior patterns characterized by the higher states of growth are infectious and lead to the affirmative stances that facilitate problem solving. Mechanical processes of implementation simply are not effective. Leaders have to model the states of growth and affirmative stances toward the environment that they hope all personnel will emulate.

Initiatives can be planned with increases in states of growth as an objective. Opportunities for growth are important. The social climate of the organization is the key, however, to capitalizing on those opportunities. Leaders and staff development personnel need to study the processes of building affirmative climates and of involving people in collaborative governance processes and in conducting training and the study of content positively and richly.

A Truism

We are what we eat, not just biologically but socially and emotionally. Rich, well-organized substance in positive circumstances makes us richer, more outreaching, and more productive. Staff development is not just the delivery of content. Inevitably it helps us grow or can shut us down by how it is conducted and by the climate we build. And the more we design environments from which people grow in *ability to grow,* the more we grow ourselves.

9

Creating Communities in Districts and Schools: The Organizational Aspects of Growth Environments

Here we examine the general literature on organizational leadership and look at the cases of two school principals, one effective as a leader of staff development and one not so effective, due to important differences in cognitions—frames of reference—about schooling and the culture of school faculties. Chapter 10 is a companion of this one. In it we look at a study that compares staff development in districts containing very high- and very low-achieving schools, consider the results of leadership cognitions by school board/superintendent teams in districts with extremely high- and low-achieving schools, and finally look at teachers' perceptions of individual-, school faculty–, and district-governed staff development.

A caveat relates to our experience. We are optimistic about the potential for good leadership in our field. In the cases in Chapter 2 that represent our work we have watched leadership development that is heartwarming. Leadership in the sense that we emphasize—creating inquiring learning communities—is best developed by learning to lead school improvement efforts, which means learning to generate the kinds of staff development that lead to student learning.

Literatures

The literature on leadership is enormous and contains considerable wise advice and well-developed procedures for creating vital organizations where attention is paid to improvement as well as to maintenance of current procedures.

That literature can be conveniently seen in terms of seven strands of inquiry that have a good deal in common. In addition to the common effort of trying to help leaders (and all personnel) balance maintenance with renewal, we can see within each strand the effort to move the ethos of the organization from an individualistic to a collaborative mode.

We begin by looking at the work of industrial psychologists and social psychologists beginning in the late 1930s, accelerating during World War II and the immediate postwar period, and continuing to the present. Lewin (1947) and his colleagues developed a cooperative action research framework that organizes workers to study their social process and productivity, a tradition that continues in education, mediated by the work of Corey (1953) and currently through the work of Calhoun and her associates (see Joyce & Calhoun, 1996). The work of the famous Edward Deming (1982) was an extension of the framework; this work has enjoyed serious applications since the early 1950s and has recently been discovered and applied to education. Social psychologists studied personality and group dynamics extensively (see Bennis & Shepard, 1964) and established the Laboratory Method for working with organizations to develop energy for making the organization better (Bradford, Gibb, & Benne, 1964). Elton Mayo and his colleagues studied the organizational climate within institutions and the types of conditions that affected productivity (generating, among many others, the famous Hawthorne study). Heinrich Adorno and his colleagues studied personality and leadership styles (for a review, see Joyce, Calhoun, & Hopkins, 1999). Later, Hunt and his colleagues (e.g., Hunt, 1971) studied conceptual systems and the effect of personality on interactive and information processing behavior and matches and mismatches between leadership personality and the personalities of persons within the organization.

In the 1960s a powerful group of researchers affiliated with the University of Chicago—Getzels, Guba, Thelen, Cunningham, Campbell, Halpin, and Croft—worked to bring research from the social and behavioral sciences to administrative theory and generated conceptual models for bringing institutions from a state of maintenance to self-renewal (see Halpin, 1966). Of particular interest to education is the concept that perceives organizations as individualistic (ideographic) or collective (nomothetic). Working from a similar framework, Lortie (1975) conducted an intensive study of teacher behavior in organizations and concluded that the individualistic is the normative mode. Most of the Chicago group held that the collective mode was both generally important for the health of the organization (school and school district) and the people in it and, concomitantly, as a necessary condition for the convergence of energy to improve it.

Since the 1950s, practitioner-researchers such as Goodlad, Anderson, Schaefer, and Shaplin (see, particularly, Schaefer, 1967) developed new structures for education, particularly dynamic models for team teaching and the Ford Foundation–supported Educational Facilities Laboratories that provided new school designs for collaborative teaching and differentiated staffing. Those structures (both the team organizations and the buildings designed for teams) favored collective action and were short-lived as the individualistic culture overwhelmed the attempt to create more collective and democratic organizations. Their legacies are the idea that self-renewing structures can be created and enhance energy to improve the organization and a clear warning that the individualistic aspect of the ethos of school culture is a major force to be reckoned with. To this day, a generation of teachers who have never experienced either team teaching or worked in an "open plan" school react with horror at the idea of either one. Many teacher candidates select education partly *because* they can work alone with little surveillance by other adults.

Democratic process (Glickman, 1993) fueled the work of several students of school renewal, who recommended that schools mirror the Constitution and strains of Jeffersonian democracy. The strain is not well researched but is nonetheless important as it affirms the development of learning communities as the heart of school renewal.

In recent years, a number of educators recommending cross-district collaboration for school renewal have developed leagues of schools and school districts that can work in tandem. Among these are Hopkins and his colleagues in the United Kingdom (see Hopkins, Ainscow, & West, 1994) and Glickman, Calhoun, and Sizer in the United States (see Calhoun & Allen, 1996, a and b). Again, they advocate collective rather than individualistic structures.

Working from research that distinguishes schools with greater school improvement from less effective schools (see Brookover et al., 1978; Mortimore et al., 1988), Lezotte and Levine have become the leading spokespersons for "effective schools" improvement efforts. Their approach—to have schools study the literature and make initiatives for improving their own settings—is attractive and straightforward, but their own studies have indicated how difficult it is to make that approach pay off (see Levine & Lezotte, 1990).

Finally, students of administrative behavior (see for example, Leithwood, 1990; Murphy & Hallinger, 1987; Spillane, Halverson, & Diamond, 2001) have administrators whose schools are presumed to be more effective learning communities. Their central purpose is to lead administrators from the mechanical, maintenance mode toward open and integrative modes of behavior oriented toward school improvement.

Adding It Up

The importance of creating a self-renewing infrastructure is the key recommendation we distill from this varied and extensive literature. Much organizational energy must necessarily be expended in keeping the schools on an even keel, keeping the community active and helpful, and dealing with the myriad bumps in the road that rise continually, like a well-tended farm where colonies of gophers and moles make determined efforts to create little holes and rises that invite attention. The organization needs to tend its personnel, ensuring reasonable calm and security and sense of direction. The energy to improve the educational environments—the core of the function of education—needs to be as firmly anchored in the infrastructure as are the elements that provide stability. Staff development and school improvement initiatives are inherently destabilizing but with benign intent.

In most school districts, central office personnel, building administrators, and teachers are better linked to maintain the organization than they are to identify opportunities to improve curriculum, instruction, and the quality of the school's social climate. Relations with parents and other community members provide an example. There *will be* report cards and parent conferences and everybody knows how to make them happen and even how to deal with the complaints that will inevitably emerge as parents examine the success of their children. Reaching out to parents, informing them, involving the shy and reluctant, and creating partnerships with the community less routine and require a special focus and energy.

Similarly, keeping the existing curriculum going is an embedded function, as is letting students know how they are doing in that curriculum *in a summative fashion, as end-of-term and year reports.* Formative feedback is less routine. Changing curriculum and instruction requires learning new things, studying together, and deliberately altering long-standing habits and beliefs.

The customary relationships among central office personnel, principals, and teachers need to be complemented by a different set of relationships, one coexisting with the traditions that generate and sustain vigorous efforts to make student learning better. Essentially, what is needed is an elevating belief system, one where the idea that schools can increase learning capability is central, rather than an accepting belief system that assumes that schools must accept the limitations of students and can do little to improve their ability.

These new sets of relationships need to be shaped so that decisions are made about what needs focus; initiatives result; adequate staff development is provided; data are collected, analyzed, and shared; and all personnel are increasingly brought together in a community of inquirers.

As Levine and Lezotte (1990; Levine, 1991) have pointed out, many school improvement efforts are organized with temporary, ad hoc arrangements that quickly disappear as an innovative effort loses steam. Even in districts where substantial improvements have been made, the limitations of the ad hoc arrangements have become apparent. Some schools of need have not participated fully even where substantial levels of financial support have been provided (Berman & Gjelten, 1983; David & Peterson, 1984). There is a constant battle to keep efforts like Read to Succeed properly staffed and implemented despite their success. Some administrators and teachers have resisted the destabilizing effects of innovative efforts. Even Just Read, on the surface the easiest initiative described in Chapter 2, can be heavily resisted in some schools of obvious need and deprecated by some of their personnel.

Our explanation is that many educators have a maintenance orientation, rationalized by a belief that the regular procedures of schools—the culturally normative—are correct and that problems of achievement are student characteristics and home problems rather than problems of curriculum and instruction.

Many state governments have proposed a series of general initiatives designed to pressure school districts and schools to take steps to improve education. These include what is called "high stakes" testing programs, voucher programs, and charter school programs, all intended to generate competition. A huge literature has developed around them, much of it written by educators decrying them. For example, in March 2001, ERIC contained more than 1,100 references, virtually all negative. The educators appear to maintain either that schools are doing all right or that the efforts by general governance agencies will have negative effects. Why should they take this position? Is it because they are protective of education *as is*? Have vouchers and charter proposals no merit at all? Vastly more articles object to the attempts by governmental entities to improve education than support initiatives made within the profession to improve it.

Here we will simply outline the propositions for leadership that we believe lay out the conditions that enable student achievement-oriented staff development to thrive. Let's begin with two frames of reference that will become apparent in an account of the work of two principals.

The "Elevating" and "Accepting" Belief Systems

We place considerable emphasis on belief systems and structures rather than on technique. Let's begin here with beliefs and the concepts of "elevating" and "accepting" that were felicitously named by our colleague Emily Calhoun, reflecting on the study of the ethos of school board/superintendent teams that is described in Chapter 10.

● In an **accepting** view, the students are accepted as they are; and their progress is viewed as a product of their characteristics, including those characteristics that are attributed to the economic and social conditions of the home. The educational system is not viewed critically; it is accepted as the normative way of educating students. Thus it is to be managed rather than changed. The limitations of the educational environment are accepted: Not all students will thrive in it.

● In an **elevating** view, the students are viewed as emerging and flexible, and the task of schooling is to enable their potential to be enhanced. The educational system is viewed critically, and opportunities to improve it are sought. Social and economic limitations of the home are challenges in the quest to enable all students to succeed.

Two Principals

Let's compare the behavior of two principals, one of whom we will call Mr. Elevating. The other is Mr. Accepting. They work in the same school district and have about the same amounts of experience. They are real people. We have known them for about two years and observed them as their district has provided resources and opportunities both for school and district to develop structures and to make initiatives for school improvement. Both schools applied for and were awarded three-year grants from the state department of education to improve K–3 curriculum and instruction in literacy. To obtain the grants all affected teachers had to agree to participate in staff development that was organized by the district for these and several other schools. In addition, the study of student learning was required, and a set of measures were adopted that were embedded in the curricular/instructional approach.

The district had also sponsored the Just Read approach and the Second Chance curriculum described in Chapter 2. Extensive staff development was an important part of the initiative, focusing on a curriculum for teaching reading, with embedded study of student learning (and certain data collected as often as weekly). The staff development began in the fall of 2000 with a four-day workshop and continued for one day a week throughout the school year. Teams from several other school faculties were involved.

The Schools

The school led by Mr. Accepting serves a K–3 student body where the judgment of teachers, the school administrators, and interpretations of test results agree that about 55 percent of the students have been unable to read effectively as they graduated from the school and entered the upper elementary grades in another school. Nearly 40 percent of the male students receive special education services without affecting the literacy picture. The annual amount of the grant received for the school is $160,000 per year. Most is budgeted for various schemes for reducing the size of instructional groups.

Mr. Elevating's school serves a K–9 student body where the judgment of teachers, confirmed by standard tests, was that about 30 percent of the students reached the middle grades with serious literacy problems. As a consequence, the faculty incorporated Second Chance into its program, and teachers and administrators staffed it. The costs of Second Chance are not included in the state grant, which focuses on the primary grades and generates a full-day kindergarten that includes a reading curriculum. Most of the $100,000 from the grant is budgeted to increase the kindergarten staff to permit the full-day program to take place.

Dynamic Cognitions: Accepting and Elevating

The story begins with attendance at meetings where the opportunity to manifest ideas began with mid-year reports from teachers in the two schools and others in the district.

Both principals attended meetings in February 2001. In one meeting, the 1st grade teachers who were also involved in the state grant program discussed the progress of their students. In another meeting, the kindergarten teachers from the same schools reported to each other the progress of their students. In both meetings data about progress were available from the teachers. The two principals came to the meetings with rather different histories with respect to the initiatives that were on the table.

Mr. Elevating attended training from the beginning and worked out arrangements with his teachers whereby he and they jointly practiced the new curricular and instructional procedures. He became a member of the district cadre and provided training for teachers throughout the district. He studied the Just Read logs for his classes and found that his school had an outstanding implemention. In addition, he studied the logs of his kindergarten and 1st grade teachers and worked with them to improve implementation. He tested students at all levels and interpreted the data relative to the initiatives and also general achievement in the school.

Thus Mr. Elevating came to the meeting knowledgeable about the initiatives and with collaborative relationships with his teachers. In the meetings, he occupied himself helping teachers interpret their data diagnostically. Nearly all the kindergarten students reached the point where they could read simple books independently. Because none of the kindergarten teachers had taught reading before, they had many questions for the consultants about how to help the students along.

On the other hand, the meetings were the first Mr. Accepting had attended. He himself had not participated in the relevant staff development. He had delegated Just Read to an assistant principal and had not studied its implementation. He had not studied the logs of his teachers.

As the meetings progressed, the reactions of the two principals were predictably different; aspects of their reactions were remarkably different.

At Mr. Accepting's school, two of the 1st grade teachers reported outstanding progress—all but two of each of their students had learned to read simple trade books during the first half of the year. The other three had not implemented the curriculum that was intended to improve the performance of their students. Those three maintained that the curriculum was not appropriate for their students, although those students had been randomly assigned to their classes from the same pool as the students who were assigned to the high-implementing teachers. In addition, teachers from other schools reported considerable success with the same 1st grade curriculum.

As indicated earlier, until the February meetings Accepting had not attended staff development sessions. He knew that several of his teachers were not using the curriculum, and they told him that the new curriculum would not "work" with their students. He had not talked to the high-implementing teachers. These February meetings were the first occasions where he heard the teachers from the other schools (or his two high-implementing 1st grade teachers) report their enthusiasm and apparent success and share their data on vocabulary development and the levels of books their classes were reading.

At the February meeting, the kindergarten teachers presented reports from 12 classes. Eight teachers were from other schools and reported good progress. The four teachers from Accepting's school reported that they had not implemented the kindergarten literacy curriculum because it was not appropriate for their students. Thus Mr. Accepting had now attended two sessions where all the teachers from the other schools and two of his 1st grade teachers were excitedly reporting success while the remainder of his teachers were, in the same meeting, reporting that they were not implementing the new curriculum.

What follows is a summary of the reactions by Mr. Accepting and Mr. Elevating to what they heard during the meetings and during subsequent interchanges between them.

1. Mr. Accepting's first statement explaining the low implementation of his seven teachers was that "top down doesn't work." He argued that the curriculum had been imposed on his teachers and therefore, despite the condition of student learning in his school, he blamed the low implementation on the central office organizers and staff development providers. *This although he knew that the faculty had applied for the money and asked for the staff development needed to carry out the proposal.* In a certain sense he was criticizing the state, suggesting that, even if the faculty had agreed to take the money, they were coerced by the magnitude of the incentive.

2. "The high-implementing teachers are unpopular." Mr. Accepting expressed the opinion that the low-implementing teachers didn't like the ones who were improving the achievement of the students. Evidently getting along with the normative social system was more important to him than success. To him, breaking the unspoken "rules" was a bad thing. Mr. Elevating, overhearing him, asked Mr. Accepting how his nonimplementers felt about the high implementers from the other schools. Mr. Accepting replied that the other schools had student populations different from his, and the teachers knew that.

3. "Change takes from 5 to 10 years." Mr. Accepting suggested that it was unreasonable to expect changes to take place rapidly. Essentially, he denied what he was hearing. From his perspective,

four generations of his students would continue to fail before improvement could be expected. He could not reconcile the rapid implementation of most of the teachers in the meetings with his belief that curricular and instructional changes require several years. The low-implementing teachers fit his concept better than did the others. Mr. Elevating said that the implementation by his K–1 teachers fit with the rapid implementation of Second Chance and its success over the last two years and suggested that Accepting was confusing broad cultural change with the implementation of initiatives. Mr. Accepting responded that initiatives just couldn't be made without making the cultural changes first.

4. "The implementation 'dip' reduces student achievement for several years." Mr. Accepting opined that innovations in curriculum and instruction reduce student achievement in the near term, misinterpreting the literature that holds that after an initial burst of energy, innovations flag for a while and then can be revived. Although he was listening to reports of gains in student achievement, he tended to believe that the gains were anomalous. He discounted them, because he believed that a lowering rather than a gain in student learning would be the initial product of a change, however well founded. Thus he believed that his nonimplementing teachers were experiencing a normal problem—that initial efforts reduced student learning. They, rather than the other teachers, were behaving correctly, because they were proceeding gradually to lessen the negative effect on student learning. Mr. Elevating couldn't believe what he was hearing.

5. "Low achievement is a function of parenting." This was a major item in Mr. Accepting's belief system. He stated again and again that the nonimplementing teachers were correct in their assessment of the children and their beliefs about the appropriateness of the curriculum. The success of the other teachers appeared to him to be an accident—a peculiar and almost random event. Students in his school would be low-achieving—success was contradictory to his beliefs; and he maintained the belief in the face of contrary evidence. He manifested considerable hostility toward his high-implementing teachers when they continued to challenge his beliefs.

6. "Enthusiastic teaching produces results." Mr. Accepting appeared to believe that even if higher achievement was occurring it was a product of a group of unusually enthusiastic teachers rather than the curriculum they were implementing. In a sense he denied that there was knowledge on which a better curriculum could be

built. Teacher personality was the key to effectiveness rather than skill in teaching. Mr. Elevating acknowledged that his teachers were enthusiastic, but the curriculum they were using was a product of training.

7. "When teachers see that others are having success, they will 'buy in.'" Mr. Accepting argued that his nonimplementers simply had not seen the success of the others for a long enough period to convince them, and the study of curriculum and agreements to implement one were not really valid—success had to be seen at close hand. He also suggested that the nonimplementers were probably correct when they argued that the high-implementing teachers had somehow gotten classes with more able students in them. Thus, there wasn't real success, just a different student body.

8. "There is too much paperwork involved in this study of student learning." As Mr. Accepting listened to the teachers and looked at the data they had brought to the sessions—data his teachers had not brought—he commented about what he saw as an overload of paperwork. He simply could not understand why, if a teacher were trying to teach the students 20 words, that teacher might want to know whether the students had learned them. His view of teaching was to follow a published package of materials and then give a standard test at the end of the year. The teacher-researcher frame of reference, the idea of embedded study of student learning, the overall idea of teaching as action research were so foreign to him that all he could see was that studying student learning was an arduous additional task that was too much to expect. In a sense, his leadership was effective—his teachers just didn't do it. Mr. Elevating pointed out that the data collection and analysis were a normal part of preparation—as was the staff development as teachers prepared units of study for their children.

A Hopeless Position Defended

What is so striking about Mr. Accepting is the complexity and strength of his belief system as it was revealed through his defenses of the low-implementing teachers and his confidence that student learning was programmed at home. He focused on defending the resistant teachers rather than celebrating the achievements of the others. For years he had presided over a failing school and had developed a rationale for failure that rejected school improvement even as it was occurring before his eyes.

Essentially, his students were products of the home and their achievement levels could not be elevated. His school was as good as it could be. He liked the low-implementing teachers. Their beliefs fit better into his frame of reference than did those of the teachers who were bringing about better achievement.

Mr. Accepting created a "Catch-22" bind for himself and his school. Success was not within the school's control because the home determined success. Getting along with others dominated. The frames of reference that he and most of his faculty had used to rationalize failure needed to be protected. As a school improvement initiative was generated, his teachers could reject even what they had agreed to and the enormous resources provided to the school could be discounted because they represented "top down" pressure for increasing student learning. The state and the district were not legitimate sources of school improvement procedures.

Fullan and his associates have pointed out that giving up beliefs and practices is more difficult than learning new ones (Fullan, 2001). We may have a case in point here. As long as our principal believes that his school is as good as it can be and parenting is responsible for student achievement—what we call an "accepting" view—he will surely not generate initiatives and will defend his teachers against change, actually disparaging the efforts of those of his faculty who are actually increasing student learning.

Changing Leadership Styles

The Accepting style is anathema to school improvement. Although Mr. Accepting is an extreme collection of beliefs that prevent him from leading his school out of its long achievement doldrums, many of his ideas are not uncommon. Our problem is how to help such leaders develop a more productive style. There are two available avenues: structure and training.

Structure

Important are regular, democratically conducted meetings of the faculty where the study of student learning is a major part of the agenda, a la the whole-school action research framework. Concomitantly, the building leadership team needs to be organized (see Wolf, 1994) to consider the health of the school and expand the leadership base. Mr. Elevating does this as a matter of course.

Organizing the faculty into peer coaching groups to study student learning and work together to implement initiatives is also important. Again, this is a natural and comfortable process for Mr. Elevating.

Mr. Accepting will be uncomfortable with these structures, but he can get accustomed to them. At some point he will have to let go of his tight hold on the idea that his school is functioning well and it is parents and students who have to change if student achievement is to rise.

Out of these structures the opportunity will develop for the faculty to begin to study the knowledge base.

Training

When initiatives are made, Mr. Accepting needs to see himself as a student, learning new procedures and practicing them. He must also support the faculty through the implementation process. Mr. Elevating would not imagine an alternative. Accepting needs to get himself into a learning mode, trying to add to his professional repertoire rather than seeing himself as complete as he is.

Surely, Mr. Accepting will need considerable assistance in implementing the structural changes and in studying new curricular and instructional options.

In Chapter 10 we will examine some recent information about leadership in high- and low-achieving schools and districts and the effects of initiatives emanating from district, school, and individual decisions.

10 *Three Studies and Their Implications for Leadership: Ethos, Ethos, and Ethos*

In this chapter we examine information from three studies. The first study focused on staff development practices in schools characterized by extremely high or low academic achievement. The second explored the belief systems of school personnel in districts containing schools with extremely high or low academic achievement. The third explored teacher perceptions of the utility of staff development chosen by individuals, faculties, or the school district. The first two studies help clarify the actions of leaders and policy makers in settings where student achievement is very different; the third helps us reflect on the design of staff development offerings where different governance modes operate—those focusing on teacher, school, and district choice.

Study #1: High and Low-Achieving Schools: Is There a Difference in Staff Development?*

The issue examined in this study is whether there is evidence that investment in staff development is associated with student learning—and, if so, what kinds of staff development characterize schools where student learning is highest. What can we learn from those schools?

The Georgia Council for School Performance approached the problem directly by conducting a study of consistently high- and low-achieving schools and examining the nature of the staff development experienced by their faculties (Harkreader & Weathersby, 1998).

Design

The design had two phases: first, selecting schools differing in student achievement while controlling for demographic factors;

---

* The report on which the following description is based was prepared by Jeanie Weathersby and Bruce Joyce, working from the original report by Harkreader and Weathersby (1998).

second, producing case studies that would enable the desired comparisons to take place.

A technical problem in the conduct of studies of effective schools and teachers is the stability of effects. Year-to-year correlations are quite low, often 0.20 or less (Brophy, 1973; Weil et al., 1984). Fortunately, the data base from the Georgia state testing program permitted following schools over a period of years. State standards provided criteria by which student achievement in schools could be judged and compared.

Data from the state testing program included curriculum-based assessments in reading, social studies, science, and mathematics at 3rd, 5th, 8th, and 11th grades. To reduce the probability that mobility was a factor, researchers selected only schools with relatively stable populations. Half of these schools had high scores for three successive years (school years 1994–95, 1995–96, and 1996–97), taking into account the socioeconomic status (SES) of the student body as measured by qualifications for free lunch. The other half had low scores for three years, controlling for socioeconomic status. The result was two sets of schools matched by socioeconomic status but displaying considerable differences in the number of students reaching state standards of achievement. Twenty high schools, 20 middle schools, and 20 elementary schools were selected, half of each level having unusually high scores for three successive years and half having unusually low scores over the same three-year period.

The differences between the high- and low-achieving schools were substantial at all levels. For example, in the highest-achieving high SES elementary schools, 91 percent of the students reached the state goals on the tests compared with 66 percent of the students in the lowest-achieving high SES schools (Harkreader & Weathersby, 1998).

Elementary schools were rated on 21 criteria. A specific example of the difference between two matched low SES schools is that the high-achieving school was in the top 20 percent on all comparisons for its SES cluster (and in the top 20 percent compared with all schools in the state), and the low-achieving matched school was in the bottom 20 percent in its cluster in all comparisons. (Note that a side effect of the study was an indication of the extent to which school or socioeconomic status is responsible for student learning. The three-year data in Georgia, organized to find consistently very high- and very low-achieving schools, is evidence that school can be the critical factor.)

Researchers developed interview guides, visited schools, and interviewed teachers, school administrators, and district officials. The members of the study staff who conducted the interviews were unaware of the status of the schools they were visiting—in other words, they did not know whether they were visiting a high- or low-achieving school. The interviews focused on the governance of staff development, its content, strategies, providers, arrangements for time, perceptions of effects, and motivation for participation. The role of district and intermediate agency personnel was also explored, as was training for leadership of staff development.

Both similarities and differences emerged. Both are important as we try to understand staff development in these consistently high- and low-achieving schools.

Similarities

The high- and low-achieving schools had about equal resources for staff development. They could draw on comparable offerings and providers from the districts and intermediate agencies, and they had similar amounts of time available for staff development and school renewal activities. In addition, and largely because they were drawing on the same pool of offerings and providers, the content (computers, curriculum areas, and teaching strategies) selected was inevitably similar. Thus the schools had much in common in over-all terms of the amount of staff development and the general nature of the content.

Importantly, the schools were not favored or neglected by their districts. The high-achieving schools did not receive exceptional technical or monetary support from their districts nor did the low-achieving schools receive less technical or monetary support than the other schools in their districts. Also, over their careers, the principals of the high- and low-achieving schools received approximately equal training in how to operate school renewal/staff development inquiries. Thus the differences that emerged were probably generated within the dynamics of the schools rather than being propelled by personnel or policies external to the schools.

Differences

If the differences were not in available resources, topics, providers, or organizational support, then what were they? What had apparently happened in the high-achieving schools constituted an elevating dynamic, one that energized the context of staff development, affected the manner of delivery, and heightened the connection between the content and classroom and student behavior and the intensity with which staff development was pursued. Working with what was essentially the same raw material, the high-achieving schools generated a synergy that magnified the potential of the content. The styles of operation were not diametrically opposed in the high- and low-achieving schools, the differences were more in terms of degree—the high-achieving schools employed certain practices either more or less often than the low-achieving schools.

Governance. The high-achieving schools were more collaborative in decision making, with more involvement of more people, and the organizers, particularly the principals, were more inclusive rather than arbitrary. Concomitantly, the principals in the high-achieving schools provided more direction and support and arranged for more support for their faculties. Consequently, the teachers in those schools were more sure that they would get support from the administrators and others. The old "top down/bottom up" distinction among leadership styles does not work here. The leadership of the high-achieving schools pushed and pulled more, involved more, and responded more.

Delivery and Focus. Bearing in mind that both categories of schools were drawing on similar pools of offerings and providers, it is interesting that the high-achieving schools were more often able to ensure that more training strategies were used, that implementation was greater, and that evidence was more often generated that indicated positive outcomes for students. The staff development, actually over very similar content, was energized and was more student- and classroom-focused. Imagine, for example, the study of the computer by the faculties of two schools. In one school, the study is closely connected to how the computer is to be used to enhance student learning. In the other school, the emphasis is on the teachers' learning of the computer and not directly connected to instructional use. That type of difference—one that brought the same content more directly into the learning environment—emerged repeatedly throughout the study.

Motivation for Participation. In the low-achieving schools, teachers were more often motivated to achieve certification requirements or to earn stipends. In the high-achieving schools, motivation was more often a matter of participation in a whole-faculty effort to improve student learning. While not reaching the levels of school-wide action research described by Calhoun (1994; Calhoun & Allen, 1996, a and b), the high-achieving schools had some of the same characteristics: the collective focus on student learning, the use of staff development to benefit the learning environment, and attention to effects.

Altogether, the differences add up to a more highly focused, collaborative effort to make education better on the part of the faculties in the higher-achieving schools, with staff development a significant part of the effort to generate a synergy that affects student learning. Contrastingly, staff development in the lower-performing schools was more a matter of an externally motivated, pro forma exercise.

Interpretation for Policy and Leadership. The state made an effort to provide increasing resources for staff development—considerably more than many states—but the amount of time and money was still much less than needed, and all the schools had to scramble for time for collective inquiry. Also, as we will see in a second study examined in this chapter, the offerings the schools have to draw on can be much improved in both content and process.

However, the differences are instructive. The high-achieving schools take the same opportunities and focus and organize them more effectively through collaborative decision making centered around a collective drive toward ever-improving student learning.

The implications for policy are probably greatest in the domain of leadership preparation. The leaders of the high-achieving schools created a more inclusive and democratic governance process, brought their faculties to a greater focus on student learning and fewer, more intensively pursued initiatives, and generated more effective staff development. Preparing leaders to generate for all schools the elevated mode of staff development found in the high-achieving schools should not be difficult. The skills needed are not exotic nor do they require remarkable degrees of charisma in the leaders. States and districts should be able to prepare their principals to do those things that are such an important part of the workplace devoted to excellence for our children.

We now turn, with the same theme, to a study of leadership at the district level, one that followed up the Harkreader/Weathersby study and focused again on ways of thinking as well as practices.

Study #2: The Iowa Association of School Boards Study of School Board/Superintendent Team Behaviors in School Districts with Extreme Differences in Student Achievement*

This investigation concentrated on linkages between the organizational behavior of school board/superintendent teams and attitudes of schools and faculties, as wholes, in districts containing exceptionally high- and low-achieving schools. Weathersby made available the data base from her study with Harkreader and identified school districts that were studied by a team from the Iowa Association of School Boards. The Iowa team did not know, as they conducted interviews in the Georgia districts, which ones contained the high- or low-achieving schools.

Design and Sample

Six Georgia school districts were identified in three pairs matched for SES and other demographic variables. One member of each pair contained exceptionally high-achieving schools and the other exceptionally low-achieving schools. Case studies were made through interviews with superintendent/board team members, administrators, and teachers. Altogether, 157 people were interviewed.

The three districts containing the high-achieving schools were termed "Moving," and the three with the low-achieving schools were termed "Stuck" after Rosenholtz's (1989) findings in studies of districts able to improve and those unable to improve. In this case the term refers to the educational environments.

All were rural districts, small (each has just one middle school), and with similar monetary resources.

All contained mixed SES populations. Free/reduced lunch in these SES clusters was about half the school population, or a little less.

In all six districts, nearly all (75–80 percent) of the professional personnel and board members grew up and were educated in the district, a nearby one, or in a similar county in the region. In several cases more than half of the teachers attended the schools where they now teach.

The research team sought information about possible differences between the Moving and Stuck districts in the organizational behavior

---

* This study was conducted by the Iowa Association of School Boards research team: Mary Delagardelle, Mary Jane Vens, Margaret Buckton, Wayne Leuders, Carolyn Johns, and Ron Rice with Bruce Joyce, Jim Wolf, and Jeanie Weathersby, consultants.

of the board/superintendent teams, including the presence of conditions favorable for school renewal.

Similarities

Among the study's key findings:

● All six superintendent/board teams appeared to have amicable relationships. Stuck district boards were as satisfied with their superintendents as were the boards of the Moving districts.

● No district was addressing the failures of the categorical programs (special education, Title I, bilingual education) in a direct way, although the high-achieving schools were doing so indirectly.

● All were using the "site-based" management policy, but in all six there was some confusion about how to reconcile the site-based policy with the role of district governance.

● Community satisfaction with the performance of the district was similar.

Differences

What, then, were some of the differences between Stuck and Moving school districts?

In the Moving districts, the "elevating" belief system was strongly present in the culture. Students were to be elevated to their potential. The system was to be elevated accordingly.

In the Stuck districts, the "accepting" belief pervaded the culture. Students were viewed by the school board/superintendent team and a majority of the school personnel as having fixed potential, and the system accepted its position as relatively powerless to influence student possibilities.

The difference can be seen dramatically in the positive and negative comments about students and parents that board members, superintendents, and teachers made spontaneously in the course of the interviews. Altogether, 156 negative comments about parents and community were made by teachers in one school of a Stuck district compared to 27 by the teachers in the Moving districts (14 of those were made by just one teacher).

Consider two illustrative quotes from school board members:

> SES is used as an excuse. We can't do that. Sometimes people say the poor students have limits. I say all kids have limits. I believe we have not reached the limits of any of the kids in our system, including the poor children.

(From an interview with a board member from a "Moving" district.)

How can you hold teachers accountable for student improvement in academics? When dealing with human beings, there's not much you can do about accountability. You can lead a horse to water, but you can't make him drink. This applies to both students and staff.

(From a board member in a "Stuck" district.)

Study #3: Things Are Not Always What They Seem: Individual, School, and District Initiatives—Perceptions of Teachers*

We often hear strong opinions about the governance structures that work best. We hear that teachers as individuals must make their own choices if staff development is to be successful. We hear that the focus should be only at the school level in keeping with site-based management practices. We hear that districts have the primary responsibility for organizing staff development and developing initiatives. We also hear that teachers are too individualistic already, that school faculties do not have the cohesiveness to engage in whole-school levels, and that the district level is ipso facto "top down" and can't get anywhere because the real world is in the schools which have unique needs or district initiatives will be resisted on political grounds.

What Is the Truth?

Once in a while somebody tries to find out. What follows is food for thought from an effort to do so.

The University City (a pseudonym for Ames, Iowa) program came about because administrators acknowledged the measures of "truth" underlying often-competing theses about school renewal and staff development—theses that provide rationale for all three governance modes. These are modes focused on individuals, schools, and district initiatives (see Joyce & Calhoun, 1996).

The *individual mode* supports the energy of individuals, developing opportunities where the locus of control is with the person whose actions will presumably be congruent with that individual's perceptual world. Individually generated staff development acknowledges the division of the workplace into units (classrooms)

---

* This study was designed and carried out by Bruce Joyce, Emily Calhoun, and Nina Carran. A longer description is included in Joyce and Calhoun (1996).

where individual teachers use their perceptions and strengths to create innovations to which they can be committed.

Schoolwide action research is supported because the curricular and social climate dimensions of the school can be addressed in a way not possible through individual or small group action alone. Further, schoolwide action research directly addresses the goal of developing shared governance modes and increasing the capacity of the faculty to inquire into and solve problems requiring concerted, democratic action.

The *districtwide initiatives* emphasize the importance of curricular coherence and the development of district faculties that embrace professional citizenship in a community where children deserve equal educational opportunity and a common core of knowledge and skills.

In the district studied, resources (up to $1,000 each year) were provided to all district faculty members to select personal staff development options. Each school was provided with discretionary monies for schoolwide action research. The district initiative is described in Chapter 2.

The three types of program were implemented as planned. The results of the district initiative were discussed in Chapter 2. Here we are concerned with teacher estimates of both satisfaction and productivity.

The Interview Study: Teacher Satisfaction and Productivity with Individual, Schoolwide, and District Initiatives

These interviews were designed to explore teachers' perceptions of the content of the initiatives and the satisfaction and productivity that emerged from each of them. Thirty-five questions were asked about the initiatives. Teachers' general perceptions were also solicited through open-ended invitations interspersed throughout the interviews.

The data presented here are taken from one round of interviews conducted between May 17 and June 7, 1993. The interviews lasted from about 15 minutes to two hours.

Information Gained/Results

The results were around three topics:

● Teachers' **perceptions of satisfaction** across the three sources of initiatives;

● Teachers' **perceptions of changes in the classroom and effects on students;** and

● **Impressions** about the introduction, reception, implementation, and effectiveness of each level of initiative.

The interviewers asked the 64 teachers to discuss each program component in detail. For cross-initiative comparisons, the critical items were four questions tapping teachers' estimates of the worth of each initiative: the Individual Growth Fund (IGF), Schoolwide Action Research (AR), and the district's Models of Teaching/Language Arts (MOT/LA). These parallel items asked whether the initiative should be continued in University City, whether they would recommend it to another school district, whether there were positive effects for students, and what their general feelings were about the initiative.

(To interpret the results shared here, it is important to know that 12.5 percent of the sample did not make use of the IGF initiative at all and that 18.5 percent used the IGF money to develop instructional plans or materials and thus did not use the resources for staff development. Another 18.5 percent had not used the IGF when the interviews were conducted but planned to use it in the summer. Most did.)

Question: Should the initiative be continued? Figure 10.1 contains the responses to the questions about continuing each initiative.

Clearly, the majority of these teachers favored the continuance of all three initiatives. The largest percentage favored continuing the MOT/LA initiative. The next largest favored the continuance of the Schoolwide Action Research initiative.

Question: Would you recommend the initiative to another district? Figure 10.2 displays the responses.

Again, the majority of these teachers would recommend each of the initiatives to people working in other districts. The differences favoring the Models of Teaching/Language Arts and Schoolwide Action Research initiatives were similar to the responses regarding whether the initiatives should be continued.

Question: Did the initiative have an effect on students?

Figure 10.3 displays the responses to this question. The results closely approximated those of the other two questions designed to

FIGURE 10.1

Comparison of Initiatives: Should the Initiative Be Continued?

Initiative	Yes N (%)	No N (%)	Don't Know or No Comment	Total N
IGF	38 (59.4%)	4 (6.3%)	22 (34.4%)	64
AR	49 (78.4%)	3 (4.7%)	12 (18.7%)	64
MOT/LA	61 (95.1%)	1 (1.6%)	2 (3.1%)	64

Notes:
IGF = Individual Growth Fund
AR = Schoolwide Action Research
MOT/LA = Models of Teaching/Language Arts

FIGURE 10.2

Comparison of Initiatives: Would You Recommend
to Another District?

Initiative	Yes N (%)	No N (%)	Unsure, Missing, or No Comment N (%)
IGF	36 (56.3%)	0	28 (43.7%)
AR	50 (76.6%)	3 (4.7%)	9 (14.1%)
MOT/LA	56 (87.5%)	3 (4.7%)	5 (7.8%)

Notes:
IGF = Individual Growth Fund
AR = Schoolwide Action Research
MOT/LA = Models of Teaching/Language Arts

obtain an assessment of the teachers' general perceptions of the three initiatives.

Question: How do you feel about . . . ? The results again are in line with those from the other three questions.

Again, the two collective components were apparently viewed very positively, and the Individual Growth Fund initiative was viewed as positive in terms of general feeling by three out of five people.

FIGURE 10.3.

Comparison of Initiatives: Did the Initiative Have an Effect on Students?

Initiative	Yes *N* (%)	No *N* (%)	Unsure *N* (%)	Missing or No Comment *N* (%)
IGF	35 (54.7%)	1 (1.6%)	2 (3.1%)	26 (40.6%)
AR	48 (75%)	8 (12.5%)	2 (3.2)	6 (9.4%)
MOT/LA	54 (84.4%)	3 (4.7%)	2 (3.1%)	4 (6.3%)

Notes:
IGF = Individual Growth Fund
AR = Schoolwide Action Research
MOT/LA = Models of Teaching/Language Arts

Experience in Teaching and Academic Background

Cross-tabulations were made between years of teaching experience and the four variables with respect to each initiative. Chi square values were computed. In no case did years of teaching experience appear to affect response to the questions exploring reactions to any of the three components of the program. Apparently, the responses were independent of the amounts of teaching experience of the respondents. Similar computations were made to explore whether the location of colleges attended was influential; the findings were identical to those exploring experience as a possible factor.

The importance of the University City study lies in the finding that the individual, school, and district governance modes can all be made to work from the perspective of the teachers. But none are automatic. Also, district initiatives can be successful—those who believe that if a district makes an initiative it will not work because it is "top down" should not be comforted by these findings or the ones discussed in Chapters 2 or 3.

A Simple Paradigm

The Nike slogan "Just do it" captures what people do who create learning communities. Beliefs power their actions. The essential one is the "elevating" perspective, and it applies to adults as well as children. Those who believe that the home bakes the cognitive cake of the students and schools just put on the icing have accepted a posture of helplessness and lifelong lassitude with respect to professional growth (the accepting perspective). Those who believe that education is a critical factor in helping students become more powerful learners (the elevating perspective) can find, through inquiry, the tools to make a massive difference. Leadership is simply the development of communities who inquire, with deep commitment, into professional growth. The details of how those leaders do that are relatively unimportant. Example and gentle persuasion are as close to a formula as we have.

Many studies have indicated that providing districts and schools with discretionary resources for school renewal has been successful with only a small proportion of those schools (see, for example, the dynamics described in the large-scale study in Florida by Joyce & Belitzky, 1999). Leadership can change that dreary picture and link staff development directly to the goal we all have—increasing student learning by making productive changes in curriculum and instruction.

National Standards: The Fit with Aspirations for Student Achievement

The national organizations in education are endeavoring to provide schools and school districts with criteria for performance (standards and benchmarks) in the various curriculum areas. The National Staff Development Council has generated standards (NSDC, 2001) for staff development that have been widely disseminated and provide educators with guides to the development of high-quality programs. As we have studied the NSDC standards and used them with school districts, we have seen them as dynamic working documents, ones that we can use as a metric against which to measure and adjust our own work. But we also see them as evolutionary, best used not as a formula but as guidelines which need to be adapted with an analytic eye. This chapter contains some of our observations.

The Structure of the Standards

The Council's standards fall into three categories: context, process, and content. Within each of these categories, guidelines suggest policy for the conduct of staff development, and specific suggestions/ examples illustrate how these policy recommendations would work out in practice (NSDC, 2001).

- Those relating to the *context* of staff development address the culture of the school and school district, including norms for continuous growth and time for collaborative professional learning, administrative leadership, and the alignment of district and school goals for student achievement.
- The *process* standards address the design of staff development— how student data are analyzed to determine need, which content is most likely to impact the identified need, how training and follow-up is organized and implemented, and how faculty understanding of organizational structure and change processes is developed.

● The *content* standards address NSDC's suggestions for topics considered appropriate for staff development (at the middle school level, for example, these topics include adolescent development, classroom management, diversity training, curriculum and instruction, expectations of students, etc.). Within the three categories the standards usually move from the general to the specific, but the content standards tend to be more specific than the others.

A question of obvious importance to us, of course, is the match between the standards and the orientation of this book. We believe that the standards as a whole certainly support our orientation, although they support others as well. The creation of professional communities that support curriculum and instruction, the emphasis on research-based staff development design, the study of implementation, and effects on student learning all fit the standards explicitly or implicitly.

Applying the Standards

In our field work we have looked at standards through a series of lenses as the districts with whom we've worked have organized to develop staff development systems and targeted programs. Our analysis of the standards reflects the kinds of concerns and issues we've faced working with educators to build the kind of system we outline in this book.

At the broadest level, we have found the standards both useful and practical. The major categories of the standards—context, process, content—can indeed operate well to inform practice in the real-world work of staff development. The context must provide clear directions for student learning and goals for improvement; school and district leadership must support norms for continuous improvement that justify an ongoing quest for new knowledge and skills targeted at student growth. We especially have found that the issue of time to learn and work collaboratively toward shared goals is a critical component that, if ignored, will defeat all the efforts to follow.

In like fashion, the second level of specificity of standards for process and content, at least in our initial trials at applying them to school improvement efforts, have proved quite useful. Given our focus on student achievement, the standards relating to the study of disaggregated student data, the selection of content, the design of training and follow-up, and evaluation of impact were easily applied. Particularly useful was the standard for selecting the content for staff development—"Staff development uses content that has proven value in increasing student learning and development."

On the other hand, our results working with the standards on developing understanding of organizations and systems thinking as well as those on the change process itself were mixed. Although we found ourselves, as staff developers, drawing heavily on knowledge in these fields, that knowledge seldom served as explicit content for staff development.

When we followed (1) the context admonition to align content with school and district goals for student achievement and (2) the process admonition to select content with a solid research base, we found that—in terms of (3) content—we had omitted everything but the curriculum and instruction areas. That may be because of our orientation, but some of the content recommendations, such as addressing diversity, seem to have meaning only in the context of the study of curriculum, instruction, and social climate.

Building a System or a Targeted Program?

Frequently, we have had a difficult time helping school districts distinguish between developing a system of staff development that embeds support for individuals, faculties, and district initiatives compared with generating a targeted initiative designed to alleviate a specific problem. The standards speak in many places to the building of staff development systems, and NSDC clearly believes that general systems should be developed. However, many of the specifics appear to be directed at targeted initiatives that might or might not be nested within a general program. In our work, we have had to supplement the standards to make the distinction clear.

In addition, we believe that staff development for individuals, for school faculties, or in support of district initiatives needs to be quite differently organized (see Chapter 10). The standards do not make such distinctions, however.

Time for Staff Development

At the greatest level of specificity, in which the NSDC standards identify particulars for process and content, we experienced some difficulty in application. While working with schools and districts (that is, planning, analysis of student data, training and follow-up, and collaborative work), we constantly struggled to ensure time for both organizational change process work (at least in a formal sense) and selection of content/planning of training and follow-up. In many of the jurisdictions where we work, at least in the beginning, the time for staff development was only 3 or 4 days a year; the districts were comfortable until they found that 10 or 12 days a year is a minimum if practice is to change enough to generate student effects.

Aside from our preferences, the three to five days that are typical frequently are organized with a wide variety of offerings that individuals can choose from. People can pick and choose from those offerings, which in many cases are heavily weighted toward elementary school practice. Aside from the inherent weakness of the brevity of the offerings, do people have to attend? Strangely, we have found that in an increasing number of districts, teachers can opt to stay in their classrooms and conduct their own personal study.

A Simple Standard

We are passionate about the conduct of staff development, believing that it is the primary vehicle for improving the knowledge and skills of both individuals and organizations and thus for increased student learning. We support the idea of a set of standards guiding the practice of staff development for the field of education because we believe they will increase our professionalism and our effectiveness.

Suppose that all educators spent 15 (paid) days in communities of professionals studying how to increase learning of various sorts. Now wouldn't that be something! How's that for a beginning standard on which many solid initiatives can be developed? For starters, the types of initiatives we have proposed in this book could be considered.

References and Bibliography

Abrams, P. (1984). Educational seduction. *Review of Educational Research, 52*(3), 446–464.

Adkins, D., Payne, F., & O'Malley, J. (1974). Moral development. In F. N. Kerlinger & J. B. Carroll (Eds.), *Review of Research in Education*. Itasca, IL: F. E. Peacock Publishers, Inc.

Allen, J., Combs, J., Hendricks, M., Nash, P., & S. Wilson. (1988). Studying change: Teachers who became researchers. *Language Arts, 65*(4), 379–387.

Allen, R. (2001, Spring). Cultivating kindergarten: The reach for academic heights raises challenges. *Curriculum Update*, pp. 1–8.

Almy, M. (1970). *Logical thinking in second grade*. New York: Teachers College Press.

Anderson, H., & Brewer, H. (1939). Domination and social integration in the behavior of kindergarten children and teachers. *Genetic Psychology Monograph, 21*, 287–385.

Anderson, H., & Brewer, J. (1946). *Studies of teacher classroom personality II*. Stanford, CA: Stanford University Press.

Anderson, L., Evertson, C., & Brophy, J. (1979). An experimental study of effective teaching in first grade reading groups. *Elementary School Journal, 79*, 193–223.

Anderson, L., & Pellicer, L. (1990). Synthesis of research on compensatory and remedial education. *Educational Leadership, 48*(1), 10–16.

Applebee, A., Langer, J., Jenkins, L., Mullis, I., & Foertsch, M. (1990). *Learning to write in our nation's schools*. Washington, DC: U.S. Department of Education.

Argyris, C., & Schon, E. (1974). *Theory into practice: Increasing professional effectiveness*. San Francisco: Jossey-Bass.

Aspy, D., & Roebuck, F. (1973). An investigation on the relationship between student levels of cognitive functioning and the teacher's classroom behavior. *Journal of Educational Research, 65*, 365–368.

Aspy, D., Roebuck, F., Wilson, M., & Adams, O. (1974). *Interpersonal skills training for teachers*. (Interim Report #2 for NIMH Grant Number 5 PO 1 MH 19871). Monroe: Northeast Louisiana University.

Atkinson, R. (1975). Nemotechnics in second language learning. *American Psychologist, 30*, 821–828.

Ausubel, D. (1963). *The psychology of meaningful verbal learning*. New York: Grune and Stratton.

Ausubel, D. (1980). Schemata, cognitive structure, and advance organizers: A reply to Anderson, Spiro, and Anderson. *American Educational Research Journal, 17*(3), 400–404.

Baker, R., & Showers, B. (1984). *The effects of a coaching strategy on teachers' transfer of training to classroom practice: A six-month follow-up study*. Paper presented at the annual meeting of the American Educational Research Association, New Orleans.

Baldridge, V., & Deal, T. (1975). *Managing change in educational organizations*. Berkeley, CA: McCutchan.

Ball, S., & Bogatz, G. A. (1970). *The first year of* Sesame Street. Princeton, NJ: Educational Testing Service.

Bandura, A. (1971). *Social learning theory*. New York: General Learning.

Bangert, R., & Kulik, J. (1982). *Individualized systems of instruction: A meta-analysis of findings in secondary schools.* Paper presented at the annual meeting of the American Educational Research Association, New York.

Barnes, B., & Clauson, E. (1973). The effects of organizers on the learning of structured anthropology materials in the elementary grades. *Journal of Experimental Education, 42,* 11–15.

Barnes, B., & Clauson, E. (1975). Do advance organizers facilitate learning? Recommendations for further research based on an analysis of 32 studies. *Review of Educational Research, 45*(4), 637–659.

Barron, F. (1963). *Creativity and psychological health: origins of personal vitality and creative freedom.* Princeton, NJ: Von Nostrand.

Barth, R. (1980). *Run, school, run.* Cambridge: Harvard University Press.

Barth, R. (1990). *Inproving schools from within.* San Francisco: Jossey-Bass.

Becker, W. (1978). Teaching reading and language to the disadvantaged: What we have learned from field research. *Harvard Educational Review, 47*(4), 518–543.

Becker, W., & Carmine, D. (1980). Direct instruction: An effective approach for educational intervention with the disadvantaged and low performers. In B. Lahey & A. Kazdin (Eds.), *Advances in child clinical psychology* (pp. 429–473). New York: Plenum.

Becker, W., & Gersten, R. (1982). A follow-up of follow through: The later effects of the direct instruction model on children in the fifth and sixth grades. *American Educational Research Journal, 19*(1), 75–92.

Bellack, A. (1962). *The language of the classroom.* New York: Teachers College Press.

Bennett, B. (1987). *The effectiveness of staff development training practices: A metaanalysis.* Unpublished doctoral dissertation, University of Oregon.

Bennis, W., & Shepard, H. (1964). A theory of group development. In W. Bennis, K. Benne, & R. Chin, (Eds.), *The planning of change: Readings in the applied behavioral sciences.* New York: Holt, Rinehart & Winston.

Bereiter, C. (1984). How to keep thinking skills from going the way of all frills. *Educational Leadership, 42,* 1.

Bereiter, C., & Englemann, S. (1966). *Teaching the culturally disadvantaged child in the preschool.* Englewood Cliffs, NJ: Prentice Hall.

Bereiter, C., & Kurland, M. (1981–82). Were some follow through models more effective than others? *Interchange, 12*(1), 1–22.

Berman, P., & Gjelten, T. (1983). *Improving school improvement.* Berkeley, CA: Berman, Weiler Associates.

Berman, P., & McLaughlin, M. (1975). *Federal programs supporting educational change, Vol. IV: The findings in review.* Santa Monica, CA: The Rand Corporation.

Block, J. (1980). Success rate. In C. Denham & A. Lieberman (Eds.), *Time to learn.* Washington, DC: Program on Teaching and Learning, National Institute of Education.

Bloom, B. (1971). Mastery learning. In J. Block (Ed.), *Mastery learning: Theory and practice.* New York: Holt, Rinehart, & Winston.

Bloom, B. (1974). Time and learning. *American Psychologist, 29,* 682–688.

Bloom, B. (1984). The 2 sigma problem: The search for methods of instruction as effective as one-to-one tutoring. *Educational Leadership, 41*, 4–17.

Bloom, B. S. (1981). *The new direction in educational research and measurement: Alterable variables.* Paper presented at the annual meeting of the American Research Association.

Bonsangue, M. V. (1993). Long term effects of the Calculus Workshop Model. *Cooperative Learning, 13*(3), 19–20.

Bradford, L., Gibb, J., & Benne, K. (Eds.). (1964). *T-Group theory and laboratory method.* New York: John Wiley & Sons, Inc.

Bredderman, T. (1981). *Elementary school process curricula: A meta-analysis.* ERIC Ed., 170–333.

Bredderman, T. (1983). Effects of activity-based elementary science on student outcomes: A quantitative synthesis. *Review of Educational Research, 53*(4), 499–518.

Brookover, W., Schwitzer, J., Schneider, J., Beady, C., Flood, P., & Wisenbaker, J. (1978). Elementary school social climate and school achievement. *American Educational Research Journal, 15*(2), 301–318.

Brophy, J. (1973). Stability of teacher effectiveness. *American Educational Research Journal, 10*(2), 245–252.

Brophy, J. (1992). Probing the subtleties of subject-matter teaching. *Educational Leadership, 49*(7), 4–8.

Brophy, J., & Good, T. (1986). Teacher behavior and student achievement. In M. Wittrock (Ed.), *Handbook of research on teaching* (3rd ed., pp. 328–375). New York: Macmillan.

Bruner, J. (1961). *The process of education.* Cambridge, MA: Harvard University Press.

Calderon, M. (1994). *Bilingual teacher development within school learning communities: A synthesis of the staff development model.* El Paso: University of Texas at El Paso.

Calderon, M., Hertz-Lazarowitz, R., & Tinajero, J. (1991). Adapting CIRC to multiethnic and bilingual classrooms. *Cooperative Learning, 12*, 17–20.

Calhoun, E. (1994). *How to use action research in the self-renewing school.* Alexandria, VA: The Association for Supervision and Curriculum Development.

Calhoun, E. (1997). *Literacy for all.* Saint Simons Island, GA: The Phoenix Alliance.

Calhoun, E. (1998). *Literacy for the primary grades: What works, for whom, and to what degree.* Saint Simons Island, GA: The Phoenix Alliance.

Calhoun, E. (1999). *Teaching beginning reading with the picture word inductive model.* Alexandria, VA: Association for Supervision and Curriculum Development.

Calhoun, E., & Allen, L. (1996a). The action network. In B. Joyce & F. Calhoun (Eds.), *Learning experiences in school renewal.* Eugene, Oregon: The ERIC Clearinghouse for Educational Management.

Calhoun, E., & Allen, L. (1996b). *Results of schoolwide action research in the League of Professional Schools.* Paper presented at the annual meeting of the American Educational Research Association, New Orleans.

Carroll, J. (1963). A model of school learning. *Teachers College Record, 64*(4), 722–733.

Carroll, J. (1977). A revisionist model of school learning. *Review of Education, 3*, 155–167.

Chall, J. S. (1983). *Stages of reading development.* New York: McGraw-Hill.

Chamberlin, C., & Chamberlin, E. (1943). *Did they succeed in college?* New York: Harper and Row.

Clark, C., & Peterson, P. (1986). Teachers' thought processes. In M. Wittrock (Ed.), *Handbook of research on teaching* (pp. 225–296). New York: Macmillan.

Clark, C., & Yinger, R. (1979). *Three studies of teacher planning (Research Series #55)*. East Lansing: Michigan State University.

Clauson, E., & Barnes, B. (1973). The effects of organizers on the learning of structured anthropology materials in the elementary grades. *Journal of Experimental Education*, 42, 11–15.

Cohen, M. (1982). Effective schools: Accumulating evidence. *American Education*, 18(3), 13–16.

Coleman, J., Campbell, E., Hobson, C., McPortland, J., Mood, A., Weinfield, E., & York, R. (1966). *Equality of educational opportunity*. Washington, DC: U.S. Government Printing Office.

Collins, K. (1969). The importance of strong confrontation in an inquiry model of teaching. *School Science and Mathematics*, 69(7), 615–617.

Comer, J. (1988). Educating poor minority children. *Scientific American*, 42(8), 43–55.

Coppel, C., & Sigel, I. (1971). *Educating the young thinker. Classroom strategies for cognitive growth*. New York: Krieger.

Corey, S. M. (1953). *Action research to improve school practices*. New York: Teachers College Press.

Crandall, D., et al. (1982). *People, policies, and practices: Examining the chain of school improvement* (Vols. I–X). Andover, MA: The Network.

CRESST: National Center for Research on Evaluation, Standards, and Student Testing. (1994). *Measurement-driven reform: The more things change, the more they stay the same*. CRESST Technical Report 373. Los Angeles: Center for the Study of Education, UCLA.

Cuban, L. (1990). Reforming again, again, and again. *Educational Researcher*, 19(1), 3–13.

Dalton, M. (1986). *The thought processes of teachers when practicing two models of teaching*. Doctoral dissertation, University of Oregon.

Dalton, M., & Dodd, J. (1986). *Teacher thinking: The development of skill in using two models of teaching and model-relevant thinking*. Paper presented at the annual meetings of the American Educational Research Association, San Francisco.

David, J. (1990). *Restructuring: Increased autonomy and changing roles*. Invited address presented at the annual meeting of the American Educational Research Association, Boston.

David, J., & Peterson, S. (1984). *Can schools improve themselves? A study of school-based improvement programs*. Palo Alto, CA: Bay Area Research Group.

Deming, W. (1982). *Out of the crisis*. Cambridge, MA: Massachusetts Institute of Technology, Center for Advanced Engineering Study.

Derry, S., & Murphy, D. (1986). Designing systems that train learning ability: from theory to practice. *Review of Educational Research*, 56, 1–40.

Dewey, J. (1916). *Democracy in education*. New York: Macmillan, Inc.

Dewey, J. (1937). *Experience in education*. New York: Macmillan, Inc.

Dole, J., Duffy, G., Roehler, L., & Pearson, P. (1991). Moving from the old to the new: Research on reading comprehension instruction. *Review of Educational Research*, 61(2), 239–264.

Donahue, P. (1999). *1998 NAEP reading report card for the nation and the states*. Washington, DC: U.S. Department of Education.

Donahue, P., Flanagan, R., Lutkus, A., Allen, N., & Campbell, J. (2001). *The national report card: Fourth grade reading 2000.* Washington, DC: U.S. Department of Education, Office of Educational Research and Improvement, National Center for Educational Statistics.

Downey, L. (1969). *The secondary phase of education.* New York: Ginn.

Drucker, P. (1988). Knowledge work and the structure of the schools. *Educational Leadership, 45*(5), 44–46.

Drucker, P. (1994). The age of social transformation. *Atlantic Monthly, 11,* 53–80.

Duke, N., & Pearson, P. (n.d.). *Effective practices for developing reading comprehension.* East Lansing: College of Education, Michigan State University.

Edmonds, R. (1979). Effective schools for the urban poor. *Educational Leadership, 37*(1), 15–23.

Ehri, L. (1999). *Phases of acquisition in learning to read words and instructional implications.* Paper presented to the Annual Meeting of the American Educational Research Association, Montreal.

El-Nemr, M. (1979). *Meta-analysis of the outcomes of teaching biology as inquiry.* Unpublished doctoral dissertation, University of Colorado.

Elefant, E. (1980). Deaf children in an inquiry training program. *The Volta Review, 82,* 271–279.

Ellis, A., & Harper, R. (1975). *A new guide to rational living.* Englewood Cliffs, NJ: Prentice Hall.

Elmore, R. (Ed.). (1990). *Restructuring schools.* San Francisco, CA: Jossey-Bass.

Elmore, R., & Rothman, R. (Eds.). (1999). *Testing, teaching, and learning: A guide for states and school districts.* Committee on Title I Testing and Assessment. Washington, DC: National Academy Press.

Englemann, S., Osborn, J., & Englemann, T. (1972). *DISTAR Language Program.* Chicago: Science Research Associates, Inc.

Englert, C., & Raphael, T. (1989). Developing successful writers through cognitive strategy instruction. In J. Brophy (Ed.), *Advances in research in teaching* (pp. 105–151). Greenwich, CT: JAI Press.

Englert, C., Raphael, T., Anderson, L., Anthony, H., & Stevens, D. (1991). Making strategies and self-talk visible: Writing instruction in regular and special education classrooms. *American Educational Research Journal, 28*(2), 337–372.

Erikson, E. (1950). *Childhood and society.* New York: Norton.

Estes, W. (Ed.). (1976). *Handbook of learning and cognitive processes, Vol. IV: Attention and memory.* Hillsdale, NJ: Lawrence Erlbaum Associates.

Evertson, C., Anderson, C., Anderson, L., & Brophy, J. (1980). Relationships between classroom behaviors and student outcomes in junior high mathematics and English classes. *American Educational Research Journal, 17*(1), 43–60.

Feeley, T. (1972). *The concept of inquiry in the social studies.* Unpublished doctoral dissertation, Stanford University.

Flavell, J. (1963). *The developmental psychology of Jean Piaget.* Princeton, NJ: Van Nostrand Reinhold.

Flesch, R. (1955). *Why Johnny can't read.* New York: Harper Brothers.

Fullan, M. (1990). Staff development, innovation, and institutional development. In B. Joyce (Ed.), *Changing school culture through staff development.* 1990 ASCD yearbook. Alexandria, VA: Association for Supervision and Curriculum Development.

Fullan, M. (2001). *The new meaning of educational change* (3rd ed.). New York: Teachers College Press.

Fullan, M., & Miles, M. (1992). Getting reform right: What works and what doesn't. *Phi Delta Kappan, 73*(10), 744–752.

Fullan, M., Miles, M., & Taylor, G. (1980). Organization development in schools: The state of the art. *Review of Educational Research, 50*(1), 121–184.

Fullan, M., & Park, P. (1981). *Curriculum implementation: A resource booklet.* Toronto: Ontario Ministry of Education.

Fullan, M., & Pomfret, A. (1977). Research on curriculum and instruction implementation. *Review of Educational Research, 47*(2), 335–397.

Fullan, M., & Steigelbauer, S. (1991). *The new meaning of educational change.* New York: Teachers College Press.

Gage, N. (1979). *The scientific basis for the art of teaching.* New York: Teachers College Press.

Gagné, R. (1962). Military training and principles of learning. *American Psychologist, 17,* 46–67.

Gagné, R., ed. (1962). *Psychological principles in systems development.* New York: Holt, Rinehart & Winston.

Gagné, R. (1965). *Conditions of Learning.* New York: Holt, Rinehart & Winston.

Gagné, R. (1965). The learning of concepts. *The School Review, 75,* 187–196.

Gagné, R., & Briggs, L. (1979). *Principles of instructional design.* New York: Holt, Rinehart and Winston.

Gallway, T. (1977). *Inner skiing.* New York: Random House.

Gamoran, A., & Berends, M. (1987). The effects of stratification in secondary schools. *Review of Educational Research, 57*(4), 415–435.

Gardner, J. W. (1963). *Self renewal: The individual and the innovative society.* New York: Harper and Row.

Garmston, R. (1987). How administrators support peer coaching. *Educational Leadership, 44*(5), 18–26.

Garner, R. (1987). *Metacognition and reading comprehension.* Norwood, NJ: Ablex.

Gaskins, I. (1999). A multidimensional reading program. *Reading Teacher, 53*(2), 162–164.

Glass, G. (1975). Primary, secondary, and meta-analysis of research. *Educational Researcher, 7*(3), 3–7.

Glass, G. (1982). Meta-analysis: An approach to the synthesis of research results. *Journal of Research in Science Teaching, 19*(2), 93–112.

Glasser, W. (1984). *Take effective control of your life.* New York: Harper & Row.

Glickman, C. (1993). *Renewing America's schools.* San Francisco: Jossey-Bass.

Good, T., Grouws, D., & Ebmeier, H. (1983). *Active mathematics teaching.* New York: Longman, Inc.

Goodlad, J. (1984). *A place called school.* New York: McGraw-Hill.

Goodlad, J., & Klein, F. (1970). *Looking behind the classroom door.* Worthington, OH: Charles E. Jones.

Goodman, R., Fulbright, L., & Zimmerman, W., Jr. (1997). *Getting there from here. School board-superintendent collaboration: Creating a school governance team capable of raising student achievement.* Arlington, VA: The New England School Development Council and Educational Research Services.

Gordon, W. (1962, August). The Nobel Prizewinners. *The Atlantic Monthly.*

Gordon, W. (1963 March). How to get your imagination off the ground. *Think.*

Gordon, W. (1970). *The metaphorical way of learning and knowing.* Cambridge, MA: S.E.S. Press.

Gordon, W., & Poze, T. (1971). *The basic course in synectics.* Cambridge: Porpoise Books.

Graves, M. F. (1992). The elementary vocabulary curriculum: What should it be? In M. J. Dreher & W. H. Slater (Eds.), *Elementary school literacy: Critical issues* (pp. 101–131). Norwood, MA: Christopher-Gordon.

Graves, N., & Graves, T. (1990). *Cooperative learning: a resource guide.* Santa Cruz: The International Association for the Study of Cooperation in Education.

Guetzkow, H., (1966). *Simulation in international relations.* Englewood Cliffs, NJ: Prentice Hall.

Guetzkow, H., & Valdez, J. (Eds.). (1966). *Simulated international processes: Theories and research in global modeling.* Beverly Hills, CA: Sage Publications.

Gunning, T. (1997). *Best books for beginning readers.* Boston: Allyn & Bacon.

Habib, F., Cook, T., Marcantonio, R., Anson, A., & Clifford, E. (1993). *The Comer middle school development program after two years.* Paper presented at the annual meeting of the American Educational Researcher Association. Atlanta.

Hall, G. (1986). *Skills derived from studies of the implementation of innovations in education.* Paper presented at the annual meeting of the American Educational Research Association, San Francisco.

Hall, G., & Hord, S. (1987). *Change in schools: Facilitating the process.* New York: State University of New York.

Hall, G., & Loucks, S. (1977). A developmental model for determining whether the treatment is actually implemented. *American Educational Research Journal, 14*(3), 263–276.

Hallinger, P., & Murphy, J. (1985). Assessing the instructional management behavior of principals. *Elementary School Journal, 86*(2), 217–247.

Halpin, A. W. (1966). *Theory and research in administration.* New York: Macmillan.

Hanson, R., & Farrell, D. (1995). The long-term effects on high school seniors of learning to read in kindergarten. *Reading Research Quarterly, 30*(4), 908–933.

Harkreader, S., & Weathersby, J. (1998). *Staff development and student achievement: Making the connection in Georgia schools.* Atlanta: Georgia State University, The Council for School Performance.

Harvey, O., Hunt, D., & Schroeder, H. (1961). *Conceptual Systems and Personality Organization.* New York: John Wiley & Sons, Inc.

Harter, S. (1982). The perceived competence scale for children. *Child Development, 53,* 87–97.

Hawkes, E. (1971). *The effects of an instructional strategy on approaches to problem-solving.* Unpublished doctoral dissertation, Teachers College, Columbia University, New York.

Hawley, W., Rosenholtz, S., Goodstein, H., & Hasselbring, T. (1984). Good schools: What research says about improving student achievement. *Peabody Journal of Education, 61*(4), 1–178.

Herman, R. (1999). *An educator's guide to schoolwide reform.* Arlington, VA: Educational Research Service.

Hertz-Lazarovitz, R. (1993). Using group investigation to enhance Arab-Jewish relationships. *Cooperative Learning, 11*(2), 13–14.

Hertz-Lazarowitz, R., & Shachar, H. (1990). Changes in teachers' verbal behavior in cooperative classrooms. *Cooperative Learning, 11*(2), 13–14.

Hiebert, E., & Taylor, B. (Eds.). (1994). *Getting reading right from the start.* Boston: Allyn & Bacon.

Hillocks, G. (1987). Synthesis of research on teaching writing. *Educational Leadership, 44*(8), 71–82.

Hoetker, J., & Ahlbrand, W. (1969). The persistence of the recitation. *American Educational Research Journal, 6,* 145–167.

Hollingsworth, S., & Sockett, H. (1994). *Teacher research and educational reform.* Chicago: University of Chicago Press.

Holloway, S. (1988). Concepts of ability and effort in Japan and the U.S. *Review of Educational Research, 58*(3), 327–346.

Hopkins, D. (1990). Integrating staff development and school improvement: A study of teacher personality and school climate. In B. Joyce (Ed.), *Changing school culture through staff development.* The 1990 ASCD Yearbook (pp. 41–70). Alexandria, VA: The Association for Supervision and Curriculum Development.

Hopkins, D., Ainscow, M., & West, M. (1994). *School improvement in an era of change.* London: Cassell.

Huberman, A. (1992). Successful school improvement: Reflections and observations. Introduction to M. Fullan, *Successful school improvement.* Toronto: University of Toronto Press.

Hrycauk, M. (2002). District weaves safety net. *Journal of Staff Development, 23*(1), 55–58.

Huberman, A., & Miles, M. (1984). *Innovation up close: How school improvement works.* New York: Plenum Press.

Huberman, A., & Miles, M. (1986). Rethinking the quest for school improvement: some findings from the DESSI study. In A. Lieberman (Ed.), *Rethinking school improvement research* (pp. 76–107). New York: Teachers College Press.

Hunt, D. (1970). A conceptual level matching model for coordinating learner characteristics with educational approaches. *Interchange: A Journal of Educational Studies. 1*(2), 1–31.

Hunt, D. (1971). *Matching models in education.* Toronto: Ontario Institute for Studies in Education.

Hunt, D. (1981). *Teachers' personal theorizing.* Toronto: Ontario Institute for Studies in Education.

Hunt, D., Butler, L., Noy, J., & Rosser, M. (1978). *Assessing conceptual level by the paragraph completion method.* Toronto: Ontario Institute for Studies in Education.

Hunt, J. McV. (1961). *Intelligence and experience.* New York: Ronald Press.

Hunter, M., & Russell, D. (1981). Planning for effective instruction: Lesson design. In *Increasing your teaching effectiveness* [Pamphlet]. Palo Alto, CA: Learning Institute.

Hurley, E., Chamberlain, A., Slavin, R., & Madden, N. (2000). *Effects of success for all on TAAS reading: A statewide evaluation.* Baltimore: Success for All Foundation.

International Reading Association. (1998). *Position statement on phonemic awareness and the teaching of reading.* Newark, DE: International Reading Association.

International Reading Association and The National Association for the Education of Young Children. (1998). *Position statement on learning to read and write: Developmentally appropriate practices for young children.* Newark, DE: International Reading Association.

Iowa Association of School Boards and Iowa State Board of Education. (1994). *School board leadership: The future*. Des Moines: Iowa Association of School Boards.

Ivany, G. (1969). The assessment of verbal inquiry in elementary school science. *Science Education, 53*(4), 287–293.

Jencks, C., et al. (1970). *Education vouchers: A report on financing elementary education by grants to parents*. Cambridge, MA: Center for the Study of Public Policy.

Johnson, D., & Johnson, R. (1975). *Learning together and alone*. Englewood Cliffs, NJ: Prentice Hall.

Johnson, D., & Johnson, R. (1999). *Methods of cooperative learning: What can we prove works*. Edwina, MN: Cooperative Learning Institute.

Johnson, D., Maruyama, G., Johnson, R., Nelson, D., & Skon, L. (1981). Effects of cooperative, competitive, and individualistic goal structures on achievement: a meta-analysis. *Psychological Bulletin, 89*(1), 47–62.

Joyce, B. (Ed.). (1978). *Involvement: A study of shared governance of teacher education*. Washington, DC: ERIC Clearinghouse on Teacher Education.

Joyce, B. (1978–79). Toward a theory of information processing in teaching. *Educational Research Quarterly, 3*(4), 66–77.

Joyce, B. (1980). *Teacher innovator system: Observer's manual*. Saint Simons Island, Georgia: Booksend Laboratories.

Joyce, B. (Ed.). (1990). *Changing school culture through staff development*. The 1990 ASCD Yearbook. Alexandria, VA: The Association for Supervision and Curriculum Development.

Joyce, B. (1991). Doors to school improvement. *Educational Leadership, 48*(8), 59–62.

Joyce, B. (1992). Cooperative learning and staff development: Teaching the method with the method. *Cooperative Learning, 12*(2), 10–13.

Joyce, B. (1999). Reading about reading. *The Reading Teacher, 6*, 1–12.

Joyce, B., & Belitzky, A. (1999). *Creating a system*. Tallahassee, FL: Florida State Department of Education.

Joyce, B., Bush, R., & McKibbin, M. (1982). *The California staff development study. The January, 1982 report*. Palo Alto: Booksend Laboratories.

Joyce, B., & Calhoun, E. (Eds.). (1996). *Learning experiences in school renewal*. Eugene, OR: ERIC Clearinghouse on Educational Management. (ERIC Document Reproduction Service No. ED 401 600).

Joyce, B., & Calhoun, E. (1998). *Learning to teach inductively*. Boston: Allyn & Bacon.

Joyce, B., Calhoun, E., Halliburton, C., Simser, J., Rust, D., & Carran, N. (1994). *The Ames Community Schools staff development program*. Paper presented at the annual meeting of The Association for Supervision and Curriculum Development, Chicago.

Joyce, B., Calhoun, E., & Hopkins, D. (1999). *The new structure of school improvement: Inquiring schools and achieving students*. Buckingham, UK, and Philadelphia: The Open University Press.

Joyce, B., Calhoun, E., & Weil, M. (2000). *Models of teaching* (6th ed.). Boston: Allyn & Bacon.

Joyce, B., & Clift, R. (1984). The phoenix agenda: Essential reform in teacher education. *Educational Researcher, 13*(4), 5–18.

Joyce, B., & Harootunian, B. (1967). *The structure of teaching*. Chicago: Science Research Associates.

Joyce, B., Hersh, R., & McKibbin, M. (1983). *The structure of school improvement.* New York: Longman.

Joyce, B., McKibbin, M., & Bush, R. (1983). *The seasons of professional life: The growth states of teachers.* Paper presented at the annual meeting of the American Education Research Association. Montreal.

Joyce, B., McKibbin, M., & Bush, R. (1984). *Predicting whether an innovation will be implemented: Four case studies.* Paper presented at the annual meeting of the American Educational Research Association, New Orleans.

Joyce, B., Murphy, C., Showers, B., & Murphy, J. (1989). School renewal as cultural change. *Educational Leadership, 47*(3), 70–78.

Joyce, B., Peck, L., & Brown, C. (Eds.). (1981). *Flexibility in teaching.* New York: Longman, Inc.

Joyce, B., & Showers, B. (1980). Improving inservice training: The messages of research. *Educational Leadership, 37*(5), 379–385.

Joyce, B., & Showers, B. (1981). *Teacher training research: Working hypothesis for program design and directions for further study.* Paper presented at the annual meeting of the American Education Research Association, Los Angeles.

Joyce, B., & Showers, B. (1982). The coaching of teaching. *Educational Leadership, 40*(1), 4–16.

Joyce, B., & Showers, B. (1983). *Power in staff development through research on training.* Alexandria, VA: Association for Supervision and Curriculum Development.

Joyce, B., & Showers, B. (1988). *Student achievement through staff development.* New York: Longman, Inc.

Joyce, B., & Showers, B. (1995). *Student achievement through staff development* (rev. ed). White Plains, NY: Longman, Inc.

Joyce, B., Showers, B., Beaton, C., & Dalton, M. (1984). *The search for validated objectives of teacher education: Teaching skills derived from naturalistic and persuasion oriented studies of teaching.* Paper presented at the annual meeting of the American Educational Research Association, New Orleans.

Joyce, B., Showers, B., Dalton, M., & Beaton, C. (1985). *The search for validated skills of teaching: Four lines of inquiry.* A paper presented to the annual meeting of the American Educational Research Association. Chicago.

Joyce, B., & Wolf, J. (1992). *Operation just read and write: Toward a literate society.* Paper presented to the annual meeting of the Association for Supervision and Curriculum Development. New Orleans.

Joyce, B., Wolf, J., & Calhoun, E. (1993). *The self-renewing school.* Alexandria, VA: Association for Supervision and Curriculum Development.

Joyce, B. R., & Wolf, J. (1996). Readerville: Building culture readers and writers. In B. Joyce & E. Calhoun. (Eds.), *Learning experiences in school renewal: An exploration of five successful programs.* Eugene, OR: ERIC Clearinghouse on Educational Management, University of Oregon.

Juel, C. (1988). Learning to read and write. *Journal of Educational Psychology, 80*(4), 437–447.

Kagan, S. (1999). *Cooperative learning resources for teachers.* San Juan Capistrano: Resources for Teachers.

Kamii, C., & Devries, R. (1974). Piaget-based curricula for early childhood education. In R. Parker (Ed.), *The preschool in action.* Boston: Allyn & Bacon.

Kaplan, A. (1964). *The conduct of inquiry.* San Francisco: Chandler.

Kerman, S. (1979). Teacher expectations and student achievement. *Phi Delta Kappan, 10,* 716–718.

Knowles, M. (1978). *The adult learner: A neglected species.* Houston: Gulf Publishing Co.

Kohlberg, L. (1983). *The psychology of moral development.* New York: Harper & Row.

Kuhn, D., Amsel, E., & O'Loughlin, M. (1988). *The development of scientific thinking skills.* New York: Academic Press.

Kulik, C. L., Kulik, C., & Bengert-Drowns, R. (1990). Effectiveness of mastery learning programs: a meta-analysis. *Review of Educational Research, 60,* 265–299.

Lara, A., & Medley, D. (1987). Effective teacher behavior as a function of learner ability. *Professional School Psychology, 2*(1), 15–23.

Lawton, J. (1977a). Effects of advance organizer lessons on children's use and understanding of the causal and logical "Because." *Journal of Experimental Education, 46*(1), 41–46.

Lawton, J. (1977b). The use of advance organizers in the learning and retention of logical operations in social studies concepts. *American Educational Research Journal, 14*(1), 24–43.

Lawton, J., & Wanska, S. (1977). Advance organizers as a teaching strategy: A reply to Barnes and Clawson. *Review of Educational Research, 1,* 233–244.

Lawton, J., & Wanska, S. (1979). The effects of different types of advance organizers on classification learning. *American Educational Research Journal, 16*(3), 223–39.

Learning Research and Development Center. (1968). *Individually prescribed instruction: mathematics continuum.* Pittsburgh, PA: University of Pittsburgh, Learning Research and Development Center.

Leithwood, K. (1990). The principal's role in teacher development. In B. Joyce (Ed.), *Changing school culture through staff development.* Alexandria, VA: Association for Supervision and Curriculum Development.

Leithwood, K. (1992). The move toward transformational leadership. *Educational Leadership, 49*(5), 8–12.

Levin, J., McCormick, C., Miller, C., & Berry, J. (1982). Mnemonic versus nonmnemonic strategies for children. *American Educational Research Journal, 19*(1), 121–136.

Levin, J., Shriberg, L., & Berry, J. (1983). A concrete strategy for remembering abstract prose. *American Educational Research Journal, 20*(2), 277–290.

Levin, M., & Levin, J. R. (1990). Scientific mnemonics: Methods for maximizing more than memory. *American Educational Research Journal, 27,* 301–321.

Levine, D. (1991, January). Creating effective schools: Findings and implications from research and practice. *Phi Delta Kappan,* 389–393.

Levine, D., & Lezotte, L. (1990). *Creating unusually effective schools: A review and analysis of research and practice.* Madison, WI: National Center for Effective Schools.

Lewin, K. (1947). *Resolving social conflicts.* New York: Harper & Row.

Lieberman, A. (Ed.). (1988). *Building a professional culture in schools.* New York: Teachers College Press.

Lindvall, C., & Bolvin, J. (1966). *The project for individually prescribed instruction. Oakleaf Project.* Unpublished manuscript, University of Pittsburgh, Learning Research and Development Center.

Lippitt, R., Fox, R., & Schaible, L. (1969). *Social science laboratory units.* Chicago: Science Research Associates.

Little, J. (1982). Norms of collegiality and experimentation: Workplace conditions of school success. *American Educational Research Journal, 42*(3), 325–340.

Little, J. (1990). *The persistence of privacy: Autonomy and initiative in teachers' professional relations.* Paper presented at the annual meeting of the American Educational Research Association, San Francisco.

Lorwayne, H., & Lucas, J. (1996). *The memory book.* New York: Briarcliff Manor.

Lortie, D. (1975). *Schoolteacher.* Chicago: The University of Chicago Press.

Luiten, J., Ames, W., & Ackerson, G. (1980). A meta-analysis of the effects of advance organizers on learning and retention. *American Educational Research Journal, 17*(2), 211–218.

Lundquist, G., & Parr, G. (1978). Assertiveness training with adolescents. *Technical Journal of Education, 5,* 37–44.

Madden, N., & Slavin, R. (1983). Cooperative learning and social acceptance of main-streamed academically handicapped students. *Journal of Special Education, 17,* 171–182.

Maeroff, G. I. (1991, December). Assessing alternative assessment. *Phi Delta Kappan,* 272–281.

Mahoney, M., & Thorensen, C. (1972). Behavioral self-control—power to the person. *Educational Researcher, 1,* 5–7.

Mandeville, G. (1989). *An evaluation of PET based on longitudinal data.* Paper presented at the annual meeting of the American Educational Research Association. San Francisco.

March, H., & O'Neill, R. (1984). Self-description Questionnaire III: The construct validity of multidimensional self-concept ratings by late adolescents. *Journal of Educational Measurement, 21,* 153–174.

Marzano, R., Pickering, D., & Pollock, J. (2001). *Classroom instruction that works: Research-based strategies for increasing student achievement.* Alexandria, VA: Association for Supervision and Curriculum Development.

Maslow, A. (1962). *Toward a psychology of being.* New York: Van Nostrand.

McDonald, F., & Elias, P. (1976). *Executive summary report: Beginning teacher evaluation study, phase two.* Princeton, NJ: Educational Testing Service.

McGill-Franzen, A., & Allington, R. L. (1991). Every child's right: Literacy. *Reading Teacher, 45,* 86–90.

McGill-Franzen, A., Allington, R., Yokoi, L., & Brooks, G. (1999). Putting books in the classroom seems necessary but not sufficient. *Journal of Educational Research, 93,* 67–74.

McGill-Franzen, A., & Goatley, V. (2001). Title I and special education: Support for children who struggle to learn to read. In S. Neuman & D. Dickinson (Eds.), *Handbook of early literacy research* (pp. 471–484). New York: The Guilford Press.

McGill-Franzen, A., Lanford, C., & Killian, J. (n.d.). *Case studies of literature-based textbook use in kindergarten.* Albany: State University of New York.

McKibbin, M., & Joyce, B. (1980). Psychological states and staff development. *Theory into Practice, 19*(4), 248–255.

McNair, K. (1978–1979). Capturing in-flight decisions. *Educational Research Quarterly, 3*(4), 26–42.

Medley, D. (1977). *Teacher competence and teacher effectiveness.* Washington, DC: American Association of Colleges of Teacher Education.

Medley, D., Coker, H., Coker, J., Lorentz, J., Soar, R., & Spaulding, R. (1981). Assessing teacher performance from observed competency indicators defined by classroom teachers. *Journal of Educational Research, 74,* 197–216.

Merrill, M., & Tennyson, R. (1977). *Concept teaching: An instructional design guide.* Englewood Cliffs, NJ: Educational Technology.

Meyer, L. (1984). Long-term academic effects of the Direct Instruction Project follow through. *Elementary School Journal, 84,* 380–394.

Miles, M. (1992). *40 years of change in schools: Some personal reflections.* Paper presented at the annual meeting of the American Educational Research Association, San Francisco.

Moore, D., & Davenport, S. (1989). *The new improved sorting machine: Concerning school choice.* Chicago: Designs for Change.

Mortimore, P. (1999). Foreword. In B. Joyce, E. Calhoun, & D. Hopkins, *The new structure of school improvement.* Buckingham, UK, and Philadelphia: The Open University Press.

Mortimore, P., Sammons, P., Stoll, L., Lewis, D., & Ecob, R. (1988). *School matters: The junior years.* London: Open Books.

Muncey, D. (1984). *Individual and schoolwide change in eight coalition schools: Findings from a longitudinal ethnographic study.* Paper presented at the annual meeting of the American Educational Research Association, New Orleans.

Muncey, D., & McQuillan, P. (1993). Preliminary findings from a five-year study of the Coalition of Essential Schools. *Phi Delta Kappan, 74*(6), 486–489.

Murphy, J. (1992). *The landscape of leadership preparation.* Newbury Park, CA: Corwin Press.

Murphy, J., & Hallinger, P. (Eds.). (1987). *Approaches to administrative training.* Albany: State University of New York (SUNY) Press.

Murphy, J., & Louis, K. S. (Eds.). (1994). *Reshaping the principalship: Insights from transformational change efforts.* Newbury Park, CA: Corwin.

Nagy, W., & Anderson, P. (1987). Breadth and depth in vocabulary knowledge. *Reading Research Quarterly, 19,* 304–330.

Nagy, W., Herman, P., & Anderson, R. (1985). Learning words from context. *Reading Research Quarterly, 19,* 304–330.

Natale, J. (2001). Early learners: Are full day academic kindergartens too much, too soon. *American School Board Journal, 188*(3), 22–25.

National Center for Educational Statistics. (1998). *Long term trends in reading performance. NAEP Facts.* Washington, DC: Office of Educational Research and Improvement, U.S. Department of Education.

National Staff Development Council. (2001). *Revised standards for staff development.* Oxford, OH: National Council for Staff Development.

National Council of Teachers of Mathematics. (1991). *Professional standards for teaching mathematics.* Reston, VA: Author.

National Council of Teachers of Mathematics. (1989). *Curriculum and evaluation standards for school mathematics.* Reston, VA: Author.

National Institutes of Education. (1975). *National conference on studies in teaching, Vols. 1–10.* Washington, DC: U.S. Department of Health, Education & Welfare.

Neuman, S., & Dickinson, D. (Eds.). (2001). *Handbook of early literacy research.* New York: The Guilford Press.

Oakes, J. (1985). *Keeping track: How schools structure inequality.* New Haven, CT: Yale University Press.

Oja, S. (1989). *Collaborative action research: A developmental perspective.* London: Falmer Press.

Orlich, D., Remaley, A., Facemyer, K., Logan, J., & Cao, Q. (1993). Seeking the link between student achievement and staff development. *Journal of Staff Development, 14*(3), 2–8.

Pearson, D. (1998). *New York State Reading Symposium.* Albany: The New York State Education Department.

Perkins, D. (1984). Creativity by design. *Educational Leadership, 42*(1), 18–25.

Perls, F. (1968). *Gestalt Therapy verbatim.* Lafayette, CA: Real People Press.

Peterson, P., & Clark, C. (1978). Teachers' reports of their cognitive processes while teaching. *American Educational Research Journal, 15,* 555–565.

Peterson, P., Marx, R., & Clark, C. (1978). Teacher planning, teacher behavior, and student achievement. *American Educational Research Journal, 15,* 417–432.

Phillips, D. (1987). *Philosophy, science, and social inquiry.* Oxford, UK: Pergamon.

Piaget, J. (1960). *The child's conception of the world.* Atlantic Highlands, NJ: Humanities Press, Inc.

Pikulski, J., & Taylor, B. (1999). *Emergent literacy survey/K–2.* Boston: Houghton Mifflin.

Pinnell, G. (1989). Helping at risk children learn to read. *Elementary School Journal, 90*(2), 161–184.

Pinnell, G., & McCarrier (1994). Interactive writing. In E. Hiebert & B. Taylor (Eds.), *Getting reading right from the start* (pp. 149–170). Boston: Allyn & Bacon.

Potter, D., & Wall, M. (1992). *Higher standards for grade promotion and graduation: Unintended effects of reform.* Paper presented at the annual meeting of the American Educational Research Association, San Francisco.

Pressley, M. (1977). Children's use of the keyword method to learn simple Spanish vocabulary words. *Journal of Educational Psychology, 69*(5), 465–472.

Pressley, M., & Dennis-Rounds, J. (1980). Transfer of a mnemonic keyword strategy at two age levels. *Journal of Educational Psychology, 72*(4), 575–582.

Pressley, M., & Levin, J. (1978). Developmental constraints associated with children's use of the keyword method of foreign language learning. *Journal of Experimental Child Psychology, 26*(1), 359–372.

Pressley, M., Levin, J., & Delaney, H. (1982). The mnemonic keyword method. *Review of Educational Research, 52*(1), 61–91.

Pressley, M., Levin, J., & Ghatala, E. (1984). Memory strategy monitoring in adults and children. *Journal of Verbal Learning and Verbal Behavior, 23*(2), 270–288.

Pressley, M., Levin, J., & McCormick, C. (1980). Young children's learning of foreign language vocabulary. *Contemporary Educational Psychology, 5*(1), 22–29.

Pressley, M., Levin, J., & Miller, G. (1981). The keyword method and children's learning of foreign vocabulary with abstract meanings. *Canadian Psychology, 35*(3), 283–287.

Pressley, M., & Woloshyn, V. (Eds.) (1995). *Cognitive strategy instruction that really improves student performance* (2nd ed.). Cambridge, MA: Brookline.

Resnick, L. (1987). *Education and learning to think.* Washington, DC: Academic Press.

Rhine, W. (Ed.). (1981). *Making schools more effective: New questions from follow-through.* New York: Academic Press.

Rimm, D., & Masters, J. (1974). *Behavior therapy: Techniques and empirical findings.* New York: Academic Press, Inc.

Ripple, R., & Drinkwater, D. (1982). Transfer of learning. In H. E. Mitzel (Ed.), *Encyclopedia of Educational Research, Vol. 4* (pp. 1947–1953). New York: The Free Press, Macmillan Publishing Company.

Roebuck, F., Buhler, J., & Aspy, D. (1976). *A comparison of high and low levels of humane teaching/learning conditions on the subsequent achievement of students identified as having learning difficulties.* Final Report: Order No. PLD 6816–76. The National Institute of Mental Health. Denton: Texas Woman's University Press.

Rogers, C. (1961). *On becoming a person.* Boston: Houghton Mifflin.

Rogers, C. (1971). *Client centered therapy.* Boston: Houghton Mifflin.

Rogers, C. (1982). *Freedom to learn in the eighties.* Columbus: Charles E. Merrill.

Rolheiser-Bennett, C. (1986). *Four models of teaching: A meta-analysis of student outcomes.* Unpublished doctoral dissertation, University of Oregon.

Roper, S., Deal, T., & Dornbusch, S. (1976, Spring). Collegial evaluation of classroom teaching: Does it work? *Educational Research Quarterly, 1*(1), 56–66.

Rose, L., & Gallup, A. (2000). The 32nd annual Phi Delta Kappa/Gallup poll of the public's attitudes toward the public schools. *Phi Delta Kappan, 82,* 1.

Rosenholtz, S. J. (1989). *Teachers' workplace: The social organization of schools.* White Plains, NY: Longman.

Rosenshine, B. (1971). *Teaching behaviors and student achievement.* London: National Foundation for Educational Research.

Rosenshine, B. (1985). Direct instruction. In T. Husen & T. Neville Postlethwaite (Eds.), *International encyclopedia of education, Vol. 3* (pp. 1395–1400). Oxford: Pergamon Press.

Rowe, M. (1974). Wait-time and rewards as instructional variables, their influence on language, logic, and fate control. *Journal of Research in Science Teaching, 11,* 81–94.

Rutter, M., Maughan, R., Mortimer, P., Oustin, J., & Smith, A. (1979). *Fifteen thousand hours: Secondary schools and their effects on children.* Cambridge, MA: Harvard University Press.

Sanders, W., & Rivers, J. (1996). *Cumulative and residual effects of teachers on future academic achievement.* Knoxville, TN: University of Tennessee Value Added Research and Assessment Center.

Santapau, S. (2001). The nation's report card: Fourth grade reading highlights (Ch. 19), *Education Statistics Quarterly, 3*(2), 167–182.

Sarason, S. (1982). *The culture of the school and the problem of change* (2nd ed.). Boston: Allyn & Bacon.

Sarason, S. (1990). *The predictable failure of school reform: Can we change the course before it's too late?* San Francisco: Jossey-Bass.

Schaefer, R. (1967). *The school as a center of inquiry.* New York: Harper and Row.

Schmoker, M. (1996). *Results: The key to continuous school improvement.* Alexandria, VA: Association for Supervision and Curriculum Development.

Schmuck, R., & Runkel, P. (1985). *The handbook of organizational development in schools* (3rd ed.). Palo Alto, CA: Mayfield.

Schon, D. (1982). *The reflective practitioner.* New York: Basic Books.

Schrenker, G. (1976). *The effects of an inquiry-development program on elementary school children's science learning.* Unpublished doctoral dissertation. New York University.

Schroeder, H., Driver, M., & Streufert, S. (1967). *Human information processing: Individuals and groups functioning in complex social situations*. New York: Holt, Rinehart & Winston.

Schwab, J. (1965). *Biological sciences curriculum study: Biology teachers' handbook*. New York: John Wiley & Sons, Inc.

Schwab, J. (1982). *Science, curriculum, and liberal education: Selected essays*. Chicago: University of Chicago Press.

Schwab, J., & Brandwein, P. (1962). *The teaching of science*. Cambridge, MA: Harvard University Press.

Seashore-Louis, K., & Miles, M. (1990). *Improving the urban high school*. New York: Teachers College Press.

Sergiovanni, T. (1992). *Moral leadership*. San Francisco, CA: Jossey-Bass.

Shaftel, F., & Shaftel, G. (1967). *Role playing for social values: Decision making in the social studies*. Englewood Cliffs, NJ: Prentice Hall.

Shanker, A. (1993, September). Ninety-two hours. *The Developer*, p. 3.

Sharan, S. (Ed.). (1990). *Cooperative learning: Theory and research*. New York: Praeger.

Sharan, S., & Hertz-Lazarowitz, R. (1980). A group investigation method of cooperative learning in the classroom. In S. Sharon, P. Hare, C. Webb, R. Hertz-Lawarowitz (Eds.), *Cooperation in education* (pp. 14–46). Provo, UT: Brigham Young University Press.

Sharan, S., & Shachar, H. (1988). *Language and learning in the cooperative classroom*. New York: Springer-Verlag.

Showers, B. (1980). *Self-efficacy as a predictor of teacher participation in school decision-making*. Unpublished doctoral dissertation. Stanford University.

Showers, B. (1982a). *A study of coaching in teacher training*. Eugene: University of Oregon, Center for Educational Policy & Management.

Showers, B. (1982b). *Transfer of training: The contribution of coaching*. Eugene, OR: Center for Educational Policy and Management.

Showers, B. (1983). *Coaching: A training component for facilitating transfer of training*. Paper presented at the annual meeting of the American Educational Research Association, Montreal.

Showers, B. (1984a). *Peer coaching and its effect on transfer of training*. Paper presented at the annual meeting of the American Educational Research Association, New Orleans.

Showers, B. (1984b). *Peer coaching: A strategy for facilitating transfer of training*. Eugene, OR: Center for Educational Policy and Management.

Showers, B. (1985). Teachers coaching teachers. *Educational Leadership, 42*(7), 43–49.

Showers, B. (1989). *Implementation: Research-based training and teaching strategies and their effects on the workplace and instruction*. Paper presented at the annual meeting of the American Educational Research Association, San Francisco.

Showers, B., Joyce, B., & Bennett, B. (1987). Synthesis of research on staff development: A framework for future study and a state-of-the-art analysis. *Educational Leadership, 45*(3), 77–87.

Showers, B., Joyce, B., Scanlon, M., & Schnaubelt, C. (1998). A second chance to learn to read. *Educational Leadership, 55*(6), 27–31.

Showers, B., Murphy, C., & Joyce, B. (1996). The River City program. In B. Joyce & E. Calhoun (Eds.), *Learning experiences in school renewal*, (pp. 13–52). Eugene, OR: The ERIC Clearinghouse on Educational Management.

Sigel, I. (Ed.). (1984). *Advances in applied developmental psychology.* New York: Ablex.

Simon, H. (1976). *Administrative behavior: A study of decision-making processes in administrative organizations* (3rd ed.). New York: Free Press.

Sirotnik, K. (1983). What you see is what you get: Consistency, persistence, and mediocrity in classrooms. *Harvard Educational Review, 53*(1), 16–31.

Sizer, T. R. (1991). No pain, no gain. *Educational Leadership, 48*(8), 32–34.

Skinner, B. (1978). *Reflections on behaviorism and society.* Englewood Cliffs, NJ: Prentice Hall.

Slavin, R. (1983). *Cooperative learning.* New York: Longman, Inc.

Slavin, R. (1990). Achievement effects of ability grouping in secondary schools: A best-evidence synthesis. *Review of Educational Research, 60*(3), 471–500.

Slavin, R., Karweit, N., & Wasik, B. (1991). *Preventing early school failure: What works.* Baltimore: Center for Research on Effective Schooling for Disadvantaged Students, Johns Hopkins University.

Slavin, R., & Madden, N. (1994). *Lee Conmigo: Effects of success for all in bilingual first grades.* Paper presented at the annual meeting of The American Educational Research Association, New Orleans.

Slavin, R., Madden, N., Dolan, L., & Wasik, B. (1996). *Every child, every school: Success for all.* Thousand Oaks, CA: Corwin Press.

Smith, K., & Smith, M. (1966). *Cybernetic principles of learning and educational design.* New York: Holt, Rinehart, and Winston.

Smith, L., Ross, S., & Nunnery, J. (1997). *Increasing the chances for Success for All: The relationship between program implementation and student achievement at eight inner-city schools.* Paper presented at the annual meeting of the American Educational Research Association, Chicago.

Smith, L., & Keith, P. (1971). *Anatomy of an innovation.* New York: Wiley.

Smith, M. (1980). *Effects of aesthetics education on basic skills learning.* Boulder, CO: Laboratory of Educational Research, University of Colorado.

Snow, C., Burns, M., & Griffin, P. (Eds.). (1998). *Preventing reading difficulties in young children.* Washington, DC: National Academy Press.

Snow, R. (1982). *Intelligence, motivation, and academic work.* Paper presented for a symposium on The Student's Role in Learning, conducted by the National Commission for Excellence in Education, U.S. Department of Education, San Diego, California.

Soar, R. (1973). *Follow through classroom process measurement and pupil growth.* (1970–71 final report.) Gainesville: Institute for the Development of Human Resources, University of Florida.

Sparks, D. (1993a). Insights on school improvement: An interview with Larry Lezotte. *Journal of Staff Development, 14*(3), 18–21.

Sparks, D. (1993b, October). Organization development in schools. *The Developer,* p. 1.

Sparks, D. (2000, Winter). Results. *Journal of the National Staff Development Council,* pp. 51–53.

Sparks, D., & Loucks-Horsley, S. (1992). *Five models of staff development for teachers.* Oxford, OH: The National Staff Development Council.

Spaulding, R. (1970). *Educational improvement program.* Durham, NC: Duke University Press.

Speer, T. (1998). *Researching for excellence: What school boards are doing to raise student achievement.* Alexandria, VA: The National School Boards Association.

Spillane, J., Halverson, R., & Diamond, J. (2001). Investigating school leadership practice: A distributed perspective. *Educational Researcher, 30*(3), 23–28.

Sprinthall, M., & Thies-Sprinthall, L. (1981). Teachers as adult learners. In G. Griffin (Ed.), *Staff development* (82nd yearbook of the National Society for the Study of Education, pp. 13–25). Chicago: University of Chicago Press.

SRI International. (1982). *Evaluation of the implementation of Public Law 94–142.* Menlo Park, CA: Author.

Stauffer, R. (1969). *Directing reading maturity as a cognitive-learning process.* New York: Harper & Row.

Stenhouse, L. (1975). *An introduction to curriculum research and development.* London: Heinemann.

Sternberg, R. (1986a). *Intelligence applied: Understanding and increasing your intellectual skills.* San Diego: Harcourt Brace Jovanovich.

Sternberg, R. (1986b). Synthesis of research on the effectiveness of intellectual skills programs. *Educational Leadership, 44,* 60–67.

Stevenson, H., & Stigler, J. (1992). *The learning gap.* New York: Summit Books.

Stone, C. (1983). A meta-analysis of advance organizer studies. *Journal of Experimental Education, 51*(4), 194–199.

Suchman, J. (1962). *The elementary school training program in scientific inquiry.* Report to the U.S. Office of Education, Project Title VII. Urbana: University of Illinois.

Suchman, R. (1964). Studies in inquiry training. In R. Ripple & V. Bookcastle (Eds.), *Piaget reconsidered.* Ithaca, NY: Cornell University Press.

Sullivan, E. (1967). Piaget and the school curriculum: A critical appraisal. *Bulletin No. 2.* Toronto: Ontario Institute for Studies in Education.

Swanborn, M. S. L., & de Glopper, K. (1999). Incidental word learning while reading: A meta-analysis. *Review of Educational Research, 69*(3), 261–285.

Sylwester, R. (1995). *A celebration of neurons: An educator's guide to the human brain.* Alexandria, VA: Association for Supervision and Curriculum Development.

Taba, H. (1966). *Teaching strategies and cognitive functioning in elementary school children.* (Cooperative Research Project 2404.) San Francisco: San Francisco State College.

Tennyson, R., & Cocchiarella, M. (1986). An empirically based instructional design theory for teaching concepts. *Review of Educational Research, 56,* 40–71.

Thelen, H. (1960). *Education and the human quest.* New York: Harper & Row.

Thoresen, C., & Mahoney, M. (1974). *Behavioral self-control.* New York: Holt, Rinehart & Winston.

Thorndike, E. (1913). *The psychology of learning, Vol. II: Educational psychology.* New York: Teachers College.

Timar, T. (1989). The politics of school restructuring. *Phi Delta Kappan, 71*(4), 264–275.

Tobin, K. (1986). Effects of teacher wait time on discourse characteristics in mathematics and language arts classes. *American Educational Research Journal, 23*(2), 191–200.

Tuttle, E. (1963). *School board leadership in America.* Danville, IL: Interstate Press.

U.S. Department of Education. (1999). *The final report of the National Assessment of Title I.* Washington, DC: U.S. Government Printing Office.

Vance, V., & Schlechty, P. (1982). The distribution of academic ability in the teaching force: Policy implications. *Phi Delta Kappan, 64*(1), 22–27.

Vellutino, F., & Scanlon, D. (2001). Emergent literacy skills, early instruction, and individual differences as determinants of difficulties in learning to read: The case for early intervention. In S. Neuman & D. Dickinson (Eds.), *Handbook of early literacy research* (pp. 295–321). New York: The Guilford Press.

Voss, B. (1982). *Summary of research in science education.* Columbus, OH: ERIC Clearinghouse for Science, Mathematics, and Environmental Education.

Walberg, H. (1985). *Why Japanese educational productivity excels.* Paper presented at the annual meeting of the American Educational Research Association, Chicago.

Walberg, H. (1990). Productive teaching and instruction: Assessing the knowledge base. *Phi Delta Kappan, 71*(6), 70–78.

Wallace, R., Jr. (1996). *From vision to practice: The art of educational leadership.* Thousand Oaks, CA: Corwin Press.

Wallace, R., Lemahieu, P., & Bickel, W. (1990). The Pittsburgh experience: Achieving commitment to comprehensive staff development. In B. Joyce (Ed.), *Changing school culture through staff development.* Alexandria, VA: Association for Supervision and Curriculum Development.

Wallace, R., Young, J., Johnston, J., Bickel, W., & LeMahieu, P. (1984). Secondary educational renewal in Pittsburgh. *Educational Leadership, 41*(6), 73–77.

Wang, M., Haertel, G., & Walberg, H. (1993). Toward a knowledge base for school learning. *Review of Educational Research, 63*(3), 249–294.

Weikart, D., et al. (1971). *The cognitively oriented curriculum: A framework for pre-school teachers.* Washington, DC: National Association for Education of Young Children.

Weil, M., Marshalek, B., Mittman, A., Murphy, J., Hallinger, P., & Pruyn, J. (1984). *Effective and typical schools: How different are they?* Paper presented at the annual meeting of the American Educational Research Association, New Orleans.

Weiss, I. (1978). *1977 national survey of science, social science, and mathematics education.* National Science Foundation. Washington, DC: U.S. Government Printing Office.

Willig, A. (1985). A meta-analysis of selected studies on the effectiveness of bilingual education. *Review of Educational Research, 55*(3), 269–318.

Wolf, J. (1994). *BLT: A resource handbook for building leadership teams.* Minneapolis, MN: The North Central Association of Schools and Colleges.

Wolf, J., &. Joyce, B. (1992). *Just Read and Write.* Materials presented at the annual meeting of the Association for Supervision and Curriculum Development, New Orleans.

Wolpe, J., & Wolpe, J. (1981). *Our useless fears.* Boston: Houghton Mifflin.

Worthen, B. (1968). A study of discovery and expository presentation: Implications for teaching. *Journal of Teacher Education, 19*(4), 223–242.

Index

Note: Page numbers followed by *f* indicate figures.